NONTRADITIONAL COLLEGE ROUTES
TO CAREERS

A detailed look at all aspects of nontraditionality in higher education with emphasis on career preparation—different degree programs, interdisciplinary and self-designed majors, multi-media learning, off-campus activities, study abroad, correspondence study, cooperative education, consortia, "University without Walls," external degrees, new and unique colleges, experiential credit, life long learning and others. A valuable source for information about nontraditional ways to prepare for a chosen career.

BOOKS BY SARAH SPLAVER

NONTRADITIONAL CAREERS FOR WOMEN

NONTRADITIONAL COLLEGE ROUTES TO CAREERS

PARAPROFESSIONS
Careers of the Future and the Present

YOU AND TODAY'S TROUBLED WORLD—
A Psychologist Talks to Urban Youth

YOUR CAREER—IF YOU'RE NOT GOING TO COLLEGE

YOUR COLLEGE EDUCATION—
How to Pay for It

YOUR HANDICAP—DON'T LET IT HANDICAP YOU

YOUR PERSONALITY AND YOU

Nontraditional College Routes To Careers

By SARAH SPLAVER, Ph.D.

JULIAN MESSNER
NEW YORK

Published by Julian Messner, a Division of Simon & Schuster, Inc.
1 West 39 Street, New York, N. Y. 10018. All rights reserved.

to
two dear friends
EVE and AL CHAIKEN
my Washington "representatives"
who embrace both the nontraditional
and the traditional in their
continuing search for enhancement of life's goals

Library of Congress Cataloging in Publication Data

Splaver, Sarah.
  Nontraditional college routes to careers.
  Bibliography: p. 237

  Includes index.
  SUMMARY: Discusses some of the changes taking place in college
education, including interdisciplinary majors, study abroad, multi-
media learning, the "University without Walls," and others.
  1. Education, Higher—United States. 2. University
extension—United States. [1. Education, Higher]
I. Title.
LA227.3.S68   378   75-1060
ISBN 0-671-32732-1
ISBN 0-671-32733-X lib. bdg.

Printed in the United States of America

CONTENTS

ACKNOWLEDGMENT

Nontraditional innovations can make a college curriculum inspiring, challenging and dynamic. This, however, can be so only if these innovations are positive and constructive and not negative and destructive. Nontraditionality in higher education is NOW. Yet, nowhere has there been a volume covering all aspects of nontraditionality in the colleges and universities throughout the nation.

To provide students and their parents, counselors, teachers, professors and the gamut of college administrators with information on the nontraditional alternatives available in the institutions of higher education in the United States, I undertook an extensive study of nontraditionality (with emphasis on career preparation through nontraditional educational routes) in American colleges and universities. To make this study as comprehensive as possible, I sent letters of inquiry to over 2,200 accredited two-year and four-year institutions of higher education in the United States and to the State, District and Territorial Commissioners of Higher Education.

The College Handbook, published by the College Entrance Examination Board, was used as the primary reference directory for the names and addresses of the colleges and universities; the latter were supplemented by names and addresses of additional institutions from government publications and miscellaneous other sources. Where necessary, there were second and third follow-up letters and telephone calls.

The response to this survey exceeded even my optimistic expectations. My sincerest thanks go out to all the college presidents, vice presidents, assistants to the vice presidents, provosts, deans, directors of special projects, directors of continuing education, professors and

7

college and university administrators with a miscellany of other titles who cooperated so thoughtfully and gave their invaluable time to write detailed reports of the nontraditional characteristics of their colleges. Unfortunately, space limitations make it impossible to include their names here.

Some of those who responded may be disappointed because their colleges may not have been included in this book or because their colleges have not been given as much space as they might have liked them to receive. I would like to assure all of these respondees that this does not in any way indicate any lack of gratefulness on my part for all of their efforts. On the contrary, I am very grateful to all who responded, for *all* of the responses in their totality enabled me to arrive at what I hope are constructive conclusions and decisions regarding nontraditionality in higher education. Thus, every response played an important role in the formulation of my thoughts on nontraditionality and in the consequent composition of this book.

Space limitations compelled me to condense and curtail, often contrary to my personal desires. In all categories of nontraditionality, I selected those innovations I considered especially significant and noteworthy and presented them as concisely as space commitments dictated, being careful always not to sacrifice essential descriptive matter for the sake of brevity. Additionally, to include in this book all of the nontraditional characteristics brought to my attention by the responses to my survey would have been to make this a massive, non-readable encyclopedic guide book; the latter is certainly not my desire. My aim has been to make this a readable, valuable volume of use to students of all ages and to all who are concerned with the subject of nontraditionality and not a guide book to gather dust on a library shelf.

I hope that this book will not only help students to locate and participate in the dynamic, nontraditional offerings that will challenge their potential and lead them onward to rewarding, fulfilling careers and lives of personal, cultural and social fulfillment, but that it will also play a role in stimulating institutions of higher education toward positive, constructive nontraditionality and away from the paths of faddish foolishness which some of them have been following in the false name of nontraditionality.

My heartfelt thanks to all who gave their precious time and gracious efforts to help make this book as all-encompassing as possible.

S.S.

1.
ONCE UPON A TIME

Once upon a time, there was a college. It had students. The students were mostly male, white, middle-class, high achievers, between the ages of eighteen and twenty-two. The students had received their high school diplomas in June and entered the college as freshmen in September and were prepared to spend four years at this college.

The academic calendar of each of the four years was on a "5-5" schedule, consisting of two five-month terms, known as semesters. The Fall semester started in September and ended in January; the Spring semester started in February and ended in late May. The students selected standard, traditional major programs of study including traditional courses (required and elective) within the confines of structured, pre-designed curricula.

Learning, hopefully, took place when the professors lectured and the students listened. The students spent their four years at college *on campus* listening to these lectures in the classrooms and the laboratories. After passing their courses and accumulating the necessary credits, the students were awarded the traditional Bachelor of Arts (B.A.) or Bachelor of Science (B.S.) four-year degree, or the Associate in Arts (A.A.) or Associate in Science (A.S.) degree if they successfully completed the two-year associate degree program of studies.

Then, with sheepskin in hand, they went out into the cold, wide world from which they had been sheltered behind the ivied walls of their soporific college.

That was TRADITION, TRADITION—once upon a time. How long ago was "once upon a time?" It was way back in 1970, and in 1972 and in 1974—and even as long ago as yesterday—and in many, many cases, even just one minute ago!

9

Now, a transition is taking place. It is taking place rapidly in some colleges, slowly in others and ever so very slowly in many others. Rapidly, slowly or at a crawling pace—what is it that is actually taking place?

NONTRADITION, NONTRADITION—Now and Tomorrow

College students are no longer the traditional "mostly male, white, middle-class high achievers, between the ages of eighteen and twenty-two." Now, there are many females in college classes along with the males. (See Chapter 16 on programs for women.) The white students are being joined by Blacks, Puerto Ricans, Chicanos, American Indians (or Native Americans, which is a more accurate appellation) and Orientals.

To the middle-class high achievers have been added students from low-income, underprivileged homes whose disadvantaged backgrounds have caused them to be underprepared for college. No longer is the undergraduate college student body between the ages of eighteen and twenty-two. Qualified high school juniors and seniors are being given the opportunity for "early admission" to college and, at the other end of the scale, mature adults and senior citizens are enrolling in college courses and degree programs in ever increasing numbers. (See Chapter 2 on nontraditional students.)

Students today are not necessarily continuing on to college immediately after their high school graduation, as was the traditional procedure. The academic calendars are no longer simply two five-month semesters; the traditional "5-5" schedule is giving way to many nontraditional varieties. (See Chapter 3 on unusual schedules.)

The standard, traditional major programs are still found in hundreds of colleges throughout the nation. But, added to these (and, in some cases, in their place) are many nontraditional versions of degree programs. (See Chapter 4 on degree programs.) Many colleges have added nontraditional courses, studies and other related offerings to their curricula. (See Chapter 5 on the latter subject.) Learning is "in" and lectures are "out" on many campuses, and multi-media instruction is a refreshing newcomer to the college scene. (See Chapter 6 on multi-media learning.)

Most students are no longer spending four years *on campus*. There are many nontraditional field work, internship and other off-campus experiences for which college students are now being granted college credits. (See Chapter 7 on off-campus experiences.) Many are taking study abroad programs for a term, a year or even as short a period as the one-month January term. (See Chapter 8 on study abroad.)

Students of all ages are accumulating credits through correspondence study. (See Chapter 9.) Others are involved in cooperative education programs which make it possible for them to earn while they learn. (See Chapter 10 on cooperative education.)

Many students are delighted with the opportunity to spend a term or a year on campus at another institution. This is now possible because of the new development of interinstitutional cooperation known as the *consortium.* Students may now take courses at any member college of the consortium to which their college belongs. (See Chapter 12 on consortia.)

Traditionally, most students who successfully completed a four-year college program were awarded either the B.A. or B.S. degree. Miscellaneous nontraditional baccalaureates are now being awarded to students who complete varied nontraditional degree programs. (See Chapter 11 on these nontraditional degrees.)

The ivied college walls no longer lock the students away from the cold, cruel world. Joshua fought the battle of Jericho and the walls came tumbling down. Students—and faculty—in the past decade have fought the battle of academe and the walls have come crumbling—if not tumbling—down. "University without walls" (and versions thereof) and external degrees are gaining in popularity. (See Chapter 13 on this subject.)

There are colleges—with and without walls—so unique and non-traditional that, like the old grey mare, they are not what colleges "used to be." (See Chapter 14 for some unusual colleges.)

No longer can learning end when the student leaves the formal classroom setting. The diploma and the degree are symbols of beginning, not ending. Life long learning is not merely an alliterative expression; it is a necessity in this rapidly changing, jet-age world of ours. Men and women of all ages must avail themselves of the opportunities of continuing education. (See Chapter 15 on life long learning.)

Credits-in-Escrow or Deferred Credits

A number of colleges have adopted the nontraditional procedure of giving intelligent high school students the opportunity to earn college credit while they are still attending high school. Some colleges call this *Credits-in-Escrow;* others call it *Deferred Credits.*

Valencia Community College (Orlando, Fla.) permits high school seniors to register for college courses and attend classes for credit if they have the approval of their high school counselors. These seniors must be capable of doing their high school work and their college studies at the same time. The credits these students acquire after successfully completing their college courses are held as *in escrow* until after their high school graduation. Then, after the students enroll at Valencia, their credits are applied toward their degrees and they are able to earn their degrees in less time than usual.

Taylor University (Upland, Ind.) also has a *credits-in-escrow* arrangement. Outstanding high school students are permitted to enroll at Taylor prior to their graduation from high school. The credits they earn in this way may be applied toward their degree programs if, at some future date, they matriculate at Taylor.

Madonna College (Livonia, Mich.) permits above average high school students to enroll in various general education courses beginning when these students are in their junior year at high school. By the time they have completed their high school graduation requirements, these talented young people may concurrently have earned a maximum of eighteen college credits and thereby reduced the time it will take them to earn their baccalaureate degree.

High school juniors and seniors who possess above average academic ability may be permitted to take freshman level courses at *Rust College* in Holly Springs, Miss. Upon the successful completion of these courses, the students are granted *deferred credits*. These credits are later recorded as regular college credits for those students who enter Rust after they have been graduated from high school.

Early Admission Program

The *State University of New York* (*SUNY*) *at Albany* has an innovative *Early Admission Program*. In 1972, the *James E. Allen Jr. Collegiate Center* was established as an integral part of SUNY at Albany to permit selected students to start their collegiate level work at the end of their third year of high school. These students are awarded a high school diploma after they have successfully completed their first year at the Allen Collegiate Center.

The students then proceed with their college studies in an interdisciplinary program which focuses on the basic institutions of society and their interdependencies. Concurrent with classroom study of the institutions of society, there may be laboratory or field experiences of some of these institutions. Many courses are "Readings" and are colloquia on class readings in each specific subject area. Thus, there are Readings courses in Anthropology, Economics, History, Literature, Philosophy, Political Science, Psychology and Sociology.

For details about this program, write to the Office of the Dean, James E. Allen Jr. Collegiate Center, SUNY at Albany, Albany, N.Y. 12203.

Deferred Admission — Leave of Absence

Another new development in institutions of higher education is flexibility in the students' attendance at college. Included in this category are *Deferred Admission* and the *Student Leave of Absence*. The "leave of absence" gives students the opportunity to "stop out" rather than "drop out."

Many students want to enter college as soon as possible. Others, however, prefer an intermission between high school and college. Some institutions of higher education have, therefore, instituted a *deferred admission* policy. *Johns Hopkins University* (Baltimore, Md.) has such a policy. After accepting a student for admission, Johns Hopkins permits those who so desire to defer entrance into the freshman class to work or travel for one or two years after high school graduation.

Johns Hopkins University also permits its students to take a *leave of absence*. This leave is an interruption of the student's college studies for personal reasons. It must not exceed a period of two years.

Like Johns Hopkins, *Newton College*, a liberal arts college for women in Newton, Mass., has a *deferred admission* policy. There are students who want to take a year off between high school and college, but want to be sure they have been accepted in the following year's freshman class. Newton permits such qualified high school seniors to complete the admission process and then defers their admission for one year with the understanding that the year will be used for work, travel or non-college related study.

Newton also permits a student to take a leave of absence. However, whereas some colleges allow their students to take a leave only for miscellaneous personal reasons, but not for study, Newton allows its students to study at an accredited college or university while on leave.

Students in good academic standing at *Central Connecticut State College* (New Britain, Conn.) are assured re-admission into the college after voluntarily leaving for at least one full semester. Those who take such leaves may use the time to travel, work, attend another educational institution or indulge in some other worthwhile activity.

Negotiated Admissions Policy

Worcester Polytechnic Institute (WPI) of Worcester, Mass., initiated a truly innovative admission procedure in September 1972, when it introduced the *Negotiated Admissions Policy*. Under this arrangement, candidates for admission who have completed four years of math and three years of science in high school judge their own chances for admission and decide whether to approve or not approve their own admission.

Applicants for admission are invited to visit the college admissions office. There they are interviewed by an admissions officer and a faculty member or upperclass student and then are taken on a guided tour of WPI. Applicants are given complete information on the nature of the nontraditional program of study at WPI, known as the WPI Plan (see Chapter 4), and other information to help them decide whether or not they have the ability to succeed at WPI.

After returning home and weighing all the information they have received against their own abilities and potentials, the applicants evaluate themselves and decide whether they believe they should or should not be accepted by WPI. Those who decide they have the proper motivation and qualifications complete the application forms, write an essay on how they relate to the WPI Plan and send these to the WPI Admissions Office. WPI then sends self-acceptance letters to these applicants.

If the Admissions Officer believes that a particular applicant is unrealistic in his/her evaluation of his/her potential for success at WPI, the Admissions Officer thus informs the applicant. If this applicant is determined and seriously wishes to attend WPI, WPI is generally willing to take a chance on this type of highly motivated prospective student.

Experiential Credit

Another nontraditional newcomer in the area of credit-earning upon a student's admission to college is *experiential credit*.

Experiential credit is credit allowed for work experience acquired in gainful employment before the student's enrollment in an institution of higher education. Work experience of a general nature is not sufficient for credit-earning purposes. Mature adults, who have worked for several years since leaving school, may have acquired substantial work experience. A college admissions committee may judge this experience as equivalent to one or more specific college courses and grant the student a specified number of credits toward the associate or baccalaureate degree.

Hillsborough Community College (Tampa, Fla.) recognizes that it would be a needless waste of time for students to repeat in formal courses what they may have already learned after a number of years on their jobs. Therefore, academic credit is granted in lieu of practicum and mid-management courses to those who have appropriate work experience in the Business Administration and Architectural Construction Technology programs.

Finch College in New York City grants a maximum of thirty-two credits toward the bachelor's degree for acceptable life/work experience. The work or life experience should have an obvious relationship to the college curriculum and to the subject area department into which this experience fits. Determination of the specific number of credits to be granted depends upon the amount of understanding and knowledge acquired in the subject area by the student through the life/work experience.

Colorado Mountain College (Leadville, Colo.) offers credit "by virtue of documented experience." The student presents all the "back-up material" as requested by the instructor of the course for which the student wishes work experience credit. If this experience meets with the instructor's approval, the instructor makes the necessary recommendation to the Chairman of the Division in which that course belongs. If the Chairman approves, the back-up material and the Chairman's recommendation are forwarded to the Curriculum Committee for final determination.

If you have satisfactory life/work experience, you may receive credit for it toward a degree at *Sacred Heart University* (Bridgeport, Conn.). This university awards academic credit for intellectual achievements or scholarly work in four general forms of life/work experience. This is for work or life activities in other than collegiate institutions and may be in any of the following four categories: 1) Professional Certified Experience—evidence of successful practice is required in work activities calling for certification, such as miscellaneous licensed business brokers, practical and registered nurses and paraprofessionals; 2) In-Service Training Program—evidence of successful practice and intellectual development in supervised on-the-job work activities in such areas as banking, computer programming, government service, insurance and military service; 3) Management Work Experience—responsible progress in a position which involved independent judgment, problem solving and an understanding of people; and 4) General Experience—the general background and sophistication of the candidate are judged and credit may be awarded for self-education which the candidate may have acquired through extensive reading, traveling and/or living in foreign countries.

Throughout this book, there is mention of other colleges that also offer degree credits for life/work experience. Some colleges grant credits to incoming freshmen for life/work experience without subjecting them to written examinations; others insist that the students pass examinations administered by the college before credit is granted.

Credit by Examination

Students can receive college credits by demonstrating proficiency in a subject (or subjects) by passing certain examinations and thereby accelerate their programs toward associate or baccalaureate degrees. They save money by eliminating the tuition costs of courses they need not take and save time in this manner. The three major varieties of such tests are the College Entrance Examination Board's Advanced Placement (AP) examinations, CLEP and the individual college's own tests.

The College Entrance Examination Board (CEEB) administers the Advanced Placement Program. This program is based on the fact that intelligent high school students with special abilities can profit from college-level studies while they are still in high school. CEEB helps secondary schools set up college-level courses. It administers and grades AP examinations for the students who take these courses in anticipation of getting college credit for them. Hundreds of colleges throughout the nation participate in this program and offer advanced placement and/or college credit to students who achieve scores of 3, 4 or 5 on the AP examinations.

If you would like to know more about this program speak with your high school counselor, if you are still in high school, or request a free copy of the latest edition of "A Guide to the Advanced Placement Program" from the Publications Order Office, College Entrance Examination Board, Box 592, Princeton, N.J. 08540.

CLEP is an acronym for College Level Examination Program. This credit-by-examination program sponsored by the College Entrance Examination Board was introduced on a national scale in 1967. CLEP examinations test the knowledge a student may have acquired through such nontraditional means as independent study, TV or radio courses, intensive reading, life/work experience and other unusual learning experiences. About 1,400 institutions of higher education throughout the United States grant credit to those who obtain satisfactory scores on these tests.

Persons of all ages may take CLEP examinations. If you have mastered the subject matter of one or more college courses, regardless of how or where or when you mastered it, it would be wise for you to take the appropriate CLEP Subject Examination. You may obtain a list and descriptions of the Subject Examinations and the General Examinations by writing to: College Entrance Examination Board, Box 592, Princeton, N.J. 08540.

A truly unique innovation in the realm of credit by examination is being pioneered at *California State College, San Bernardino.* Students are given the opportunity to acquire a full quarter's worth of credit by means of one examination. This nontraditional program is called "Comprehensive Examinations: An Alternative to Multi-Course Classroom Instruction."

This one examination covers the contents of three courses. Students who pass it are awarded fifteen quarter units of credit, which is equivalent to one quarter's full load. (Cal. State San Bernardino is on the quarter schedule.) To pass this comprehensive examination, however, students must do a great deal of independent study. A variety of audio-visual materials, videotape cassettes and written guides are available to help students who wish to participate in this program.

This radical departure from traditional learning procedures is not just an alternative means of helping the traditional college students hasten their progress toward the baccalaureate degree, but is also a novel option for those who live far from the college campus, or for evening session or part-time students or for varied nontraditional students. If you have any questions you would like to have answered about this program, contact the Dean of Academic Planning, California State College—San Bernardino, 5500 State College Parkway, San Bernardino, Calif. 92407.

Career Education

This chapter has put the spotlight on many significant aspects of nontraditionality in higher education. As you proceed in reading this book, you will find many components of the nontraditional routes to degrees and careers described in greater detail.

The bulk of nontraditionality in higher education and the nontraditional college routes to careers are very young. There are colleges and universities that have as yet made only one or two changes, and perhaps even minor ones at that, in their traditional curricula. Some have made innovative changes only in their admissions procedures, or only in their methods and/or places of instruction, or only in their academic calendar or only on their degree programs or curricular offerings. Then, there are a limited number of institutions of higher education that have nontraditional programs of such scope that they are housed within one "umbrella" unit of the institution. Thus, the *University of Northern Colorado* (Greeley, Colo.) houses its many nontraditional activities in its Center for Nontraditional and Outreach Education; you will find these activities discussed in several chapters in this book.

What do all these innovations and alternatives that come under the large umbrella of nontraditionality add up to? In the final analysis, in the final quarter of the twentieth century, they add up to the most recent innovation, *career education*. That's where the action really is in higher education today.

Essentially, the concept of career education proclaims that schools and colleges, in addition to their many other functions, should assume their responsibilities in helping their students prepare for productive, constructive careers. As you will note in the chapters that follow, colleges are employing many nontraditional routes to stimulate career awareness in their students and to provide their students with opportunities for career exploration and preparation.

In the 1960s, theoretical and abstract courses were popular on the college campuses. Now, as we head toward the 1980s and onward, the students are more concerned about courses and programs leading to comfortable careers. Even those who take liberal arts programs rather than specific career-directed majors, such as accounting and engineering, have opportunities for vocational preparation by means of such routes as exploratory field work and internships. A liberal arts education provides students with a great deal of flexibility in the routes they pursue toward the careers in which they will engage during their lifetimes.

In addition to their major programs or areas of concentration, all students would be wise to take elective courses that stimulate and develop their individual intellectual interests, for with bold imagination these too could lead to exciting, challenging occupational opportunities.

Every high school and college student should peruse the U. S. Department of Labor's Bureau of Labor Statistics' *Occupational Outlook Handbook* and then carefully read the sections about the occupations which are of interest to them. The 1974–75 edition of this encyclopedic *Handbook* discusses more than 850 occupations considered to be of greatest interest to young people. You should be able to find a copy of this *Handbook* in your school library or local public library, or ask your school counselor if you may look at the copy in the Guidance Department library.

Now, let us look at today's nontraditional college students.

2.
COLLEGE STUDENTS ARE NOT
WHAT THEY USED TO BE

Traditionally, college students, in the main, have been white, male, between the ages of 18 and 22, high-achievers, who have performed above average academically in high school and are well prepared for college.

In recent years, increasing numbers of nontraditional students have been enrolling in colleges and universities throughout the nation and matriculating for college degrees. These nontraditional students are non-white, from varied ethnic groups, female, over 22 years of age and/or inadequately prepared for college.

In Chapter 5, you will find information about Black Studies, Afro-American Studies and studies relating to miscellaneous ethnic groups. Programs designed specifically for women students are discussed in Chapter 16.

Large numbers of men and women beyond the age of twenty-two, having become aware of the value of post-secondary school education, have been attending regular day session college classes. There are those who prefer to attend evening session classes and participate in Continuing Education programs (see Chapter 15), but there are many "overaged" students who are sitting right next to and joining with the regular day session students.

Many young people do not do as well in high school as their native talents would permit because their home and community environments are impoverished and lacking in many of the advantages which the traditional college students often have taken for granted. These disadvantaged students may very well be college material, but they are "underprepared" for college. Many colleges have established special programs, in addition to the many varied versions of Upward Bound and Education Opportunity programs, to improve these students' readiness for college and to aid them along the way educationally and financially.

This chapter contains the highlights of those programs for these "overaged" and "underprepared" students which I consider especially worthy of note.

A. "OVERAGED" STUDENTS

In this category, there are programs for "mature adults" and those exclusively for "senior citizens."

I. *Mature Adults*

The Deferred Degree Program

Adults who do not possess all of the qualifications and, therefore, would find it impossible to enter a degree-granting program, may have the opportunity to do so via the *Deferred Degree Program* of the Continuing Education Division of the *University of Maine at Portland-Gorham.*

This is a reduced-load academic program consisting of evening session freshman level courses. After successfully completing a prescribed number of credit hours with specific grades, the student in this program will be accepted as a degree candidate in the day or evening session and granted appropriate advanced standing on the basis of the courses already completed.

The prescribed number of freshman level credit hours which the student must complete varies with the academic major and degree which the student has chosen to pursue. There are deferred degree programs leading to the Bachelor of Arts, Bachelor of Science in Business Administration, Bachelor of Science in Economics, Bachelor of Arts in Economics, Associate of Science in Business Administration, Bachelor of Science in Elementary Education, Bachelor of Science in Secondary Education and Bachelor of Science in Nursing degrees.

For further information about these programs, write to: Deferred Degree Counselor, Continuing Education Division, University of Maine at Portland-Gorham, 96 Falmouth St., Portland, Maine 04103.

ABLE

ABLE is an acronym for *Adult Baccalaureate Life Experience*. This is the *Adelphi University* (Garden City, N.Y.) new, nontraditional program for adults. It is administered jointly by the College of Arts and Sciences and the Division of Continuing Education.

Designed with the adult in mind, this program is ideal for many different types of persons who are 25+ years of age. Among the latter may be working men and women who seek to advance on their jobs, adults who would like to prepare for new careers, housewives who wish to re-enter the working world, the older adult who is preparing for retirement, recently discharged servicemen and servicewomen and other adults whose education was interrupted or who previously were unable to attend college.

The basic components of ABLE are: 1) the ABLE seminars, 2) regular university course offerings, 3) independent study, 4) life experience credits and 5) transfer credits. The seminar offerings are in the Humanities, the Arts, Social Sciences, Behavioral Sciences, Life Sciences and Communication Skills. ABLE students may choose from seminars held in the mornings, afternoons and evenings. Each seminar carries six credits, meets three hours weekly and requires about ten hours of outside study per week.

Participants in the ABLE program may take any of the regular undergraduate course offerings of any of the schools of Adelphi University, day or evening session. Unlike the ABLE seminars, in which all the students are older adults, in the regular courses, ABLE students sit in classrooms together with the traditional undergraduate students. This is of benefit to the ABLE students as well as the traditional undergraduates, for it provides a favorable, healthy climate of learning for all.

After they have completed their first semester, ABLE students are permitted to take a maximum of three credits in independent study per semester. The independent study projects must be approved by a faculty advisor and may be related to the students' employment, special interests or volunteer commitments.

ABLE students may be granted a maximum of thirty life experience credits based upon their past living or working experiences. A Life Experience Committee judges the ABLE student's past, including employment, avocational reading, facility with languages other than English, extensive travel, non-credentialized study seminars or workshops, community volunteer work or other valuable life experiences, and then decides how much experiential credit to award to the student. ABLE students may also be awarded transfer credits for credits earned at other institutions as well as for credits earned through any of the variety of testing programs.

ABLE students may have an "area of concentration" in their programs in place of the traditional major. Their annual academic calendar consists of three twelve-week sessions. A Child Activity Center is available for those students who need this service.

If you would like further details and an application to this program, write to: Director, ABLE Program, Division of Continuing Education, Adelphi University, Garden City, N.Y. 11530.

Mature Adult Program (M.A.P.)

The *State University College at Brockport* (Brockport, N.Y.) has two programs for the nontraditional older student. There are the *Mature Adult Program* and the *Bachelor of Arts in Liberal Studies,* which is an adult degree program (see Chapter 15).

The Mature Adult Program (M.A.P.) is a unique residential program that offers learning-living experiences on the Brockport campus to men and women in their middle years. Whereas most of the innovative programs for persons beyond the traditional college age range are designed to help them acquire college credits via various forms of off campus study, this program brings them onto the campus. It has apartment and residence-hall housing and food services available to M.A.P. participants. They have the opportunity to take part in the activities and events of a full-fledged campus community.

M.A.P. rejects the traditional idea that campus resources and facilities should be only for the traditional young college student and makes these available to the mature adult as well. Since M.A.P. students have varied backgrounds and goals and come from all walks of life, some mature adults enroll because they want to change occupations and/or embark on second careers, others are retired persons who wish to cultivate creative life-styles rather than accept traditional forms of retirement and yet others want to work toward college degrees while at the same time acquiring high school diplomas which they did not get when they were younger.

M.A.P., therefore, has three academic components—the career component, the retirement component and the degree-diploma component—to meet these different needs of these students. The career component is for those who want to start anew and they may choose from among thirty-three undergraduate majors in the areas of Education, Fine Arts, Humanities, Human Services, Natural and Mathematical Sciences, Physical Education and Recreation and Social Sciences; an organized program of career investigation will assist them in developing career goals if they have not arrived at any career choice.

The retirement component aims to aid retirees who seek creative life-styles based on their personal, educational and social development. The degree-diploma component is designed for those who want to pursue college degrees while simultaneously getting their high school diplomas; they may be awarded credit for relevant life experience and then embark upon degree programs similar to those in the career component.

The mature adults in this program have an unusual opportunity to combine learning activities, living experiences and special counseling services on the Brockport campus. A full range of cultural, recreational and social activities on the campus are open to them. For those who might like to work part-time while participating in M.A.P., there is a "Gaining Resources for Older Workers" (GROW) office on the Brockport campus. This is a non-profit employment agency for citizens fifty-five years of age and older.

If you would like details about this program and an application form, contact the Director, Mature Adult Program, State University College at Brockport, Brockport, N.Y. 14420.

Degree Program for Experienced Adults

The *College of St. Rose* in Albany, N.Y., established a *Degree Program for Experienced Adults* in 1971. This program is essentially for persons who are twenty-eight years of age and over and cannot attend classes on campus on a full-time basis to earn the college degree they now desire.

The Degree Program for Experienced Adults is flexible and students may be awarded college credits for acceptable life-work experience, community involvement, proficiency in a foreign language and achievements in art, music or writing. Students choose an area of concentration and with the help of an advisor they plan a program that will lead them to their B.A. or B.S. degree.

Credits may be earned through independent study projects, directed reading, participation in faculty-student seminars and, for those who wish and are able to do so, attendance at regular day or evening session classes. Students must come to the campus at least once each semester to plan that semester's program of study. Thereafter, during that semester, they may work at their studies wherever they may be. They may take advantage of the learning facilities of libraries, museums, lecture series, television courses and courses and/or resources of member colleges of the Hudson-Mohawk Association of Colleges and Universities (see Chapter 12).

After completing their semester study projects, students return to the college campus for evaluation and further planning. The number of semesters needed to fulfill the requirements for the bachelor's degree will vary depending upon the amount of credit granted to the student for past experience and the pace at which the student acquires knowledge. The minimum amount of time that a student is required to be in this program before earning the bachelor's degree is one year. However, it takes most students at least two years to complete their proposed programs of study to the satisfaction of their advisors and to be nominated for graduation.

If you have any inquiries about this program, address them to the Director, Degree Program for Experienced Adults, The College of Saint Rose, 432 Western Ave., Albany, N.Y. 12203.

Project A.W.A.R.E.

A.W.A.R.E. stands for Adults Who Are Returning to Education. *Project A.W.A.R.E.* at *Mercy College* (Dobbs Ferry, N.Y.) aims to aid adults who wish to enter or return to college. Mature adults may come to Mercy for career advancement, vocational preparation, cultural enrichment and personal fulfillment. Mercy grants adults credit for life experience up to a maximum of fifteen credits.

Day and evening classes on a year-round basis are available to Project A.W.A.R.E. students. There are flexible schedules and programs for these students. Details about Project A.W.A.R.E. may be obtained from the Director of Admissions, Mercy College, 555 Broadway, Dobbs Ferry, N.Y. 10522.

Program for Educational Renewal – PER

Rosary Hill College (Buffalo, N.Y.) has a special program for men and women beyond the average college age who may wish to begin or return to college for a bachelor's degree or who want to take certain courses without aiming for a degree. The *Program for Educational Renewal* – PER – is designed to help these adults integrate their college classes with their everyday life. Efforts are made to arrange college schedules with the students' job and home commitments in mind.

PER students may attend Rosary Hill on a full- or part-time basis. A faculty advisor is available to assist those who have been away from formal classroom study for quite some time. For details about PER, write to: Director of Admissions, Rosary Hill College, 4380 Main St., Buffalo, N.Y. 14226.

Second Careers Program

The *Second Careers Program* was inaugurated at *Montclair State College* (Upper Montclair, N.J.) in September 1974. This program is designed to encourage adults over the age of twenty-five to enter or return to a program of higher education. Students admitted into this program are required to enroll in a special two-credit, one-semester Re-Entry Seminar.

After successfully completing one semester's work of at least six semester hours, students in this program may apply for evaluation of their prior learning experiences. Credits are awarded to Second Careers students for acceptable significant personal or occupational learning experiences from which these students acquired knowledge or competencies equivalent to those gained in one or more college courses. Credits are also awarded to them for passing certain subject examinations. The credits awarded to a Second Careers student for experiential learning and for passing examinations may together not exceed a total of sixty-four credits.

Special advisement and counseling are available through the Second Careers Office to facilitate the entry of these students into the college world. This office is open to them for consultation services throughout their college years. The standard graduation requirements and academic criteria apply to the Second Careers students as they progress toward their degrees.

Further information about this new program may be obtained by writing to the Second Careers Program Director, Montclair State College, Upper Montclair, N.J. 07043.

Degree Completion Program

In 1969, *Antioch College* opened its *Baltimore Center for Social Research and Action* in Baltimore, Md., as an experimental endeavor. In the 1973–74 academic year, Antioch/Baltimore started its *Degree Completion Program.* This is an individually planned program for adults who are committed to social change. It is an educational alternative for those who believe that people have the right to shape their own destinies. Their learning activities are directed to those situations where they seek to have an impact.

A significant aspect of this program is the granting of college credit for life/work experience. Credits may be earned through formal classroom attendance, tutorials, independent study, projects and life/work experience. The college year consists of four quarters. Students may major in any of the following areas: Social Research and Strategies, Human Resources, Legal Studies, Media Studies, Theatre and Performing Arts and Creative Writing and Literature.

For details about this program, write to: Coordinator, Degree Completion Program, Center for Social Research and Action, Antioch College, 635 St. Paul Place, Baltimore, Md. 21202.

Three Years of Auditing Courses

Transylvania University in Lexington, Ky., has a unique program for persons twenty-five years of age and older. These adults are permitted to come to the campus and audit courses at audit fees. After *three years of auditing courses,* the student may enroll as a regular student and the credits earned at the reduced auditing fees may be applied toward the student's baccalaureate degree program.

General Studies for Adult Students

Iona College (New Rochelle, N.Y.) recently introduced an innovative program for adults to give them a second chance at continuing their education. This program is called *General Studies for Adult Students.* Applicants for admission to this program must be at least twenty-one years of age, and preferably older. Many, for a variety of reasons, never had the opportunity to go to college. Others may have started some years back and, due to the weight of family responsibilities, employment and/or other factors, dropped out. Because they often could not devote the necessary time to their school work, the "index" (grade average) of the drop-outs was not always indicative of their ability. This program grants "Index Amnesty" to such former students.

The curriculum leading to the Bachelor of Science in General Studies is interdisciplinary. There are no core requirements and students are free to select courses from the following five general areas of concentration: 1) Behavioral Sciences (Psychology, Sociology and Political Science); 2) Communication Arts (Speech, Journalism, Theatre/Acting and the Film); 3) Humanities (Fine Arts, Literature, Philosophy and Religious Studies); 4) Social Sciences (History, Geography and Economics); and 5) General Business (Accounting, Finance Management and Marketing), or they may select courses from the following five elective areas: Modern Languages, Written Communication, Science and Math, Computer Science and Education.

Courses are offered in the late afternoon and evening under circumstances convenient to the adult students. Students in this program may be awarded credit for life experience. This refers here to the acquisition of college-level skills and information from work, travel or other means than standard college courses. Depending upon the nature of the life experience and the amount of knowledge acquired from it, as much as forty credits (one third of the amount needed to obtain a degree) may be obtained for life experience.

If you would like to know more about this program, write to the Director, Division of General Studies, Iona College, New Rochelle, N.Y. 10801.

Senior Adult Program

Continuing Education and Community Services of *Catonsville Community College* (Catonsville, Md.) has a comprehensive *Senior Adult Program,* designed especially for adults fifty-five years of age and over. The program is designed to help mature adults retain their independence, expand their knowledge and use their leisure time to best advantage. Most of the courses and seminars are offered at no charge in various locations throughout Baltimore County.

Among the offerings in this Senior Adult Program are: Armchair Travelogue, Art Appreciation, Beginning Genealogy, Book Discussion, Communication Skills, Consumer Education for the Older Adult, Creative Writing, Food and Health Frauds, Games People Play (Bridge, Chess, Checkers), Gardening, Health Seminar, Home Mechanics, Legal Considerations of the Aged, Lip Reading, Major

Religions, Marriage in Later Years, Music Appreciation, New Ideas in Science, Oil Painting—Ceramics—Watercolor—Sculpture, Participating in Political Action, Philosophies of Life and Living, Political Discussion, Safety in the Home, Senior Power, Sex and the Older Adult, Sign Language for the Deaf, Vigor after Sixty, Volunteerism and Wills-Estates-Income Tax.

The *Life Fitness Program* is a special physical fitness and health program designed for senior adults. The *Pre-Retirement Seminar* is invaluable to persons intending to retire in the near future. The seminar entitled *Care of the Aged Patient* is designed to train nurse's aides or others caring for the elderly ill patient. The *Autumn Players* is a drama group made up entirely of adult "actors" past the age of sixty.

Would you like to know more about this Senior Adult Program or to register for any of these courses or seminars? If so, write to the Coordinator of Programs for the Aging, Division of Continuing Education and Community Services, Catonsville Community College, 800 S. Rolling Road, Catonsville, Md. 21228.

II. *Senior Citizens*

Self-fulfillment and self-enrichment await the senior citizens who take advantage of the many opportunities available to them to start college or to return to college courses from which they may have dropped out many years ago. These courses may be taken to help these citizens embark on new careers on a part-time (or perhaps even full-time) basis or for purely cultural and enjoyment purposes.

Waiver of Tuition

Increasing numbers of institutions of higher education are waiving tuition for senior citizens. Here are some noteworthy examples:

The *Senior Scholar Program* of *Whitworth College* (Spokane, Wash.), begun in the Fall of 1972, offers retired persons sixty-five years of age or older the opportunity to take one or two regular daytime courses for credit or audit at no tuition cost. The Senior Scholar may enroll in any course in any of the academic departments, attend classes with the traditional college students and participate in many of the undergraduate campus activities. A high school diploma is not required.

Whitworth also has started a program in which senior citizens who have had successful careers in specialized fields can give courses about these specialties to other retired persons (including some not yet sixty-five) who are interested in these subjects. Although these courses are to be given on campus, they are generally of shorter duration than a full semester and these senior citizen students are under less academic pressures than the Senior Scholars, for they are not competing with the traditional college students. In 1974, a qualified retired teacher conducted a course in Creative Writing for senior citizens. If you would like further information about Whitworth's programs for senior citizens, write to the Associate Director of Student Development, Office of Student Development, Whitworth College, Spokane, Wash. 99208.

At the *John C. Calhoun Junior College and Technical School* (Decatur, Ala.) older adults are encouraged to come and attend classes, but the college does not as yet have the funds to provide these older students with books as well as tuition.

The *University of Maine* has approved a waiver of tuition for persons sixty-five years of age or older who wish to register for any undergraduate courses on a non-credit arrangement at any campus of the University of Maine.

The *Community College of Baltimore* in Baltimore, Md., permits Baltimore residents who are sixty-five years of age or more to take courses which interest them without paying any tuition or other fees if the payments would be a hardship for them.

Franklin and Marshall College in Lancaster, Pa., has a *New Dimensions Program* which is open to all residents of Lancaster County who are sixty-five years of age or older. Qualified residents may attend day or evening courses as auditors, free of charge, on a space-available basis with the permission of the course instructor.

York College (York, Pa.) offers free tuition to all senior citizens enrolling in courses at this college.

The *"17–65" Program* at the *Sacred Heart University* (Bridgeport, Conn.) is an interesting idea. It permits superior secondary school students, ages sixteen or seventeen, to take a maximum of six semester hours of credit at the university gratis. These credits are held in escrow for them until a later date. When they are graduated from high school and are admitted to Sacred Heart as matriculated students, these credits are applied toward their bachelor's degree. Additionally, this program enables persons past the age of sixty-five to enroll on the same basis for a maximum of six semester hours per semester for credit. They could attend classes as a "retirement activity" or be admitted as matriculants.

Reduced Tuition

At *Roosevelt University* in Chicago, Ill., the tuition rate for senior citizens is less than one-half the price that other students pay. A Medicare card or other identification is needed to prove that the student is sixty-five years of age or older.

There are many non-credit Continuing Education opportunities available to persons sixty-five years of age or over for a fee of $3.00 at *Indiana State University's Division of Continuing Education and Extended Services*, Terre Haute, Indiana. This fee is much less than the amount charged to all others who enroll in these courses at ISU. The non-credit courses open to senior citizens at this small fee include: American Art Traditions in Perspective, Techniques of Drawing, Oil Painting as a Pastime, Water Color, Beginning Accounting, Estate Planning, Securities and Investing, Physical Fitness for Adults, Karate, German, Spanish, Introductory Numismatics, Creative Writing, Photography (Darkroom Techniques) and Needlepoint.

Senior citizens pay only $3.00 to take non-credit University Extension classes at the *University of Minnesota*. Senior citizens living in the Minneapolis area who would like further information and a free bulletin about these courses should phone 373-3195.

At *Southampton College* (Southampton, N.Y.), persons sixty years of age and over receive a fifty per cent tuition reduction if they wish to take any of the non-credit continuing education courses.

Diversified Short Courses

Many retirees have moved to Florida to enjoy the warm climate. Many among them are eager to take non-credit college courses—not just for cultural enrichment and enjoyment, but often to acquire a skill which will enable them to get part-time employment to supplement their social security checks.

At *Hillsborough Community College* in Tampa the Community Services Department offers *diversified short courses* to men and women who wish to explore new fields or increase their competency in a certain field. Included among these courses are: Blueprint Reading, Car Care for Women, Certified Professional Secretary, Commercial

Floristry, Folk Guitar, Home Landscaping, Insurance, Interior Design, Managing the Small Business, Nursing, Painting and Drawing, Photography, Private Pilot Course (Ground School), Puppetry, Rapid Reading, Real Estate, Stocks-Bonds and Mutual Funds and Writing for Fun and Profit.

B. "UNDERPREPARED" STUDENTS

Concentrated Approach Program

The *Concentrated Approach Program* (CAP) of *North Dakota State University* (Fargo, N.D.) aims to aid the student with a weak academic background. Students with limited or inadequate academic preparation need help to overcome the initial hurdles of college life and this one-year program is designed to provide this help.

CAP freshmen take year-long developmental courses in place of the regular freshman program. The classes are small and each CAP student is provided with an upperclass student who serves as a tutor-counselor throughout this year. Upon successful completion of their CAP year, students receive a full freshman year of credit and continue on into regular sophomore classes.

CAP was originally intended for recent high school graduates who needed academic assistance and special counseling. Now, some mature adults whose education was interrupted are asking to be admitted to the Concentrated Approach Program; they are being accepted and are meeting with success.

If you would like to know more about CAP, write to: Concentrated Approach Program, College of Arts and Sciences, North Dakota State University, Fargo, N.D. 58102.

Project Access

In the Summer of 1969, *Johnson State College* (Johnson, Vt.) started its *Project Access* to give an opportunity to students who would like to attend college but who could not gain admission due to borderline high school grades. In the six-week Summer session, these students have a chance to prove that they are "late bloomers" capable of handling college-level courses.

Project Access students take two college courses, each in a different academic department, during the Summer session. In addition, they are required to take a non-credit *Communications Skills* course including *Remedial Reading* and *Writing Skills*. Students who receive acceptable grades in these courses are approved for admission as fully matriculated freshmen in September.

Tutor-counselors assist Project Access students on an individual basis. They aid these students with their problems, whether these problems are academic, emotional or social. They make every effort to help the students adjust to the college experience and succeed in the Summer program.

SUCCES

In the Fall 1971 term, *Hillsborough Community College* (Tampa, Fla.) inaugurated a program of compensatory, remedial education for students who were classified as "underprepared" for college work. The program is called SUCCES (Students Under Constant Challenge for Educational Success). Each student works under the guidance of a team of specialists dedicated to enhance the student's self-concept by providing a college level success experience. The student is then channeled into the program—academic, career or technical—which best suits his/her needs.

Would you like details about SUCCES? If you would, then write to: Vice President, Management Information Services, Hillsborough Community College, P.O. Box 22127, Tampa, Fla. 33622.

The Challenge Program

The Challenge Program of the *University of Michigan-Flint* is designed to broaden the educational opportunities of young men and women from the state of Michigan. The UM-F Challenge Program was begun in 1969 when it became all too obvious that many high school students do not perform as well in high school as they could on the basis of their native intelligence.

Poverty, lack of motivation, disadvantaged environment, illness at home and a variety of other personal and family circumstances often cause some students' school marks to be far below their potential, making it impossible for them to gain admission to college. The Challenge Program is a combined effort of the University of Michigan-Flint, Office of Special Projects and high school counselors. Together, they search for capable students who need help to improve their academic skills and raise their level of academic achievement.

Challenge I, the first phase of the UM-F Challenge Program, is called the *Pre-College Summer Seminar (PCSS)*. PCSS is a five-week program open to selected high school sophomores, juniors and seniors. During this program, the students are tested to determine their academic problems. This is followed by orientation, counseling, remedial and tutorial assistance, field trips, art seminars, theater and sessions in basic communication skills designed to upgrade the academic performance and skills of these students. When the students return to school in the Fall, their progress is followed; there are school and home visits and student conferences.

Challenge II, the *Challenge Scholar Program (CSP)*, is the second phase of the Challenge Program. CSP aims to assist Challenge Scholars by providing continued educational help to them after they have entered college. It offers these students the following six supportive services: 1) Tutorial assistance in any subject area in which a student is having difficulty; 2) Counseling to aid each student in selecting goals and directions; 3) Communications skills program; 4) Study skills class to improve the students' study techniques; 5) Bi-monthly group encounter sessions of freshman Challenge Scholars to increase their self-awareness; and 6) Reading improvement classes.

Early participation of high school students in the UM-F Challenge Program is recommended since they will then have one or two years during which to improve their academic skills and receive remedial help where needed. Students who would like to participate should speak with their high school counselors or contact the Office of Special Projects, University of Michigan-Flint, 1321 E. Court St., Flint, Mich. 48503.

The Prefreshman Program

Since 1959, *Dillard University* in New Orleans, La., has had an eight-week Summer pre-college program known as *The Prefreshman Program*. Dillard should be commended for having been so far ahead of the times, for even today a program such as this must certainly be considered innovative.

It was the success of this Prefreshman Program that brought about the development of the Upward Bound program on a national scale. The Summer Prefreshman Program aims to give students a head start on their collegiate programs. No college credit is given for attendance in this program. However, the special instruction and individual counseling given to Prefreshman students give them a clear advantage when they enter Dillard as full-time students in the Fall term. During the Summer program, they receive help in improving their reading skills, in developing their ability to write, in learning to concentrate, in acquiring better speech and listening habits and in becoming acquainted with the use of science materials and mathematical concepts, all of which will aid them in the college years which lie ahead of them.

Degree Program for Youth with Learning Disabilities

The Experimental Division of *Westminster College* (Fulton, Mo.) has initiated an unusual *Degree Program for Youth with Learning Disabilities*. This is an individualized, challenging program, but it is non-threatening. There are no required courses and the students are free to choose what they want to study to earn the B.A. degree.

Students are permitted to learn at their own pace. They may enroll in a combination of regular courses and tutorials. The *Autotutor,* a programmed learning machine, is used instead of regular courses and tutorials or to supplement the latter. Films, talking books, cassette tapes and similar devices may be used in lieu of or to supplement textbook assignments.

This program is flexible in order to help all of the students admitted to it to develop their potentials to the fullest extent possible. Students are accepted on the basis of their special interests, motivation, the extent of the learning disability, special resources or equipment needed and/or available and the decision as to whether or not they will benefit from this program. Details about this program may be obtained from the Director, Experimental Division, Westminster College, Fulton, Mo. 65251.

Adult Exemplary Cooperative Program

The *Moberly Area Junior College* (Moberly, Mo.) has an unusual program for the disadvantaged. This is the *Adult Exemplary Cooperative Program,* which started in July 1973.

To be considered "disadvantaged" and thus eligible for this program, the applicant must be in at least one of the following categories: 1) a member of a family with income less than the minimum standard level fixed by the U. S. Department of Labor; 2) a person with meagre education, whose educational deficiencies are basically responsible for this person's inability to succeed in the working world; 3) a member of a racial or ethnic minority of low socio-economic status; 4) a predelinquent—one whose history of antisocial behavior indicates that he/she may become a public offender; 5) a person on probation; 6) a person on parole; or 7) a person who has completed a sentence in a correctional institution.

Students pay no fees, since the program is funded by the federal government. On-the-job training is provided in work sites specifically chosen to meet the needs of each individual trainee. The teacher-trainee ratio is low allowing for close supervision, advisement and counseling.

The occupations for which training is included in this program are: 1) Health Services—Nurse Aide, Orderly Trainee, Medical Records Clerk, Ward Clerk; 2) Food Service—Hostess/Cashier, Short Order Cook, Waitress, Cook's Helper, Baker; 3) Mechanics—Industrial Maintenance, Automotive Engine Programs. These programs vary in length from eight to sixteen months.

If you would like details about this program, write to the Director of Special Programs, Moberly Area Junior College, College and Rollins Streets, Moberly, Mo. 65270.

Behind the Walls

While the "University Without Walls" concept is growing in popularity, there are also an increasing number of uniquely nontraditional students attending classes "with walls," for these students are firmly ensconced "behind the walls" of correctional institutions.

Since September 1966, *Ashland College* (Ashland, Ohio) has sent instructors into the Ohio State Reformatory (Mansfield, Ohio) and offered college level courses for credit "behind the walls." Neither the inmates nor the state of Ohio are charged tuition for these courses. After their release from the Reformatory, many of these students have gone on to complete their studies toward a college degree at Ashland and various other colleges.

Project NewGate

The School of Community Service and Public Affairs of the *University of Oregon* administers *Project NewGate*, which aims to help prisoners get a college education. Inmates at the Oregon State Penitentiary may engage in college preparatory studies and, upon successful completion of these, embark upon a regular college program.

When these inmates are ready for this "outside" phase, they are placed on "school release status."

At the University of Oregon, these students live at a special Campus Center, a facility designed to prepare them for the next phase, namely, parole and independent living. Intensive counseling and other supportive services are offered to these students throughout Project NewGate.

3.

UNUSUAL SCHEDULES

The traditional student is accustomed to the usual schedule of two semesters, the Fall semester and the Spring semester, followed by a Summer session. In an effort to enrich the college student's educational experiences, many colleges have begun to experiment and introduce innovations to their academic calendars. Thus, nontraditional schedules are appearing in increasing numbers on the campuses throughout the nation. Let us look at some interesting, truly unusual schedules.

4-1-4 Schedule (January Month)

One of the most popular innovations is the "4-1-4" calendar. This consists of a four-month Fall term, a one-month January term and a four-month Spring term. The January term carries many different titles and its format and course content vary too with each college and university; some have modified January terms of less than one-month duration.

DePauw University in Greencastle, Indiana, is one of the institutions of higher education with a 4-1-4 schedule. The four-week January term is here known as the *Winter Term*. During the Winter Term, students are encouraged to concentrate on one specific project, either their own or a faculty-initiated project. Students may work individually or on a group project, as long as the project is imaginative and innovative.

Among the more than one hundred Winter Term projects in which DePauw students may participate are the following especially challenging ones: Brief Survey of Beethoven Sonatas, Theological Interpretations of Freedom, Communicative Disorders, Drugmobile, Amateur Radio Communication, Welding Sculpture Workshop, How to Read and Write Chinese, Special Projects in Mental Health, Recent Themes in Soviet Foreign Policy, Community Action (Getting involved with the Hispano-American Center and Operation Breadbasket in Indianapolis), Tragedy, Jewelry Design, Science Laboratory Experience, New Trends in American Diplomacy, Science Fiction: Art and Commentary, Research Topics in Psychology, Experiments in Theatre, Biblical Hebrew and Freedom and Determinism.

Lincoln College in Lincoln, Illinois, is another college that operates on the 4-1-4 calendar and calls its January term, the *Winter Term.* During the Winter Term, concentrated college courses are available on and off campus.

Courses are available off campus in Lincoln's Winter Term in Geology (4 credits), Marine Biology (3 or 4 credits), Music (2 credits), Comparative Governments and Culture and Survey of European Art (5 credits) and Skiing (1 credit). On campus in the Winter Term, students have a choice from among the following three-credit courses: Principles of Investments, Principles of Finance, Introduction to Special Education, English Composition (Expository Writing), Studies in Literature, World Economic Geography, Fine Arts Survey, American Folk Music, Asian Studies, Fundamentals of Math, Logic, Sociology, Conversational Spanish and Children's Theatre. For two credits, there are: History (Life of Lincoln), First Aid—Safety and Ceramics.

An additional nontraditional aspect of Lincoln's Winter Term is the opportunity to obtain credit for "home reading." By reading certain prescribed books and passing examinations thereafter, students can obtain one credit each in Readings in Biology, Readings in Business Administration, Political Science (The American Presidency) and/or Parapsychology (Borderline of Science).

The month of January is the *Winter Term* at *Wells College* (Aurora, N.Y.) too. Wells has been operating on the 4-1-4 academic calendar since 1969. Students carry one course during the Winter Term, in contrast to four courses during the Fall and Spring terms. Among the four-week courses that have been given in the Winter Term are: Acting, Art of Picasso, Black Writers of the Spanish Language, Culture of the North American Indians, Fundamentals of Radioactivity, Music and Poetry, Rural Confrontation, Surrealism in France, Urban Confrontation and Zen and Existentialism.

Lee College (Cleveland, Tenn.), operating on the 4-1-4 schedule, calls its month of January the *Mid-Winter Term*. Students may take only one course during the Mid-Winter Term and receive credit for this course equal to the credit gained for a course in the regular semester. On-campus studies, off-campus studies, independent studies and exchange classes with cooperating institutions on a 4-1-4 schedule are available to Lee students during the Mid-Winter Term.

Among the offerings open to students in Mid-Winter 1974 were: Man and His Environment (Human Ecology), Modern Western World (European Travel Seminar), Role of Women in the Church, Secretarial Development, Travel Seminar in Education and Psychology (Travel Study Program Concentrated in England and Switzerland) and Winter Sports (Skiing, Ice Skating, Hiking, Hockey). (See Chapter 7 for information about the course on a Mediterranean cruise ship.)

Marywood College in Scranton, Pa., has a four-week *Winterim* session in January. The Winterim enables students to engage in unusual learning opportunities through travel-study groups, independent projects, extended field trips and nontraditional courses. Among the nontraditional offerings are: Anatomy for the Artist, Eros and Thanatos, Law and the Modern Woman and The Occult Revolution.

In the 1974 Winterim, the Art and Classics Departments sponsored a "Tour of Our Western Classical Heritage: Greece and Italy," the English Department sponsored a "Trip to Ireland" and the Foreign Languages Department sponsored a three and one-half week session for American students of French at Laval University (Quebec City, Canada) and a three-week program in Spain.

At *Saint Olaf College* in Northfield, Minn., the *January Interim*, as it is called, is a period of four weeks of intensive study in one course area. Students have opportunities to conduct individual research and intensive creative work not generally possible in the normal classroom situation. Students may work alone or with one or more students, depending upon the nature of the projects in which they participate. Many projects are conducted off campus, and this may make it necessary for the student-participants to go to various parts of the United States, the Americas and abroad. The *January Interim Catalog* lists and describes the many and varied Interim offerings of Saint Olaf.

Colby College-New Hampshire (New London, N.H.) inaugurated its 4-1-4 calendar in the Fall of 1970 and its first *January Interim Winter Term* took place in January 1971. Its January Interim is four weeks long and students generally take one course during this term.

Colby is basically a traditional school with on-campus courses, but, during the January Interim, students have numerous nontraditional approaches available to them, such as off-campus courses, study at some other college, career apprenticeships, internships, field research and independent study and travel abroad.

Among the offerings in the 1974 Interim were courses in Ceramic Sculpture, Clues to Keyboards (Piano, Harpsichord, Organ), Mythology, "Witches and Warlocks and Things That Go Bump in the Night" (Study of the Occult), "The Oriental Mind" (Oriental Culture), Perspectives on Human Sexuality and Scientific Research in Transcendental Meditation.

The 4-1-4 academic calendar is increasing in popularity at *Newberry College* (Newberry, S.C.). Each year, a larger number of students engage in independent study projects during the *Interim Term*. Students may also earn credit for work experience, travel and self-directed study courses during this term.

The *January Interim* at *Thiel College* (Greenville, Pa.) has included a course entitled "June in January" since 1973. Students indicate the field in which they wish to work for the month of January to help them determine whether that is the field they wish to pursue as their post-college career. They are then placed in appropriate off-campus internship programs with local or, in some cases, distant agencies and businesses. Students work as regular employees, but receive no remuneration. Instead, they receive credit for one course after getting a "passing" evaluation by an on-the-job supervisor and writing a paper describing their internship experiences.

Anna Maria College in Paxton, Mass., also has a 4-1-4 calendar with a *January Interim*. Students suggest the subjects for interim study. The topics for such short courses have ranged from Home and Auto Mechanics to tours abroad. Academic credit is granted for the successful completion of these courses.

At *Westminster College* (New Wilmington, Pa.), several travel seminars have been conducted in the *January Interim*. These study abroad programs carry one course unit of credit. Programs have taken place in England, France, Germany, Italy, Japan, Mexico and Spain. Westminster also had field experience and internship opportunities in the January 1974 interim in the Art, Biology, Business, Chemistry, Education, English, History, Music, Physics, Political Science, Psychology, Religion and Sociology departments.

The four-week *January Interim* started in 1971 at *Oklahoma Baptist*

University (Shawnee, Okla.), and since then students have had the opportunity to take many unusual courses and trips. In the 1974 Interim, some students traveled to Mexico to explore the contrast of life styles within the Mexican culture in a course entitled "From Then Till Now in Mexico." Other students enrolled in "Broadway or Bust," a drama-music course which included a trip to New York City where students viewed varied professional stage works, plays, operas and concerts.

Some unusual courses in this Interim were "So You Want to Be An Admiral" (a study of the fundamentals of sailing), "A Raku Happening" (a ceramic study of the Japanese art of raku pottery), "State Legislative Internship" (political science students served as interns for state legislators in Oklahoma City), Communications or Manipulation?—The Public Relations Profession, Creating Material for Children to Read, Gourmet Cooking and Workshop in Creative Children's Drama.

The month of January is used as an *Independent Activities Period* at the *Massachusetts Institute of Technology* (MIT) in Cambridge, Mass. More than 600 special activities are available to students during this period. These activities include individual projects, seminars, mini-courses, films, labs, workshops, lectures on campus and such off-campus activities as field trips and academic projects abroad. The Independent Activities Period was established in 1970 to add a new dimension to the students' programs between their first and second terms each year. While many students use this period for study and research in their field of interest or in a new field, others use it for travel, relaxation and exploration.

Franklin Pierce College (Rindge, N.H.), a young, liberal arts college, adopted the 4-1-4 academic calendar in 1969 and has since then been making many exciting experiences available to its students in the January four-week "mini-semester," which it calls the *January Intersession*. Students are encouraged to exercise their imagination and creative talents by getting involved in innovative projects and experiences in the areas of their personal interest.

Four successful January Intersessions must be completed by Franklin Pierce students to fulfill their graduation requirements. During these Intersessions, students may work alone in cooperation with a faculty sponsor on an independent study project, participate in a group activity leading to collective confrontation with a problem, work in close relationship with a sponsoring faculty member on a directed study project or serve an internship in a learning-working situation. Under the "January Exchanges" arrangements, students are free to take on-campus courses or engage in off-campus projects at any of the other colleges which function on the 4-1-4 academic calendar.

On-campus January Intersession programs at Franklin Pierce include African Literature, Experimental Parapsychology, Glass Workshop, House Plants, Imagery in the Theater, Methods and Materials of Oil Painting, Needlework, Raku Workshop, Sexism and Weaving. Among the off-campus programs that involve travel abroad are such trips as: 1) "A Musical Tour of Europe," 2) "Benedict Arnold's March on Quebec," 3) "Colombia: From the Spanish Main to the Amazon," 4) "Dickens and His World," 5) "Germany Today," 6) "High Adventure in History—Antigua and Thereabouts," 7) "Intersession à Paris," 8) "Ireland," 9) "Mexican Caravan" and 10) "Spain: The Land and Her People."

Another college with a 4-1-4 calendar and a *January Intersession* is *Harriman College* (Harriman, N.Y.). Here the Intersession is three weeks long. Regular students may participate in the offerings of this Intersession without paying any additional tuition.

Johns Hopkins University (Baltimore, Md.) also has a *January Intersession* of about three weeks in length. Students and faculty may engage in voluntary activity during this Intersession. Many students use this period for innovative activities, including independent projects, field trips, theater workshops and "language" trips abroad. Students who wish to take credit courses during this Intersession may take a maximum of three credits, for which no tuition fee is charged.

In January 1975, *Adrian College* (Adrian, Mich.) started a *January Interim* program which, like the Harriman and Johns Hopkins Intersessions, is just three weeks long. This is a three-week experience during which students concentrate on one course and study it in depth. Each Interim course carries two semester hours credit at no additional cost, unless the student selects an off-campus course, in which case there is an extra charge.

Culver-Stockton College in Canton, Mo., in 1969 inaugurated a three-week *January Interim* during which many courses are offered on campus and off campus for credit. Included among these courses are: Contemporary Economic Problems, Contemporary Theatre Workshop, Contemporary Urban Issues, Development of American Jazz and "Pop" Music, History of Twentieth Century China, Literature of Fantasy and Science Fiction, Mark Twain Seminar, Political Power in

America, Problems of Contemporary Business Management, Seminar in Drugs and Drug Abuse, Seminar on Alcoholism, Twentieth Century Opera, United Nations Seminar, Violence in America and Writing Workshop and Clinic.

The academic calendar of *Northern State College* (Aberdeen, S.D.) includes an *Interim* of a maximum of three weeks. Many diverse options for one-, two- and three-week study opportunities are available during the Interim program. Tours, individual study projects and other special courses are among the Interim offerings.

Bennett College (Millbrook, N.Y.) operates on a 4-1-4 schedule. However, its one-month *Winter Term* consists of three weeks in January and one week in February, extending as it does from the second week in January through the first week in February. Students at Bennett are required to complete a Winter Term course or project each year. This four-week term gives the students the opportunity for intensive work in a single course, project or independent study.

Although Bennett is a two-year college for women, both male and female students from other colleges on 4-1-4 calendars are welcome to enroll in any of the Winter Term offerings. Among the four-credit offerings are: Advanced Horsemanship, Children's Theatre, Fashion Design, Interior Design, Seminar in Photography and Independent Projects in each of the following subjects: Art, Biology, Child Study, Mathematics and Physical Science. There is an interesting three-credit course in Science Fiction.

In the 1974 Bennett Winter Term, there were the following two unique study abroad opportunities: 1) Creative Writing in Spain for four credits in Mojacar, Almeria, Spain to give students the opportunity to explore and develop their creative potential under the stimulus of the Spanish countryside, and 2) Linguaski, a three-credit, four-week stay in France, one week of which is in Paris and the other three weeks in the Alps where the students participate in daily skiing and French language classes.

Mount Saint Mary College in Newburgh, N.Y., has a fifteen-day *January Term* generally extending from January 2nd through January 18th.

The *Interim Session* at *New Mexico State University* (Las Cruces, N.M.) occurs during the first two weeks in January for a ten-day period. Interim courses carry one or two credits each. Among the one-credit courses are Basic Welding, Business Machines, Child Psychology for Youth Workers, Clouds and Rainmaking, Elementary

Chinese, Jazz Performance, Quake Prediction and Specialized Shorthand Dictation and Transcription. Among the two-credit Interim courses are Broadcast Copyright Law, Children's Theatre Tour, Classroom Media, Essentials of Alchemy, Films and Literature, Organizational Psychology and Management and Women's Studies.

The *Liberal Arts College of Fordham University at Lincoln Center* in New York City functions on the 4-1-4 schedule and has an active January term, here called the *January Program*. In this January Program, there are many course offerings in the form of seminars and individual and group projects. Students have the chance to concentrate on studies which are of special interest to them. They can conduct particular projects, on or off the campus, which could not be undertaken during the regular sessions. One project is a full-time program for the month of January, and successful completion of this project entitles the student to credit for one course.

January study at *Widener College* (Chester, Pa.) is also called the *January Program*. Students must complete a specified minimum number of January Programs to fulfill the requirements for graduation. The opportunity to concentrate on one in-depth independent study project is especially attractive to many students. This enables these students to give vent to their creative talents in their areas of special interest.

Some unique offerings in the January Program at Widener are: 1) "January Experience at PARC," which involves working with students at the Work Training Center of the Philadelphia Association for Retarded Children (PARC); 2) "Instructional Television Production," which considers many facets of television production and in which each student participates in a group end-of-term TV production; 3) "Noise and Man," which is an in-depth exposure to the field of noise pollution; 4) "Photography in the Laboratory," which is an introduction to the use of photography in the scientific laboratory; and 5) "Study Tour of American Art Museums," which includes trips to a number of outstanding American art institutions.

Franklin and Marshall College (Lancaster, Pa.) has a *January Studies Plan* between the two semesters, and students have the chance to take one course during each annual January term. Experimental courses are encouraged during this term. In January 1974, students were able to earn four credits for one course chosen from among about thirty on-campus offerings, four off-campus travel programs or an independent study project pursued either on or off campus.

The off-campus travel courses and the departments which offered them included Mexican Field Expedition (Anthropology), Modern British Theater Practice (Drama), Contemporary Political Problems in Britain and France (Government) and Spanish Conversation and Composition in Spain (Spanish). Some rather unique on-campus January courses at Franklin and Marshall are Museology, Nautical Astronomy and Celestial Navigation, Greek and Roman Comedy, Philosophies of Punishment, Mysticism and Spiritual Practices and Pentecostal Movements.

4-1-4-1 (January and June Months)

Mitchell College (Statesville, N.C.) operates essentially on an unusual 4-1-4-1 schedule. In addition to the one-month *January Interim*, there is also a one-month *June Summer Session*. Additionally, a number of courses have been completely individualized and for these courses a flexible academic calendar is in operation. This means that students may register for and complete these courses at any time during the year.

May Term

The *Experimester* is a unique mini-semester in the month of May at *Geneva College*, Beaver Falls, Pa. Special courses from one to four weeks in duration are offered on an optional basis on and off campus. This brief session is an experimental innovation designed to encourage new modes of learning.

At *Lycoming College*, Williamsport, Pa., there is also a four-week term in May called simply the *May Term*. A wide range of credit-granting courses are offered. There are on-campus independent study projects, on-campus traditional and nontraditional courses and off-campus nearby, distant and foreign travel opportunities.

Among the nontraditional offerings at Lycoming, there have been the following: Fisheries Management, Field Ornithology, Indian Archaeology, Speleology, Thought Transference and the Cosmic Theatre. The Bermuda Biological Station for Research at St. Georges was the site of a course entitled "Introduction to Marine Biology and Biological Oceanography." "Field Experience in Sociology—Anthropology" was based in the tri-cultural community of North Central New Mexico. "The Washington Minimester: A Course in Practical Politics" was based in Washington to analyze the workings of our national government.

Weekend College

A recent addition to alternatives in college schedules, and indeed a most welcome alternative, is the *Weekend College.*

The *C. W. Post Center of Long Island University* in Greenvale, Long Island, N.Y., started its *Weekend College* in 1971. Weekend College is designed to meet the needs of persons who are unable to attend classes during the week—working men and women of all ages, housewives who could not otherwise go to college, students who seek professional growth and/or personal enrichment, students who wish to return to college after a time lapse and academically talented high school students who seek to accelerate their progress toward a college degree.

Students may earn three credits per Weekend College schedule. Classes are held during the following time periods: a) Six Saturdays, from 9:00 a.m. to 3:00 p.m. (including lunch); b) Six Sundays, from 10:00 a.m. to 4:00 p.m. (including lunch); and c) Two intensive weekends, Saturdays from 9:00 a.m. to 5:00 p.m. (including lunch) and Sundays from 9:00 a.m. to 5:00 p.m. (including lunch). Students may attend six Saturdays only, six Sundays only, six Saturdays and Sundays, or two intensive weekends. The amount of credits earned and the length of time it takes to complete the requirements for a degree will vary according to the students' schedules.

C. W. Post Weekend College degree programs include the Associate of Arts in General Studies, the Associate of Arts in Humanistic Studies and the Bachelor of Science in Nursing. The A.A. in General Studies may in itself serve as the students' academic goal or it may serve as a stepping stone toward other fields of interest and toward the baccalaureate degree. The Associate of Arts in Humanistic Studies is a recently added innovative program which aims to respond to an expressed interest by industry to enhance the humanistic awareness of its staff. It provides adult men and women with an opportunity for study of the humanities. Students in this program may be awarded up to twelve credits for acceptable life experience. After earning the A.A. in Humanistic Studies, students may continue on toward the B.A. degree at C. W. Post. The Bachelor of Science degree with a major in Nursing is an upper division program for registered professional nurses which enables them to learn while they are earning a salary in their professional careers.

C. W. Post Weekend College has a unique feature called "Spouse Tuition." Thus, if a husband and wife enroll in the same course, one pays the full tuition price while the other receives a special discount rate. For further details about this and all other features of this Weekend College, write to the Registrar, Weekend College, C. W. Post Center, Long Island University, Greenvale, N.Y. 11548.

Mercy College in Dobbs Ferry, N.Y., has a *Weekend College* arrangement for those who are unable to attend classes on weekdays in the morning, afternoon or evening. By taking courses on Saturdays and Sundays exclusively, these students at Mercy, after a period of years, may complete a program leading to the Bachelor of Science degree with a major in Business Administration or Behavioral Sciences. Further information may be obtained by writing to the Director of Admissions, Mercy College, 555 Broadway, Dobbs Ferry, N.Y. 10522.

For those people who would like to go to college or return to college to resume their education, but who complain that they are too busy for school during the weekdays, *Charles Stewart Mott Community College* in Flint, Mich., has initiated the *Weekender*. Courses are offered Friday evenings, Saturday mornings and afternoons and Sunday afternoons. Students—housewives, working people, retired workers, senior citizens or anyone eighteen years of age or older—may attend classes on any one, two or all three days. Courses may be taken for the purpose of advancing on one's job, for enjoyment and culture or to obtain an associate degree. This degree can be earned in only about three years by taking courses on the "Weekender" style. Child care facilities are available to permit mothers of young children to attend Weekender classes.

Among the courses offered at Mott Community College on this "Weekender" style are: Accounting, Algebra, American Government, Applied Psychology, Art Education, Biology Fundamentals, Blueprint Reading, Business, Business Math, Electrical Circuits, English Composition, Flight Theory, History of the United States, Land Surveying, Math, Music Appreciation, Police Administration, Reading Improvement, Refrigeration and Air Conditioning, Sociology, Speech Fundamentals, Technical Math, Typing, Welding and Women's Judo.

Would you like to know more about the Weekender? If you would, contact the Office of the President, Charles Stewart Mott Community College, 1401 E. Court St., Flint, Mich. 48503.

Saturday College

There are some so-called "Weekend Colleges" where classes are given on Saturdays only; these are actually *Saturday Colleges.*

The *Penn Valley Community College* (Kansas City, Mo.) has such a "Weekend College," which is really a *Saturday College,* for it permits students to earn an associate degree by attending classes on Saturdays only. There are two sixteen-week terms, just as there are in regular day and evening sessions. The classes in this Weekend College are given in two Saturday time blocks: 8:00 a.m. to 10:40 a.m. and 10:50 a.m. to 1:30 p.m. Students may earn six credit hours per term in this manner. Details may be obtained from the Director of Admissions, Penn Valley Community College, 560 Westport Rd., Kansas City, Mo. 64111.

In September 1969, *Edward Williams College,* a two-year liberal arts division of *Fairleigh Dickinson University* (Hackensack, N.J. & Wayne, N.J.) established its *Saturday College.* The Saturday College is a college for adults. The average age of the students is about thirty-five years of age, ranging from twenty-one for the youngest to a student past sixty who is the oldest. There are no formal admission requirements. Adults who have the desire and the ability to succeed in college level studies, but did not have the time, opportunity or inclination to go to college when they were younger, have a unique opportunity to do so here.

The academic year of the Saturday College consists of four terms, three of which are fifteen weeks in length and the fourth four weeks in length. Students who attend classes Friday evenings and Saturdays during all four terms could accumulate thirty credits in a calendar year. In two years, they could thus complete the entire sixty credits needed to be awarded the Associate in Arts (A.A.) degree. They can earn this degree in all liberal arts and business areas and can then transfer to the four-year baccalaureate degree programs at Fairleigh Dickinson University.

For details, write to the Director of Admissions, The Saturday College, Edward Williams College of Fairleigh Dickinson University, University Park, Hackensack, N.J. 07601.

Husson College in Bangor, Maine, offers a program which is titled an "External Degree Program," but which would more appropriately be called a "Saturday College" since the students attend classes on Saturdays only. Individuals who have been unable to go to college due to family responsibilities, work schedules or geographic location are given the opportunity to do so through Husson's Saturday College.

It is possible for a student to attend Saturday College (including Summer sessions) and thereby earn an Associate in Business Science degree in two years and a Bachelor of Science in Business Administration in four years. Through Saturday classroom sessions and independent study, a student may earn twelve credits in the Fall semester, twelve credits in the Spring semester and six credits in the Summer session, accumulating thirty credits annually. To enable persons throughout the state of Maine to participate in this program, Saturday College classes are held at Deering High School in Portland, Schenk High School in East Millinocket and Caribou High School in Caribou.

Would you like to obtain further information about this Saturday College? If you would, contact the Coordinator, Office of Continuing Education, Husson College, Bangor, Maine 04401.

Varied Nontraditional Schedules

Coker College (Hartsville, S.C.) has a college calendar which carries the unique title, "*3-3-3-1-2-2 system.*" This consists of ten-week academic quarters in the Fall, Winter and Spring, plus an Interim term of three weeks from mid-May to early June and two five-week Summer vacations. Students generally take three courses in each of the Fall, Winter and Spring quarters, one course during the Interim and two courses in each Summer Session.

There are many colleges that now operate on the *quarter schedule.* The *University of Montana* in Missoula, Mont. is an example of this. At Montana each quarter is approximately ten weeks in length. The Fall quarter starts in mid-September and runs until mid-December, the Winter quarter runs from early January through mid-March, and the Spring quarter from the end of March to early June. The Summer Session is made up of two four-and-a-half week half-sessions and a concurrent nine-week full session. At *Saint Francis College* in Biddeford, Maine, the academic calendar consists of *three ten-week terms.* Many students claim they learn more when they concentrate on a lesser number of courses at a time. Instead of students at Saint Francis taking five or six courses in each of two fifteen-week semesters in the traditional manner, the students concentrate on two or three courses in each of the three ten-week terms.

Madonna College in Livonia, Mich., has an unusual *"tri-term"* schedule which makes it possible for students to complete the bachelor's degree in three years. Term I (Fall Term) is fifteen weeks long, from September through December. Term II (Winter Term) is fifteen weeks long, January through April. Term III may be a twelve week combination of the Spring and Summer Terms or six weeks (Spring, May-June) and six weeks (Summer, June-July).

Hanover College in Hanover, Indiana, has an unusual schedule known as the *Hanover Plan*. Under this Plan, the academic calendar consists of a fourteen-week Fall Term, a fourteen-week Winter Term and a five-week Spring Term. Students take three courses each during the Fall and Winter Terms and only one course during the Spring Term. The Fall Term runs from September through December, the Winter Term from January through April and the Spring Term during May and June. This Plan gives students unusual opportunities for in-depth study and off-campus experiences. (See Chapter 12 for more information about the latter.)

Susquehanna University in Selinsgrove, Pa., has an annual calendar of three terms plus a Summer session. The First Term extends from September through November, the Second Term from December through February and the Third Term from March through May. Students are required to take three courses in each of the three terms and, as a consequence, this schedule is entitled *"Three Courses—Three Terms."* The granting of degrees at Susquehanna is not based on the accumulation of credits but on the successful completion of courses. Students must complete thirty-five courses in order to earn the baccalaureate degree.

A most unusual schedule exists at *Keuka College* (Keuka Park, N.Y.). Here, in 1972, a new *"10-5-10-8"* calendar was introduced. This consists of a ten-week Fall Term (September to mid-November), a five-week Field Period (Off-Campus Study, mid-November through December), followed by Christmas Recess, then a ten-week Winter Term (January to mid-March), a one-week Spring Recess and an eight-week Spring Term (end of March to mid-May). In the Fall and

Winter Terms, the students take three courses; in the Spring Term, they may take two courses concurrently for eight weeks or two four-week intensive study courses. The five-week Field Period is credited for the equivalent of one course.

In September 1971, *Whittier College* (Whittier, Calif.) introduced an innovative academic calendar. The schedule consists of seven sessions. There is a Fall Term composed of three five-week sessions, a four-week January Interim and a Spring Term of three five-week sessions.

Western College (Oxford, Ohio) has an unusual *modular arrangement* of its academic calendar. This modular arrangement is explained in the following chapter on degree programs, in which Western's non-traditional program is discussed.

4.

DEGREE PROGRAMS—INDIVIDUALIZED, DUAL AND DEFINITELY DIFFERENT

The traditional college has not only a traditional academic calendar, but also traditional predesigned major programs of study. Recently, varied nontraditional programs have been introduced in institutions of higher education throughout the nation. Majors have been undergoing minor and major changes in their titles, design and composition. There are now: A) individualized or self-designed major degree programs, B) dual degree programs and C) programs that could best be described as definitely different.

A. INDIVIDUALIZED DEGREE PROGRAMS

Many colleges have begun to permit their students to design their own programs. These individualized programs are varied in nature and have a variety of names. Let us examine some especially significant ones.

Freedom with Responsibility

Western College (Oxford, Ohio) was for many years a small, traditional liberal arts college. In 1970, many reforms were introduced and Western embarked upon a program called *Freedom with Responsibility* to permit students and professors the greatest possible freedom to act in a creative and effective fashion within the college community.

Students are free to design their own academic programs. This they do in consultation with their tutors. Every student has a professor with whom the student has a tutorial relationship. The tutor assists the student with program planning and all other aspects of the academic program. However, basically, the selection of individual learning experiences and determination of the specific direction of the student's program are the student's responsibility.

There are no "major" or "minor" fields of concentration in this program. There are "learning units." A learning unit may be a course, internship, seminar, travel-study program or other form of learning experience. The usual full-time academic program consists of three learning units. This full-time program, agreed upon by the student and tutor for a specified time period, is called a *contract*. The time period is known as a *module,* and the students, to remain in good standing, must live up to the terms of their *modular learning contracts.*

Western's academic calendar, a most nontraditional one, consists of four disparate time modules designed to permit maximum flexibility in program planning. The calendar and modular lengths are as follows: Module I—12 weeks; Winter Vacation—3 weeks; Module II—4 weeks; Module III—6 weeks; Spring Vacation—2 weeks; and Module IV—10 weeks. Generally, students take three learning units in each module, with the exception of Module II, which consists of the four weeks in January and is designed for independent study and intensive work in a single project (single learning unit).

To qualify for the Bachelor of Arts degree, the student must satisfactorily complete sixteen time modules, consisting of four each of Modules I, II, III and IV. In 1974, Western became a division of Miami University. This has made available to the students many more modular learning experiences with additional course, internship and study-abroad opportunities.

Details about this new, experimental program may be obtained from the Vice President for Academic Administration, Western College, Oxford, Ohio 45056.

The IDP at Trinity

The *Individualized Degree Program (IDP)* at *Trinity College* in Hartford, Conn., offers highly motivated, intellectually mature students the opportunity to benefit from self-designed, self-paced learning. The IDP went into operation in April 1973. It is a flexible program geared to the needs of each individual student.

By means of the IDP, a student may complete the requirements for the bachelor's degree in as little as three years or as much as ten years depending upon the pace at which each student can proceed according to individual circumstances and needs. The program is open to residential undergraduates and to non-resident older persons (above the age of twenty-two) in the Connecticut Valley region; these older students may hold full-time employment and/or maintain home and family responsibilities while studying toward their undergraduate degrees.

The curriculum of the IDP consists of the general education (the "non-major") phase followed by the more specialized studies (the "major") phase. Requirements of the non-major phase are achieved by completing twenty-four Study Units plus specific integrative projects. Faculty members are available to discuss the subject matter of the Study Units with IDP students and to help them define their projects, conduct the research and prepare the final work.

In the "major" phase, IDP students select a major from among any of the following departmental and interdisciplinary major programs: Art History, Biochemistry, Biology, Chemistry, Classics, Comparative Literature, Economics, Engineering, English, History, Intercultural Studies, Mathematics, Modern Languages (French, German or Spanish), Music, Philosophy, Physics, Political Science, Psychology, Religion, Sociology, Studio Arts, Theatre Arts and Urban-Environmental Studies.

These programs emphasize independent study culminating in comprehensive examinations and/or major projects. Little, if any, formal class activity is required, with the exception of the sciences and languages where some laboratory and classroom work are mandatory. Each student is assigned a departmental IDP advisor who offers guidance in how the major requirements are to be fulfilled. For more detailed information about the IDP at Trinity, write to: Director, Individualized Degree Program, Trinity College, Hartford, Conn. 06106.

Colgate II Proficiency Based Degree Program

In 1974, *Colgate University* in Hamilton, N.Y., inaugurated a nontraditional *Proficiency Based Degree Program,* otherwise known as *Colgate II.* Colgate II is a flexible undergraduate degree program which offers motivated students the opportunity to design for themselves programs to meet their specific needs and interests.

"Fields" rather than separate courses serve as the core of this alternative program. Colgate II students may choose from a variety of fields open to them. A "field" is an organized plan of study leading to the mastery of a discipline or an interest that may cross disciplinary boundaries. Students must use their own initiative to decide how they will master their chosen fields; there are various options available to them, such as self-study by reading books and other materials, conducting independent study projects, participating in tutorial groups and even taking regular Colgate courses.

Upon being accepted into Colgate II, students are assigned individual tutors from the fields closest to the center of their interests. The tutors serve as principal advisors to their Colgate II students. To a great extent, the success of this program depends upon the effectiveness of the relationship between student and tutor.

All Colgate students have a common freshman year. Admission in Colgate II takes place in the sophomore year, and the most important criterion for admission is the ability of the student to endure a program of independent study. Students may work at their own pace. However, they must be guided by the fact that the total time to complete their program may not exceed five years nor be less than three years.

Each student must choose three (or four) of the fields in Colgate II. After becoming proficient in these fields at the introductory level, the student may proceed to the intermediate level in three of the fields. The advanced level follows after proficiency has been achieved at the intermediate level. However, the student chooses one of the three fields, the field of primary interest, and takes only that one field through the advanced level.

The fields available to Colgate II students include: 1) Canada Studies; 2) History and Society in the Indian Ocean Basin; 3) The Sociology of Development in Historical and Comparative Perspective; 4) The Development of Civilization: Problems of Process and Causality; 5) Comparative Socio-Economic Systems; 6) Quantitative Economics; 7) General Integrative (Systemic) Theories and Methods, and Their Applications to Future-Oriented Planning and Management of Individual and Social Change; 8) Musical Studies; 9) Fine Arts: Practice and Theory of Contemporary Art; 10) Medieval and Renaissance Studies; 11) Romance Studies I: The Contemporary French Novel; 12) Romance Studies II: Theatre in France; 13) Romance Studies III: The Spanish Theatre of the Golden Age; 14) The Philosophy of Religion; 15) Formal Systems and Their Application; 16) Computer and Information Science; 17) Mathematics: Techniques for Applications; 18) Human Information Processing: Developmental and Social Aspects; 19) Chemistry; 20) History of the Earth; 21) Greek

Civilization; 22) The History of Modern and Contemporary Western Philosophy; and 23) Oceanography.

Would you like to know more about Colgate II? If so, write to the Provost, Colgate University, Hamilton, N.Y. 13346.

FLEX

FLEX, "a new format for higher education," is the recently initiated program at *Limestone College* (Gaffney, S.C.), which requires the students to design their own programs of study and to choose the subjects which will constitute their degree programs. The students do this while working closely with the faculty sponsor who was assigned to them when they were admitted to Limestone. The sponsors aid the students in choosing a curriculum and advise them regarding state teacher certification and graduate and professional school requirements. FLEX thus helps to insure that the students' individual programs are consistent with their capabilities, needs, prior achievements and interests.

FLEX is designed to produce a strong independent studies program. Limestone operates on a 4-1-4 schedule. The January Interim offers students the opportunity to work on independent study projects of particular interest to them. In the Interim, they can also participate in travel abroad study programs and explore with groups of students special subjects of current interest and relevance.

If you would like to receive details about the FLEX program, write to the Director of Admissions, Limestone College, Gaffney, S.C. 29340.

Kaskaskia Plan

The *Kaskaskia Plan* at *Northeastern Illinois University* in Chicago aims to give undergraduates a four-year experience in designing their own curricula. It is a program option open to all undergraduates. It enables them to pursue coherent educational programs that will serve their individual goals better than the existing standard programs. Kaskaskia students must develop a good, working relationship with a faculty member who serves as their advisor, since adequate advisement is considered to be the key element to the success of these individually designed programs.

All Kaskaskia students are encouraged to participate in PIE projects (see Chapter 5), field work, independent study, internships and similar activities as normal components of their programs. They are excused from the basic thirty hours required of all other under-graduates and from the traditional academic major. However, to assure some degree of intellectual discipline and academic rigor, Kaskaskia students in pursuit of their Bachelor of Arts degree must choose and design, in consultation with their advisor, any one of three alternative channels, namely, 1) general studies, 2) concentration or 3) major.

If you would like to learn more about this program, contact the Kaskaskia Plan Coordinator, Center for Program Development, North-eastern Illinois University, Bryn Mawr at St. Louis Ave., Chicago, Ill. 60625.

Open Curriculum

Bradford College, a small liberal arts college in Haverhill, Mass., which basically offers a two-year program leading to the Associate in Arts degree, has an *Open Curriculum.*

The Open Curriculum at Bradford is known as "the interest route." Students design their own programs, selecting courses from over eighty offerings in the Arts, Humanities, Natural Sciences and Social Sciences. They may choose workshops, interdisciplinary seminars and arrange their own independent research projects according to their individual interests. Only one course is a required one and that is a year-long freshman tutorial that combines English composition with directed independent research.

Bradford accepts "accelerated students," that is, students who have completed only three years of high school. The January Interim in Bradford's 4-1-4 calendar gives students the opportunity to do con-centrated, independent work in projects of their own choosing.

In December 1971, Bradford was authorized to grant a baccalaureate degree with a major in Urban Studies. The program for this degree involves intensive study and is so compactly arranged that students can earn the degree within fifteen months after receiving their Asso-ciate in Arts degree. This acceleration is accomplished through the use of two summer terms. The second summer session is spent in London to give the students the opportunity to study urban phenomena in a non-American setting.

For further information about Bradford's Urban Studies and other programs, write to: President, Bradford College, Haverhill, Mass. 01830.

Personal Major

At *Saint Francis College* in Biddeford, Maine, there is the *Personal Major*. Students who do not wish to take any of the traditional major programs may design their own individual, nontraditional, interdisciplinary or multi-disciplinary majors and have their own Personal Major.

Special Studies Major

The *Special Studies Major* at *Central Connecticut State College* (New Britain, Conn.) enables students to develop their own individualized academic programs drawing upon regular course offerings from many academic departments according to each student's personal interests and future career needs.

Educational Discovery

Freshmen at *Simmons College* (Boston, Mass.) may participate, if they wish, in the *"educational discovery"* program. Instead of enrolling in regular classes, the students in this program work together with faculty advisors to design their individual programs and projects. The latter may include films, independent reading, small seminars, listening to visiting speakers and volunteer work.

Simmons aims to prepare its students for "a life-long career after graduation." Many of its programs and projects, including off-campus field work, are geared to helping the students define their career goals.

If you have any inquiries about the educational discovery program, send your questions to the Admissions Office, Simmons College, 300 The Fenway, Boston, Mass. 02115.

Curriculum for Self-Determined Studies

Herbert H. Lehman College of the City University of New York introduced the "Experimental Curriculum" in 1969. The name has since been changed to *Curriculum for Self-Determined Studies* (CSS). It is for those who seek to acquire more intellectual and personal satisfaction from their college years than might otherwise be possible.

CSS is designed for students who possess the ability to work independently and the maturity to plan their own programs for intellectual growth. Students may enter CSS either at the start of their freshman year or after they have earned one semester's worth of credit. There is a strict selection process for admission into CSS and those who wish to enter directly from high school must have an academic average of not less than 85 per cent and/or a combined verbal and mathematical SAT score of 1,110. Those who seek to enter CSS after they have completed one semester at Lehman need two letters of recommendation in place of the minimal high school average and SAT scores.

The five basic elements of CSS are: 1) seminars, 2) free choice of courses, 3) special sections, 4) extra-credit options and 5) interdisciplinary areas of specialization. Thus, CSS students may originate their own seminars when subjects of special interest to them are not offered in the regular Lehman curriculum. Although they must complete the basic courses in their area of concentration, beyond this, CSS students are free to select whatever courses they desire to satisfy their career interests. They may enter special sections of basic courses that cover a certain subject more fully. By means of the extra-credit option available to them, CSS students may complete a project or written assignment and receive extra credit as a reward for their initiative and effort beyond what is required. They may select an interdisciplinary program if the area of specialization in which they wish to concentrate requires expertise in more than one academic department.

It can be said that CSS gives students the advantages of attending a small college while belonging to and retaining the facilities of a larger institution. They are free to test the extent of their abilities and to immerse themselves thoroughly in their favorite subjects.

Would you like to know more about CSS? If so, contact the Office of the Curriculum for Self-Determined Studies, Lehman College, Bronx, N.Y. 10468.

Student Initiated Majors

In 1971, *Keuka College* (Keuka Park, N.Y.) introduced its new curriculum with *Student Initiated Majors*. Students are responsible for their own academic pursuits and are free to design their own programs based on their individual interests, experiences and goals, unrestricted by general course requirements. They have the opportunity to combine courses and independent studies from two or more academic departments and create a sequence of courses consistent with their special career goals.

Some students have initiated majors in such combined areas as Drama, English and Music; History, Philosophy and Religion; and Biology and Chemistry. There are a multitude of possible course combinations for student initiated majors based on the individual student's interests. Keuka College also has a unique five-week Field Period (see Chapter 7) which permits students to participate in challenging experiences related to their vocational goals.

If you would like details about the new curriculum at this college for women, write to the Office of Admissions, Keuka College, Keuka Park, N.Y. 14478.

Experimental College Program

Minot State College (Minot, N.D.) has established an *Experimental College Program* which offers a four-year bachelor's degree program in Science Education with Earth Science emphasis, a two-year liberal arts program which meets the general education requirements for many of the bachelor's degree programs at Minot State and special courses and projects.

In this program, students are encouraged to assume responsibility for their own education. Interdisciplinary approaches are promoted. Individualized instruction is emphasized. A stimulating learning environment is fostered by a close student-faculty relationship.

About thirty to fifty short courses—*minicourses*—dealing with a single concept or skill and generally carrying one quarter hour of credit are offered during each quarter. Short and long field trips, faculty initiated projects and study groups, special lectures, single class sessions on topics of special interest, off-campus experiences and miscellaneous student initiated offerings are all part of the Experimental College Program. This program should have special appeal to those who are interested in Science, particularly in Earth Science.

If you would like a brochure and further information, contact the Director, Experimental College Program, Minot State College, Minot, N.D. 58701.

Guided Free Choice Experiment

Increasing numbers of colleges are giving their students the opportunity to select the courses they wish and organize a four-year curriculum of their own choice and liking. At *Saint Meinrad College* (St. Meinrad, Ind.), the authorities began to wonder whether students truly benefit from having the freedom to make their own course and curriculum choice. They, therefore, set up the Saint Meinrad College *Guided Free Choice Experiment*. This is a research project that aims to determine whether permitting students to choose their academic programs by guided free choice yields any difference in their general intellectual achievement, motivation and attitudes.

The Saint Meinrad Experiment involves two groups of students—a control group taking the regular prescribed program of studies and an experimental group with no required courses. Freshmen who entered Saint Meinrad in September 1972 and September 1973 belong to the experimental group. These students are exempt from any prescribed program of studies. Throughout their four years of college, on the basis of their individual academic strengths, weaknesses, interests and goals and with the guidance of a faculty advisor, they select of their own free choice those courses they wish to take. They receive the Bachelor of Arts in Liberal Studies after the successful completion of this four-year free choice program.

Members of Saint Meinrad's entering freshman classes of September 1971 and September 1974 belong to the control group. Their four years of college consist of the standard prescribed program of studies. Extensive testing is involved in this experiment with members of the experimental and control groups given a series of tests at the start of their freshman year and then again at the end of their freshman, sophomore and senior years.

With more and more colleges yielding to external and internal pressures to exempt students from certain traditional academic requirements and permit them to choose their courses as they wish, there is great need for an educational experiment of this kind. The results of the Guided Free Choice Experiment will be much welcome by all who are concerned about future directions of higher education and Saint Meinrad College is to be commended for conducting this experiment. Details may be had by contacting the Academic Dean, Saint Meinrad College, Saint Meinrad, Ind. 47577.

B. DUAL DEGREE PROGRAMS

Dual Degree Program

Berry College in Mount Berry, Ga., offers its students an interesting *"dual degree program."* This program makes it possible for a student to attend Berry for about three academic years and the *Georgia Institute of Technology (Georgia Tech)* for about two academic years and, after the successful completion of these courses, receive a bachelor's degree from both Berry and Georgia Tech. Georgia Tech awards the following bachelor's degrees in this program:

A) from its College of Engineering: the Bachelor of Aerospace Engineering, Ceramic Engineering, Chemical Engineering, Civil Engineering, Electrical Engineering, Engineering Economic Science, Engineering Science, Industrial Engineering, Mechanical Engineering, Nuclear Engineering, Science in Textile Chemistry, Science in Textiles and Textile Engineering.

B) from its General College: the Bachelor of Science in Physics and Information and Computer Science.

C) from its College of Industrial Management: the Bachelor of Science in Behavioral Management, Economics, General Management, Industrial Management and Management Science.

If you have any questions about the dual degree program, address your questions to the Academic Dean, Berry College, Mount Berry, Ga. 30149.

B.S.-M.D. Six-Year Program

Wilkes College (Wilkes-Barre, Pa.) offers a *six-year program* in conjunction with *Hahnemann Medical College* which leads to both the Bachelor of Science and Doctor of Medicine degrees. The program is designed to prepare Family Physicians. For details about this program, write to: Dean of Academic Affairs, Wilkes College, Wilkes-Barre, Pa. 18703. If you would like information about other colleges and universities which offer similar six-year programs, write to the Council on Medical Education, American Medical Association, 535 N. Dearborn St., Chicago, Ill. 60610.

Dual Degrees and Submatriculation

At the *University of Pennsylvania* (Philadelphia, Pa.), students may arrange to study for *two undergraduate degrees*. Thus, they may be matriculated for programs which yield a degree from the Wharton (Business), Engineering or Allied Medical Professions schools in addition to a liberal arts degree.

Students may also decide to undertake an intensified major program resulting in their earning *both the bachelor's and master's degrees* after only four years of study. In such cases, the students *"submatriculate"* in the Graduate School of Arts and Sciences or in the University's other graduate and professional schools. Students generally apply for submatriculation toward the end of their junior year and some of their senior year course work is counted toward the fulfillment of both degrees.

For further information about these dual degree programs, write to: Vice-Provost for Undergraduate Studies, University of Pennsylvania, Philadelphia, Pa. 19174.

C. DEFINITELY DIFFERENT PROGRAMS

The Racine Plan

In 1973, the *College of Racine* (Racine, Wisc.) introduced *The Racine Plan*. The academic calendar in this plan is certainly most nontraditional. There are six terms per year and each is seven weeks long. Thus, for example, the 1974–75 year was as follows: 1) September 9, 1974–October 25, 1974; 2) October 28, 1974–December 18, 1974; 3) January 6, 1975–February 21, 1975; 4) March 3, 1975–April 18, 1975; 5) April 21, 1975–June 6, 1975; 6) June 23, 1975–August 8, 1975. Students may attend college year round and receive their degree in less than four years or, they may select whichever term(s) they wish for vacation purposes.

A degree program must contain a minimum of thirty-two courses. A full-time student in the Racine Plan may take two courses each term and thus complete a minimum of eight or a maximum of twelve courses for the academic year. The thirty-two courses are of three kinds, namely, 1) "Life Studies," 2) "Major Studies" and 3) "Electives." A minimum of seven or eight courses are devoted to *Life Studies*. Most majors consist of nine or ten courses. The remaining courses are electives and these may be devoted to the development of a "minor" area of interest, preparation for career certification or whatever else the student wishes.

Would you like to know more about the Racine Plan? Then, write to the Dean, College of Racine, 5915 Erie St., Racine, Wisc. 53402.

The WPI Plan

Worcester Polytechnic Institute (WPI) of Worcester, Mass., introduced its innovative WPI Plan in 1971. Instead of taking the traditional program of required courses needed to earn a Bachelor of Science degree in the area of technical education, students in this new program, *The WPI Plan*, earn their degree by demonstrating their competence as problem solvers in their chosen career fields.

There are no required courses in the WPI Plan. In consultation with a faculty advisor, each WPI Plan student designs an individual program of study in conjunction with the student's career plans. Essentially, to earn a degree under the WPI Plan, a student must successfully accomplish the following: 1) a qualifying project in the major field, 2) an interactive project which relates the major field to social needs, 3) pass a sufficiency examination in the humanities and 4) an overall competency examination when the undergraduate program has been completed.

Students in the WPI Plan accept considerable responsibility for their own scholastic progress and, therefore, must be highly motivated. There are four seven-week terms between September and May and a fifth term in the Summer. Three courses are usually taken each term; about one-third of the students' time is devoted to subjects not in their major fields. Students may enter at the start of any of these terms. There is also a January Intersession of three weeks' duration during which a large variety of minicourses and workshops are offered.

Students may attend all of these terms and complete their degree requirements in less than four years. If they wish, however, they may choose not to attend college during certain terms in order to vacation or to work to earn money for college costs.

The WPI Plan includes innovative teaching techniques, including *Individually Prescribed Instruction (IPI)*. Under IPI, learning takes place through programmed instruction, video-taped lectures and reading. The students thus study on their own and set their own pace. They meet with their instructors to clarify any matters they may not understand and to determine whether they are qualified to proceed to the next unit of work.

As they plan their programs, students select courses of value in providing them with the necessary background for their individual projects. A student may work alone on a project or, more typically, a project may involve several students, sometimes even freshmen working with upperclassmen. These projects may be conducted on or off campus; many projects involve off-campus internships.

An additional attractive aspect of Worcester Polytechnic Institute's program is the stress it places on a technical education "as the liberal education for a technological society." It recognizes the interaction of the humanities and technology. This feature and the WPI Plan may very well be the cause of WPI's maintaining an essentially constant enrollment at a time when engineering colleges throughout the country have been experiencing dramatic decreases in their enrollments. WPI is now coeducational, inasmuch as women have been admitted since 1968.

Among the major areas of concentration available to WPI students are: Actuarial Science, American Studies, Astronomy, Biochemistry, Biomedical Engineering, Business, Civil Engineering, Computer—Commercial Applications, Computers in Medicine, Construction Engineering and Management, Design Engineering, Drama, Ecology and Technology, Electrical Engineering, Electronics—Computer Design, English Literature, Environmental Engineering, Financial Management, Fire Protection Engineering, Food Technology, Industrial Engineering, Manpower Planning, Marketing and Product Development, Molecular Biology and Microanatomy, Nuclear Engineering, Physics, Pre-Law Studies, Pre-Medical Studies, Quantum Electronics, Statistics, Transportation, Urban Studies and Western Ideas and Values.

Would you like further information about this fascinating educational experiment? If so, contact the Office of Admissions, Worcester Polytechnic Institute, Worcester, Mass. 01609.

Paracollege

St. Olaf College in Northfield, Minn., has within it a small, experimental unit called the *Paracollege,* which started in 1969. Essentially, the Paracollege is a four-year program. It is an open, flexible program which stresses interdisciplinary study and independent study. It is a liberal arts institution within an institution, but it offers students an alternative approach to the study of liberal arts.

The tutorial arrangement of instruction is used. Each student has a faculty tutor, who is generally in the student's major field. The tutors are professors from various departments at St. Olaf. Students must attend regular tutorials each semester. They generally meet with their tutors at least a half-hour every other week. The tutors serve as advisors to the students and offer them all sorts of academic help.

The Paracollege does not offer its own degree. Its graduates are awarded the Bachelor of Arts degree from St. Olaf. There are no traditional "required courses." Instead, there are seminars, lectures and discussions. There are required examinations. Progress in college study is measured by reaching certain competency levels for both general studies and specialization. The examinations are used to test the students' progress in certain extensive programs of study.

To earn the B.A. degree, Paracollege students must complete certain primary and secondary requirements. The primary requirements include: 1) Passing the General Examination, which tests the student's competency in the Humanities, Social Sciences and Natural Sciences and Mathematics; 2) Passing the Comprehensive Examination in a particular concentration or major; and 3) Completing a Senior Project, such as a thesis, an extensive experiment, a recital, a studio show or other approved accomplishment in the major field of study. The secondary requirements include the freshman and senior seminars and varied independent study projects, discussion groups and miscellaneous other academic activities to fill out the students' total programs.

Those who would like to obtain further information about this program should write to: Senior Tutor of the Paracollege, St. Olaf College, Northfield, Minn. 55057.

Liberating Arts

A nontraditional program of educational experiences in the *liberating arts* was begun in September 1974 at *Nazareth College at Kalamazoo* (Nazareth, Mich.). Emphasis is on professional competence in the *Human Services*. The Liberating Arts form the core from which the professional competence develops. The major drive of this program is the acquisition of competencies in seven areas of *Human Development*.

These seven areas are: 1) Communication (competency in the written, reading, oral and aural forms of the native language); 2) Aesthetic awareness and creative expression; 3) Ethical value and religious meaning; 4) Man and his relatedness (relationship of man to his environment in its historical, psychological and anthropological dimensions); 5) Inquiry (experimental methodologies in the Natural and Social Sciences); 6) Self-direction (immediate and long range life of learning); and 7) Profession (competencies needed for a career in a Human Service profession).

The program provides students with the skills and competencies needed for entry into a Human Services career or for further study leading to a profession in the Human Services. Preparation is offered for professional competence in the following four Human Service areas: 1) Health Services, such as Nursing, Medical Technology or other student-created, related programs; 2) Social Services, such as Social Work, Behavioral Science or other student-created, related programs; 3) Education, such as Learning Disabilities, Elementary Education or other student-created, related programs; and 4) Management and Administration, such as Accounting, Business Administration, Health Service Administration or other student-created, related programs.

The student has the privilege and responsibility of creating or choosing a variety of learning experiences and developing a personalized curriculum. There are no specific required courses. Instead, there are learning contracts, which are agreements between a student and a faculty member. Additionally, a variety of learning modes are utilized. The students select those modes most suited to their individual needs and goals. Different types of learning experiences on and off campus are available and curricular, calendar and scheduling flexibilities are permitted. College credits are awarded to the students when their learning contracts are fulfilled.

This program is so new that surely changes will take place during the process of putting it into full practice. If you would like complete details on this exciting new nontraditional college adventure, write to the Office of the Academic Dean, Nazareth College at Kalamazoo, Nazareth, Mich. 49074.

Competency Curriculum

A small, rural liberal arts college in Kansas, *Sterling College,* has initiated an interesting innovative curriculum in which "competencies" replace the traditional major-minor requirements. The philosophy behind the *Competency Curriculum* is that a college graduate should be able to demonstrate competency in certain selected areas. The freshman class of the Fall of 1972 was the first class to start under the Competency Curriculum requirements. Students enrolled in this curriculum are required to demonstrate their ability in nine areas of competency before they are qualified to receive their degrees.

The following are the nine competencies. Students must prove that they have the ability to:

    I. Comprehend the Christian Heritage and Its Relevance to Life and Community.

II. Demonstrate Awareness of One's Own Values and Commitments, of Others' Values and of the Alternatives.
III. Demonstrate How to Acquire Knowledge and How to Use It.
IV. Comprehend the Artistic and Aesthetic Dimensions of Culture.
V. Comprehend the Relationship of Man to His Physical and Social Environment.
VI. Demonstrate Proficiency in at Least One Discipline in Depth.
VII. Demonstrate Competency in Verbal Communication.
VIII. Demonstrate Physical Skill in and Knowledge of One or More Recreational Activities.
IX. Be Able to Work in Groups in Studying, Analyzing and Formulating Solutions to Problems and in Acting on Them.

Competency in these areas is achieved by passing certain selected academic courses and by Sterling's new "Field Experience." This Field Experience may occur out-of-class, or it may take place inside the classroom. Examples of the latter are participation in the College Band or Choir, Art laboratory classes, such as Ceramics or Painting, Science laboratory projects and Theater Arts performance classes. Independent study pursuits and reading programs related to an area of competency may also be included in the Competency Curriculum.

Older students who enroll in the Competency Curriculum may receive "life experience" credit for significant post-secondary experiences. This credit replaces some of the academic courses these students might otherwise be required to take.

Interwoven into the Competency Curriculum are career education programs in Small Business Management, Educational Youth Leadership (Boy Scouts, Girl Scouts, Campfire Girls, 4-H and Christian Youth Programs), Health-related fields, Local (and County) Government and Arts for Rural America. For further details, write to the Academic Dean, Sterling College, Sterling, Kans. 67579.

The Kalamazoo Plan

A unique, creative program of liberal arts education developed by *Kalamazoo College* (Kalamazoo, Mich.) carries the obvious name, the *Kalamazoo Plan*. This Plan focuses on the individual and combines nontraditional on-campus and off-campus experiences.

The college calendar consists of four eleven-week quarters each year. In no year does the student spend more than three quarters on campus; only three courses are carried in each of these quarters to enable the student to concentrate fully and do as much independent study on each course as desired.

Freshmen spend their Fall, Winter and Spring quarters on campus and the Summer quarter on vacation. They take an exploratory seminar, introductory courses in different departments and an FIP (Freshman Individualized Problems) course, in addition to participating, if they wish, in all co-curricular activities including athletics, music, theater and government. Sophomores devote their Spring quarter to an off-campus Career-Service experience. This is the students' first off-campus experience, and it enables them to gain practical experience in a job related to their chosen profession, explore a career opportunity or pursue a service project. This experience is under the auspices of Kalamazoo College, but the students do not earn any college credit for it. Some jobs provide the students with a stipend, some include only room and board and others are strictly voluntary.

During their junior year, the students spend their Fall and Winter quarters in Foreign Study abroad. The students have many opportunities available to them to study in colleges and universities in France, Germany, Spain and other nations. The Kalamazoo Plan allows for flexibility. Thus, students who wish may take their Foreign Study in their sophomore year and the off-campus Career-Service experience in their junior year.

In their senior year, the students spend their Fall and Winter quarters off campus on their SIP (Senior Individualized Project), generally under the auspices of the department in which they have been majoring. The project usually integrates the experiences acquired in Career-Service, Foreign Study and their on-campus classes and seminars into a major sophisticated product, such as a thesis, scientific research study or creative arts composition. The final quarter of the students' four years at college is spent on campus.

The Kalamazoo Plan permits the students to find their personal values through the interrelationship of miscellaneous learning experiences, including individualized study, Foreign Study, Career-Service, on-campus residential living, seminars and co-curricular activities. There are a number of options and variations available to the students to meet their individual needs. As Kalamazoo College is a member of the Great Lakes Colleges Association (see Chapter 12), the students are able to participate in additional courses and programs.

If you would like more details about the Kalamazoo Plan, write to the Office of Admissions, Kalamazoo College, Kalamazoo, Mich. 49001.

The Beloit Plan

The Beloit Plan was introduced at *Beloit College* (Beloit, Wisc.) in 1964. During the past decade, the program has been refined and made more relevant to present needs. The nontraditional academic calendar and program are flexible to permit students to plan an education suitable to their special interests.

The year-round, trimester calendar consists of a September-December Fall Term, a January-April Winter Term and a May-August Spring-Summer Term. The terms are fifteen weeks long; each term is split into two seven-week modules with a week-long reading period between the modules. There is a two- or three-week vacation period between the terms.

Beloit's four-year college degree program is uniquely divided into three periods, namely, 1) the Underclass Year, 2) the Middleclass Period and 3) the Upperclass Year. The Underclass Year consists of three "credit terms" (Fall Term, Winter Term and Spring-Summer Term) on campus; during this year, the students experience an intensive educational counseling program in addition to the academic program. The Middleclass Period consists of five terms (Fall Term, Winter Term and Spring-Summer Term, followed by a second Fall Term and Winter Term). Normally, only two of these five terms are "credit terms," i.e., terms devoted to work for academic credit on campus; one term is a required Field Term of work, service or research off the campus and away from home; the remaining two terms may be used for vacation purposes if the student so desires. The Upperclass Year consists of three "credit terms" (Spring-Summer Term, Fall Term and Winter Term). Commencement takes place in April.

The academic curriculum at Beloit is organized into four areas: Man's Physical, Social and Artistic Environments, and Man's Intellectual Foundations. There are twenty-nine prescribed fields of concentration. Students may choose from among the latter or set up their own programs of study. They may start their degree programs at Beloit in September, January or May.

Would you like to know more about the Beloit Plan? If so, write to the Director of Admissions, Beloit College, Beloit, Wisc. 53511.

Academic Contract Plan

Learning contracts are slowly becoming more popular in colleges throughout the country. A learning contract is a paper drawn up by a student and a faculty advisor stipulating exactly what that student is expected to learn in a specified period of time and the methods whereby this learning shall take place.

The *Academic Contract Plan* at *Notre Dame College* (St. Louis, Mo.) is designed for those students who want to plan their own program of studies. Students must have completed the traditional freshman year before entering the contract plan. Each student plans an individual contract curriculum in cooperation with and with the consent of the contract plan committee. This committee consists of the student's contract advisor and two faculty members, all selected by the student. With this plan of studies, the student includes a statement of goals, a selection of experiences leading to the achievement of these goals and a description of an evaluation procedure for the total plan.

Students on the contract plan must complete at least two academic Theology courses and must have a distribution of courses and/or experiences among the following five areas: 1) Quest for Ultimates, 2) Social Relation and Heritage, 3) Natural Environment, 4) Humanities and 5) Language Skills.

Would you like to know more about this Contract Plan? If you would, then write to: Academic Dean, Notre Dame College, 320 East Ripa Ave., Saint Louis, Mo. 63125.

Time Shortened Degree Programs

The traditional baccalaureate degree programs call for four years of college study and attendance. A limited number of colleges have begun to offer *time shortened degree programs* which enable students to complete the baccalaureate requirements in three years. *Bethany College* (Lindsborg, Kans.) has such a *three-year Bachelor of Arts degree program.*

This program aims to enable intellectually superior students who have chosen their educational and vocational goals to complete their undergraduate studies in three years. Students who would like to participate in this program should so indicate when they are admitted to Bethany. Would you like more information about this time shortened program? If so, contact the Academic Dean, Bethany College, Lindsborg, Kans. 67456.

At Bethany College too, a student whose goals cannot be met by a regular traditional major, but can best be achieved by a combination of work on and off campus, may draw up a contract, with the advice of faculty members, stipulating the program which will constitute the student's major.

The *College of St. Francis* in Joliet, Ill., in September 1972 inaugurated a new *three-year academic program* leading to a Bachelor of Arts (B.A.) degree. Anyone who qualifies for admission to St. Francis may embark on this program. Students have maximum freedom in planning their own educational experiences. The two basic components of this new program are: 1) a major field of concentration in one of the college departments, and 2) a largely self-designed set of learning experiences, designed to involve the student in real life rather than academic situations. The student, under the direction of a faculty advisor, has the basic responsibility for planning, evaluating and completing the three-year program.

The fields of concentration include: Art, Behavioral Science (Psychology, Sociology, Social Work), Education (Elementary, Secondary), English, History, Law and Government, Mathematics, Modern Foreign Languages (French, German, Spanish), Library Science, Music, Natural Science (Biology, Chemistry, Medical Technology), Philosophy, Religious Studies, Speech and Drama (Speech Pathology, Children's Theatre, Communications, Theatre Arts), Therapeutic Recreation and Pre-Dentistry, Pre-Law and Pre-Medicine.

Details about this three-year degree program may be obtained from the Admissions Office, College of St. Francis, 500 N. Wilcox St., Joliet, Ill. 60435.

The College of St. Francis interestingly also offers a Bachelor of Science in Professional Arts (BSPA) degree to Registered Nurses and Medical Technologists. In both cases, the College of St. Francis recognizes up to ninety-six hours of academic credit toward this degree for previous academic, professional and clinical experiences. In Chapter 11, we will look at some other new, nontraditional degrees.

Whittier College (Whittier, Calif.) recently began to emphasize educational innovation and among the latter it includes time-shortened routes to a baccalaureate degree. The alternatives by which this can be accomplished are early admission, credit-by-examination, the judicious use of course overloads and/or year-round attendance (Summer school and/or extended day sessions).

Bilingual Degree Programs

The *Bilingual Degree Program* of *Texas A & I University* (Kingsville, Texas) makes it possible for bilingual students to receive a great deal of their instruction in the Spanish language. Students with demonstrated ability in oral and written Spanish may register for this program in Agriculture, Business Administration and Engineering. Except for the bilingual aspect, the curricula are the same as for all other students. In addition to their regular baccalaureate degrees, these bilingual students are awarded *Bilingual Certificates* upon graduation. For details about this program, write to the Director, Bilingual Program, Texas A & I University, Kingsville, Texas 78363.

The *University of Puerto Rico* (Rio Piedras, P.R.) has an Extension Division in which it offers a "Spanish as a Second Language" program. Spanish for non-native students is available in the form of credit and non-credit courses. Most of the students take these courses to help them adapt to the environment and perform better in their classes rather than for credit purposes. The program of Spanish as a Second Language is composed of six levels, each level corresponding to one semester's work.

5.
NONTRADITIONAL COURSES, STUDIES AND RELATED OFFERINGS

Not only are you able today to prepare for specific careers and obtain your undergraduate degree by means of nontraditional educational methods, but additionally many colleges and universities are offering nontraditional courses, studies and related offerings. Some of these are credit-carrying toward your college degree; others are non-credit for enjoyment, cultural enrichment and/or career advancement.

Acting-Dance-Theater

Are you interested in a professional career in the field of *dance?* Then, the *Bachelor of Fine Arts in Dance-Theatre* degree program of *Marygrove College* (Detroit, Mich.) is designed for you.

This program was started at Marygrove in the Fall of 1973. The dance-theater majors receive training in both classical ballet and modern dance during their freshman, sophomore and junior years and specialize in their senior years, in addition to receiving four years of a solid liberal arts foundation. These students have available to them such courses as Introduction to Dance, Dance Workshop, Ballet, Modern Dance, Dance-Theatre Performance, Ballet Technique, Historical Dances, Tap Dancing, Jazz Dancing, Folk Dance and Principles of Choreography.

High school students who would like to enroll in this program must audition for admission in the Spring term of their senior year. For details of this B.F.A. Dance-Theatre degree, write to: Director of Dance, Marygrove College, 8425 W. McNichols Rd., Detroit, Mich. 48221.

One of the "career education" programs at *Central Connecticut State College* (New Britain, Conn.) is its well-developed *theater program* leading to the Bachelor of Fine Arts (B.F.A.) degree. Students in this program receive preparation for professional careers in the theater, including acting, directing and the technical areas of lighting and costuming. A course in playwriting and a Summer Theatre Workshop are also offered here. The college has Welte Hall for musical programs, the College Theatre with about 450 seats, Theatre 123 (an intimate facility used for theater classwork and production) and a proscenium theatre in the Georgian style.

Area and Ethnic Studies

Many colleges now have *Black Studies* courses and some offer major programs in Black Studies. *Trinity College* in Hartford, Conn., additionally has Beginning Black Music and Advanced Black Music courses for degree credits. The origins of Afro-American music from its earliest African beginnings up through its development in America from the 1600s to the present are studied.

The *Center for Area and Interdisciplinary Studies* at *Central Connecticut State College* (New Britain, Conn.) offers noteworthy nontraditional programs in Afro-American Studies, East Asian Studies and Latin American Studies.

DePauw University in Greencastle, Ind., has a comprehensive area major program in African Studies. Facilities are available to the students to learn specific African languages. Additionally, there is a slide collection of African art, an African record library and an expanding teaching library for African studies. There is also an interdisciplinary Black Studies program at DePauw that aims to introduce the students to the gamut of contemporary thinking in reference to the culture and history of Black Americans. In September 1973, DePauw started to offer an area minor in Black Studies. See Chapter 8 for information on DePauw's international programs in the areas of African and Black Studies.

Western Kentucky University in Bowling Green, Ky., has a *Center for Intercultural Studies* which encompasses and gives direction to Afro-American Studies, American Studies, Folk Studies and Latin American Studies. Students may minor in any of the latter, all of which are crosscultural and interdisciplinary approaches to the understanding of the total human experience.

The *Liberal Arts College of Fordham University at Lincoln Center* in New York City has comprehensive major programs in Black Studies, Puerto Rican Studies and Urban Studies. These programs are of special value to students who plan to enter upon careers of service to the urban community.

Afro-American Studies, Latin American Studies and Urban Studies are among the interdisciplinary programs available to students at *Shippensburg State College* (Shippensburg, Pa.).

The *College of Arts and Sciences at the State University of New York at Albany* (Albany, N.Y.) has such nontraditional, interdepartmental and interdisciplinary offerings as Asian Studies, Peace Studies and Urban Affairs. There are also comprehensive majors in Afro-American Studies, American Studies, Chinese Studies, Hispanic and Italian Studies, Inter-American Studies, Judaic Studies and Puerto Rican Studies.

The *College of Arts and Sciences of Roosevelt University* in Chicago, Ill., offers to its undergraduates commendable African, Afro-American and Black Studies Programs. Students who concentrate on the latter two programs should find that these studies strengthen their preparation for jobs in various community service and social-welfare agencies. Among the courses in these programs are: Africa, African Language, African Art, African Folklore and Literature, African Music and Dance and African Politics. Additionally, there are: Afro-American Literature, Afro-American History, Politics of Black Americans, White Racism in the United States, Black Psychology, American Minorities, and Race and Ethnic Relations.

Roosevelt's College of Arts and Sciences also offers a program in Jewish Studies. In cooperation with *Spertus College of Judaica,* it has established a joint program with a major in these studies leading to a bachelor's degree. There are six areas in this program, namely, 1) Hebrew Language, 2) Bible and Biblical Literature, 3) Talmudic Literature, 4) Hebrew Literature, 5) Jewish Culture and 6) Jewish History, including Zionism.

Spertus College of Judaica in Chicago has this cooperative, consortium arrangement not only with Roosevelt University, but also with *Chicago Theological Seminary, DePaul University, Central YMCA Community College, Mundelein College, Northeastern Illinois University* and *University of Illinois at Chicago Circle,* all in Chicago, *Northern Illinois University* (DeKalb, Ill.) and *Northwestern University* (Evanston, Ill.). The students at these schools may take courses in Judaic Studies at Spertus and Spertus students may take general education and other courses at the consortium member colleges. Those who have successfully completed the undergraduate requirements at Spertus are awarded the B.A. degree; additionally, those who fulfilled the requirements for the Judaic Studies curriculum receive the *Bachelor of Judaic Studies (B.J.S.)* degree and those in the Hebraic curriculum receive the *Bachelor of Hebrew Literature (B.H.L.)* degree.

Middlesex County College (Edison, N.J.) also offers a program of Judaic Studies in cooperation with the *Institute of Judaic Studies.*

The *University of Montana* in Missoula has programs in Black Studies and in American Indian Studies.

A comprehensive program in American Indian Studies is offered by the *College of St. Scholastica* in Duluth, Minn. Included in this program are courses in American Indian Literature, Ojibwa Indian Language, American Indian History, American Indian Music and Dance, American Indian Arts and Crafts, Contemporary American Indian Art, Urban Indians, Native American Law and Government and Native American Liberation.

Almost all liberal arts colleges have Art departments, but *Newton College* (Newton, Mass.) has such nontraditional courses as Islamic Art, a study of the art and culture of Islam, and Buddhist Sculpture in India, China and Japan, a course which traces the development of the Buddhist image from its origins in India.

Johns Hopkins University (Baltimore, Md.) has a rather unique department of Near Eastern Studies. This includes the following four main areas: Egyptology, Assyriology, Arabic Philology and Islamic Studies and Northwest Semitic Languages and Literatures. Among the courses in this department are: Introduction to the New Testament, Introduction to the Old Testament, Religion and Magic in Babylonia and Assyria, Elementary Akkadian, Aramaic and Persian.

The Spanish American Area Studies program of *South Dakota State University* (Brookings, S.D.) is an all-university, vocationally-oriented program administered by the College of Arts and Sciences. It aims to expand job opportunities for students who look forward to working in Latin American countries, particularly in the fields of nursing, engineering, sociology, agronomy or home economics. This program is of value too for those who will be working in sections of the United States where large numbers of the people speak Spanish. Students who so desire may combine their first major with the Spanish American Area Studies program and thus have a second major and a Spanish minor.

Bioengineering

Bioengineering is the application of mathematical methods and the experimental techniques of engineering and the physical sciences to the understanding and solution of biological and medical problems. This is a new field, and *Johns Hopkins University* (Baltimore, Md.) offers a major program in it leading to the *Bachelor of Engineering Science (B.E.S.)* degree. Graduates of this program may work in biomedical or engineering centers or in industry.

Environmental Studies

Susquehanna University (Selinsgrove, Pa.) has an interdisciplinary program in Environmental Studies. The program is administered by the Institute for Environmental Studies and aims to acquaint the students with the economic, governmental and sociological issues involved in the utilization of natural resources. The following departments participate in this program: Biology, Chemistry, Economics, Geological Sciences, Mathematics, Physics, Political Science and Sociology. Details about this program may be obtained from the Director, Institute For Environmental Studies, Susquehanna University, Selinsgrove, Pa. 17870.

Gerontology

A program leading to an Associate in Art degree in Gerontology is offered by *Leicester Junior College* (Leicester, Mass.) for those planning to enter the field of long term care as Nursing Home Administrators and related occupations. A course in Remotivation involves training in the techniques of basic group therapy to equip the students to help long term chronic patients who are not making efforts to improve.

A student may earn a certificate of achievement, an associate degree or a bachelor's degree in Gerontology at *Madonna College* (Livonia, Mich.). Training is offered toward a variety of paraprofessional, pre-professional and professional positions in service to the aged.

The *School of Public Affairs and Community Services* of the *University of Nebraska at Omaha* created a Gerontology program to improve the quality of life of Nebraska's senior citizens. Gerontology is viewed here as a multi-disciplinary specialty and, therefore, the University of Nebraska offers courses in this field but does not offer a degree program.

Horsemanship

In September 1974, *Bennett College,* a two-year college for women in Millbrook, N.Y., introduced a three-year program in Horsemanship. This program consists of the general requirements for the associate degree plus the major in Horsemanship. Students who wish may also include the course requirements of a second major in their program of studies.

The Horsemanship major includes courses in Riding, Care and Knowledge of the Horse, Theory of Stable Management, Theory of Equitation and Theory of Teaching. The third year of the Horsemanship program is an internship at the College Riding Center or at an approved off-campus stable. The student receives a certificate as part of her professional credentials after she has completed this internship. This certificate is in addition to the A.A. degree awarded for the successful completion of the first two years of the program. For details about the Horsemanship program, write to the Dean of the College, Bennett College, Millbrook, N.Y. 12545.

A degree-credit course in Horse Care and Management has been offered by the *Maple Woods Community College* in Kansas City, Mo. The course has been given off campus and students have gone from one stable to another to acquire the desired information and training.

International Studies

Wilkes College (Wilkes-Barre, Pa.) has just instituted a baccalaureate program in International Studies, an interdisciplinary program organized around four of Wilkes' Social Science departments. The students thus get a more comprehensive background in world affairs than they could from any one of the departments alone. The interdisciplinary aspects of this program prepare the students for careers in such diverse fields as foreign service, other governmental work, international business, international finance and law.

Neglected Languages

Kalamazoo College (Kalamazoo, Mich.) has a rare area in its curriculum known as the *Neglected Languages Program.* This enables students to study certain languages generally not found in college curricula. Included among these languages are Chinese, Japanese, Portuguese and Swahili. Efforts are made to combine the study of these languages with a foreign study experience.

Chinese, Hindi and Japanese are offered at *Wells College* in Aurora, N.Y., through their *Critical Languages Program*. The students do independent study aided by the use of tapes and native language speakers. Wells, a liberal arts college for women, also has a comprehensive Italian Studies field of specialization.

Orthoptics

Among its Professional Studies curricula, *Simmons College* (Boston, Mass.) offers a concentration in Orthoptics. This young science has been called "the physical therapy of the eyes." Students who major in this field take three years of study in the physical sciences at Simmons and then spend their fourth year at the Massachusetts Eye and Ear Infirmary. This fulfills the academic requirements for the baccalaureate degree. However, those who wish to qualify as candidates for the examination for certification of the American Orthoptic Council must serve an additional six months internship if they wish to be certified to work with ophthalmologists in diagnosing and treating diseases and defects of the eye.

Most of the programs at *Colby College—New Hampshire* (New London, N.H.) lead to the associate degree. Additionally, however, Colby does offer a *four-year Bachelor of Science degree program in Orthoptics*. In addition to the on-campus program of required and elective courses, a minimum of fifteen months of study in an approved hospital is required by Colby for this degree.

Parapsychology

A student can earn one course credit for completing Introductory Parapsychology at *Trinity College* (Hartford, Conn.). Telepathy and clairvoyance, precognition and retrocognition, psychokinesis, apparitions and poltergeists, astral projection, reincarnation, mediumship and unorthodox healing are discussed in this course.

You can also take a survey course in Parapsychology at *Georgia State University* (Atlanta, Ga.) and learn about ESP (extra-sensory perception), reincarnation, karma and auras.

PIE

It's not PIE in the sky, but PIE in Higher Education at *Northeastern Illinois University* in Chicago. PIE is an acronym for *Program for Interdisciplinary Education.* PIE is not a degree program, but it includes nontraditional offerings in the area of interdisciplinary studies.

PIE was started for the purpose of encouraging innovation and interdisciplinary studies. It stimulates faculty members and students alike to depart from the traditional academic program and initiate curriculum change by crossing disciplinary and departmental lines.

No student may take more than forty-five hours of credit under PIE. It is possible for students to earn from three to eighteen units of credit over a period of one or more trimesters for each PIE project successfully completed. Whether student-initiated or faculty-initiated, the prime emphasis of a PIE project is its interdisciplinary nature.

The PIE *Criminal Justice Projects* enable students to gain insight into the criminal courts, the police and correctional institutions. The students visit criminal courts; they interview persons arrested the previous night and attempt to have their bail reduced or eliminated. They investigate reports of medical and psychological experimentation on prisoners and brutality at penal institutions. The students also contribute their thoughts and efforts toward penal reform and work for greater non-white police recruitment. Students who successfully conclude this PIE program earn fifteen credit hours.

In the Winter 1974 trimester, PIE offered a *Kibbutz Project.* This gave students the opportunity to live, work and learn on an Israeli Kibbutz. They travelled through Israel, discussed Middle East issues, learned about the Kibbutz way of life and "kibbutzniks," performed productive work in the Kibbutz according to each student's abilities and needs of the Kibbutz and attended weekly seminars at Haifa University. In return for the work done in the Kibbutz, the students were supplied with meals, room, medical care and "small needs." After the successful completion of the Kibbutz Project, students were granted from twelve to fifteen credit hours, depending upon how they implemented an interdisciplinary project while on the Kibbutz.

Poetry, Novel and Short Story Writing and Criticism

The Arts at *Marlboro College* (Marlboro, Vt.) include "Writing and Criticism." The latter, in turn, include a Poetry Workshop, consisting of a single long class each week devoted to discussion and analysis of the students' poems, a Short Story Workshop and a Novel Workshop.

Poetry lovers will want to note too an interesting nontraditional feature at *Central Connecticut State College* (New Britain, Conn.) known as the *Poet-in-Residence* program. The poet participates in a Poetry Workshop and in a unique relationship among the college's English Department, the student teaching personnel, student teachers, cooperating teachers from nearby Newington High School and the Connecticut Commission on the Arts.

Suburban Studies

The *Institute of Suburban Studies* was established at *Adelphi University* (Garden City, N.Y.) in 1974. It is the first institute of its kind in the United States. In view of the fact that the trek toward the suburbs started a number of years ago, after World War II, the establishment of such an institute to study the consequences of millions of urbanites becoming suburbanites is long overdue. An interdisciplinary bachelor's degree program in Suburban Studies is offered by the Institute. Details about this program may be obtained from the Director, Institute of Suburban Studies, Adelphi University, Garden City, N.Y. 11530.

Miscellaneous Courses, Studies and Related Offerings

A number of nontraditional courses on the subject of sex roles are beginning to appear in college curricula throughout the nation. *An Interdisciplinary Approach to Sex Roles in America* is offered at *Trinity College* (Hartford, Conn.). The disciplines of Economics, Psychology, History, Philosophy, Political Science, Religion and Sociology are involved in discussions here as the implications of sex roles are investigated.

Did you think you could take a course in Yiddish in Arizona? Well, you can—and for degree credits too—at the *University of Arizona* in Tucson. Also at the University, there are such non-credit offerings as: 1) The Folklore of India, where you can learn about the myths, legends, customs, beliefs, rituals and rites of birth, marriage, death, etc.; 2) Acrylic Painting, designed to introduce the students to the methods of working with acrylic media; 3) The Art of Murder: Contemporary Suspense Literature, which includes the study of recent detective stories, spy thrillers and psychological chillers; and 4) Wine Appreciation, to help in selecting wine in restaurants and shops and in serving it at home.

Middle Georgia College (Cochran, Ga.) offers among its two-year career programs a major in Sacred Choral Music leading to the A.A. degree and a major in Teacher Assistant Program leading to the A.S. degree. It also offers one-year career programs leading to certificates in Clerical Specialization, Drafting, Fashion Merchandising, Stenographic Specialization, Surveying and Teacher Aide Program.

At *Cochise College* in Douglas, Arizona, you can take courses in Coed Billiards, Coed Scuba Diving and Coed Yoga and receive degree credits for them. Here too, you could participate in archaeological digs. The college is located in Cochise County, which takes its name from the famed Apache Indian Chief. There are many valleys in this county and at least two or three have been living areas for Native Americans (American Indians) for thousands of years. There is a wealth of materials here for archaeological excavations. You might dig up part of a dinosaur or some other prehistoric animal. The college's *Archaeology Resource Center* provides laboratory and classroom facilities for interested students and encourages students to participate in field digs. American Indian students are trained to serve as aides or technicians for excavation in Indian country or elsewhere. A two-month field dig takes place during the Summer months; students from colleges throughout the nation are attracted to these Summer digs and receive degree credits from their home colleges after successful participation in a dig.

How would you like to learn about Chinese Calligraphy? The Division of Special Studies of *Georgia State University* (Atlanta, Ga.) teaches the basic styles and techniques of Chinese Character brush strokes. Here too, you can take Jazz—Its Origin and Development as an Art Form and learn about many jazz artists and composers beginning with early Black music and progressing to the "now sound" of contemporary jazz and rock. You might also like to enroll in Hatha Yoga and T'Ai Chi and study these two ancient systems of body awareness.

Five Towns College (Merrick, N.Y.), a new, two-year, private institution offers associate degree programs in Contemporary Music—Jazz and Music Instrument Technology. The latter includes such courses as Woodwind Instrument Repair, Brass and Percussion Repair, String

Instrument and Guitar Repair, Electronic Instrument Repair and Piano Tuning and Repair.

Many students are eager to major in Psychology. But, have you ever heard of Psychobiology? *Ripon College* (Ripon, Wisc.) offers a major in Psychobiology. This major is for students who plan to do graduate work in interdepartmental fields such as, behavior genetics, ethology, neurobiology, psychopharmacology and psychophysiology. Among the required courses in the Psychobiology major at Ripon are: Biological Structures and Processes, Human Anatomy and Physiology, Genetics, General Psychology, Descriptive and Inferential Statistics, Research Design and Methodology and Physiological Psychology.

You will find many additional nontraditional courses, studies and related offerings in Chapter 15, which deals with Continuing Education.

6.
"OUT" WITH LECTURES
—"IN" WITH (MULTI-MEDIA) LEARNING

The traditional form of college instruction is the lecture. Down through the years, professors and students—facetiously, but aptly—have defined the college lecture as the passage of information from the notebook of the professor to the notebook of the student without passing through the heads of either.

Alternative forms of instruction have arisen recently in attempts to overcome this situation. Learning is much more likely to occur when students actively participate rather than merely passively listen. Now, nontraditional multi-media methods of instruction may change students from lecture listeners to positive participants.

Miscellaneous multi-media methods and materials—television, radio, tapes, cassettes, motion picture films, slides, records, newspapers and varied other audio-visual means—have tremendous potential as alternatives to the traditional classroom lecture. Especially important is the fact that these nontraditional alternatives enable the students to engage in independent study, going at their own best possible pace.

Self-paced learning is the best form of learning, for only the students themselves truly know when they have actually assimilated the information. Some students can learn one specific subject faster than other students can and, conversely, need more time to learn another subject. Nontraditional self-paced learning allows students to proceed as quickly or as slowly as they need in order to learn the subject matter.

Self-paced Learning

Many audio-visual materials facilitate *self-paced learning* at *New River Community College* in Dublin, Va. There are, for example, no

86

lectures in their Machine Technology courses. Instead, the students view and hear on sound/slide programs the information they would usually receive by means of traditional lectures. This individualized form of instruction permits the students to work and learn at their own best rate of speed and complete their entire degree program at their own pace.

The Geology courses at New River are also supplemented with taped commentaries on slide presentations. The presentations are viewed in the college's Learning Resource Center and students may look at them individually as many times as they wish. The courses in Drafting, Electricity, English and Mathematics have similar materials for individualized instruction. Videotape instruction is being used effectively in Choral Direction, Chorus and Physical Education. If you would like more information about New River's nontraditional methods of instruction, contact the Dean of Instruction, New River Community College, Drawer 1127, Dublin, Va. 24084.

Self-paced labs in Chemistry allow students at *California State College, San Bernardino,* to work more effectively at their own pace. New videotape cassettes are used to deliver the professor's instructions for carrying out the experiments and for evaluating results. The tapes not only allow students to proceed at their own speed, but also are of benefit to students who were absent and, in a traditional laboratory situation, would have missed the instructions and other information given to the class by the professor.

Portland Community College (Portland, Ore.) also has a *Learning Center* where tape recordings enable students to progress at their own pace. Thus, for example, a student completed a one-year course in Biology in four weeks and never attended a class. The Biology Department's audio-tutorial concept of learning made this possible. At the Learning Center, microscopes, experiment kits and tape recordings are available. The lecture tapes have been prepared, written and recorded by members of the teaching staff. If individual assistance is needed, two teachers are always present at the Center to provide such help.

Drexel University (Philadelphia, Pa.) has video tapes and slide-audio cassette systems for a number of courses, including Calculus, Chemistry and Engineering Graphics. This enables students to take these courses in a self-paced manner.

An *Audio-Visual Tutorial Center* was installed in *MacCormac Junior College* in Chicago in 1972. This A-V-T Center consists of twenty-one student learning stations. These stations are superb means of permitting students to become skilled in business subjects at their own rate of learning. Each learning station has a casette tape player and headphones for the "audio" system and a rear screen projection system and slide projector for the visual materials. The students learn from viewing the screen and listening to the tapes. They then proceed at their own pace and do not go to the second lesson before mastering the first one. Students seeking skills in Typewriting, Secretarial Work and Court Reporting may start a course on any working day of the year.

In the Summer of 1973, the *Department of Educational Media Services* of *Drake University* (Des Moines, Iowa) used varied forms of electronic and audio-visual media to develop a new concept in learning facilities. Thus, the *Dial Access Learning Center* was established on the ground floor in the Language Laboratory of the Cowles Library, with sixty-four study carrels equipped for independent study. (A carrel is a booth in which a student can study in private.) There are also about seventy individual study carrels in the Library proper which are hooked up to the Dial Access System.

The Dial Access Learning Center contains equipment and facilities for viewing 8mm and 16mm motion pictures, sound filmstrips using either synchronized disk or cassette tape recordings, 2″ × 2″ slides with synchronized cassette recordings, "live" broadcast television programs and videotape programs produced on the Drake campus. Students may also listen to audio programs and simultaneously record them on cassettes for use on their own recorders.

About forty-six study carrels are located in the dormitories. These too are directly linked to the Dial Access System, enabling students to tune in for a particular program without leaving their dormitories.

Drake also utilizes closed circuit television extensively. Television and radio programs for campus and public broadcasting on local commercial stations emanate from one of the production centers, which serves as a laboratory for the School of Journalism. Video-camera facilities are used abundantly in Drake's Teacher Education Program and in the Educational Media Services Center, where faculty members may use them for their individual departments.

Anyone who would like to have more information about these or the Dial Access Learning Center should write to: Director, Educational Media Services, Drake University, Des Moines, Iowa 50311.

The Mabee Learning Center of *Oklahoma Christian College* (Oklahoma City, Okla.) is the first in the nation to contain an individual study carrel for each student. The student is assigned the carrel for the trimester and can use it at any time from early morning until almost bedtime. Students decorate their carrels according to their individual tastes and keep their books and other materials in them. They spend about fifteen hours weekly in their carrels and do most of their studying there. They read, type and use a number of the latest learning media such as audio tapes, film projectors and other visual materials in these carrels. An electronic dial access system enables the student in the carrel to have access, via a computer, to a library of tapes. There are about 3,500 tapes in the college library. These tapes are programmed each week and scheduled by the professors as they need them for their course work.

Multi-Media Methods of Instruction

The *Central Florida College Television Consortium* is dedicated to bringing innovative educational opportunities to the students in the member colleges of this consortium and to the public. The first offering was a televised three-credit course on Human Ecology in the Fall of 1973. Man and Environment was the title of the course and it was presented on open-circuit and on-campus television for students and for the general public.

Fifteen half-hour documentaries augmented by a variety of printed materials, including a text and local supplement, yielded an effective visual multi-media approach to learning. The documentaries were shown on several television channels at different times to enable viewers to select the time most suitable for them. Only a limited number of visits to the campus was necessary. To receive credit for courses taken in this manner, the student must pass a mid-term and final examination.

There are exciting offerings in store for participants in this consortium. For a complete schedule of broadcast events and other details, write to any one or more of the following member colleges: Brevard Community College (Cocoa, Fla. 32922); Hillsborough Community College (Tampa, Fla. 33622); Lake-Sumter Community College (Leesburg, Fla. 32748); Manatee Junior College (Bradenton, Fla.

33507); Pasco-Hernando Community College (East Pasco Office, Dade City, Fla. 33525; West Pasco Office, New Port Richey, Fla. 33552; Hernando Office, Brooksville, Fla. 33512); Polk Community College (Winter Haven, Fla. 33880); Seminole Junior College (Sanford, Fla. 32771); St. Petersburg Junior College (St. Petersburg, Fla. 33733); Valencia Community College (Orlando, Fla. 32811).

The *University of Georgia* television station, WGTV—Channel 8, located in the Georgia Center for Continuing Education (see Chapter 15), is on the air seven evenings per week for the fifty-two weeks of the year. There is no schedule of course work by television, but many of the WGTV programs are complementary to independent study. A monthly program guide may be had by writing to: Georgia Television, The Georgia Center, Athens, Ga. 30601.

Are you tired of getting busy signals every time you make a phone call? Well, you can be sure of not getting a busy signal when you call in on the *Telenet System* to take a Telenet course. Telenet credit and non-credit courses are available to undergraduate and graduate students at the *University of Kansas* (Lawrence, Kans.) through its Division of Continuing Education.

Not only students at the University of Kansas, but also students at other Kansas colleges, may take courses through the Statewide Continuing Education Network, as the Telenet System is officially titled. This Network is a system whereby classroom instruction is conducted by means of telephone lines which link classrooms in twenty-three communities. *Fort Hays State College, Kansas State College of Pittsburg, Kansas State Teachers College, Kansas State University* and *Wichita State University* in addition to the University of Kansas are part of the Statewide Continuing Education Network and develop and sponsor network credit and non-credit courses.

There are Network locations in the following cities in Kansas: Chanute, Concordia, Dodge City, El Dorado, Emporia, Garden City, Goodland, Hays, Hutchinson, Independence, Johnson County, Lawrence, Liberal, Manhattan, Norton, Paola, Pittsburg, Sabetha, Salina, Stockton, Topeka, Wellington and Wichita. The voices are sufficiently amplified over the telephone lines so that instructors and students can converse freely. In each location, a "monitor" is present to operate the equipment, supervise enrollment and exams and coordinate supplementary class materials.

Undergraduate courses are offered in Occupational Education, Real

Estate, Characteristics of the Learning Disabled, Understanding and Dealing with Juvenile Delinquency, Correctional Communities, Identification of Children with Learning Problems within the Regular Classroom, Referral Procedures and Courses of Outside Help for the Regular Classroom Teacher in Dealing with Children with Learning Problems, Effectively Educating Children with Learning Problems within the Regular Classroom, Behavioral Analysis of Winning and Income Tax for Laymen.

Would you like to know more about present and up-coming Telenet courses? Then, contact the Director, The Statewide Continuing Education Network, Umberger Hall, Kansas State University, Manhattan, Kans. 66506.

Mount Saint Mary's College, Emmitsburg, Md., uses tapes and cassettes in conjunction with textbooks in its language laboratory. Closed circuit television is used by the Education Department in the classes on Methods of Teaching. Computer instruction is offered by means of a computer which is tied in by telephone to a larger computer in the National Institute of Standards in Washington, D.C.

The country's first two-way education telecommunications network went into operation in Michigan in September 1973. Sponsored by the *Michigan State Board of Education,* the network is known as the *Adrian (Mich.) Cable Consortium.* It is composed of *Adrian College, Siena Heights College, Saint Joseph's Academy* (a private girls' school), *Lenawee Vocational Technical Center,* the state of Michigan's *Adrian Training School* (a public coeducational correctional institution for youth) and *Adrian Public Schools,* all located within a radius of about four miles.

These public and private educational institutions, ranging from elementary school through college level, are linked with two-way audio, video and digital signals. The instant feedback from the classrooms is a most welcome feature of this television system of bi-directional, multi-channel cable communications. This means that an instructor addressing a class in one school can be seen and heard in classrooms in the schools which are members of this Cable Consortium and the students from the member schools can ask questions, hear the instructor's answers and join in the discussion.

These telecommunications facilities offer tremendous opportunities for experimenting with varied programs and other electronically-assisted educational efforts for students of different capabilities, ages and academic levels. If you would like to keep up with the developments and achievements of the Adrian Cable Consortium, write to: Telecommunications Director, Adrian Public Schools, 204 East Church St., Adrian, Mich. 49221.

There are more than a dozen colleges participating with the *Maryland Center for Public Broadcasting College of the Air*. TV Channels 67 and 73 in Baltimore and Channel 28 in Salisbury transmit the programs.

During the September 1973 through February 1974 semester, three credit courses in English Literature I, Data Processing, American History II and Child Development were telecast at specified morning, evening and weekend hours. The participating colleges were *Salisbury State College* in Salisbury, *Ocean City College* in Ocean City, *Howard Community College* in Columbia and *Catonsville Community College, Community College of Baltimore, Dundalk Community College, Essex Community College, Harford Community College* and *Morgan State College*, all in Baltimore.

A three credit course entitled *ITV-Utilization* was an upper division (junior and senior years) undergraduate and graduate level course that centered on planning for the multiple uses of instructional television with students. The participating colleges were: *Bowie State College* (Bowie), *Coppin State College* (Baltimore), *Frostburg State College* (Frostburg), *Morgan State College* (Baltimore), *Salisbury State College* (Salisbury), *Towson State College* (Towson) and *University of Maryland* (Baltimore and College Park). A first-year, two credit course in Hebrew was telecast for twenty weeks with *Baltimore Hebrew College* in Baltimore as the participating college.

The *University of Maryland* in College Park was the participating college for two eighteen-credit courses, namely, the thirty-six week course in Humanities and the thirty-four week course in The Man-Made World (Technology). Both of these were intensive, independent study programs made available through the cooperation of England's Open University and the University College of the University of Maryland.

To enroll in any of the courses presented by the College of the Air, students must do so during the participating college's regular period of registration. All of the courses require supplementary reading and written assignments. The students must pass the same examinations as those given for these same courses on campus. The credits earned from these telecast courses are applicable toward the baccalaureate degree.

If you would like detailed information about the courses telecast via the College of the Air, write to the Maryland Center for Public Broadcasting, Owings Mills, Md. 21117.

The Continuing Education and Extension Division of the *University of Minnesota* offers television classes for credit. During the 1973-1974 year, Human Sexual Behavior (3 credits) was presented from September 24th through December 12th, Political Theory and Utopia (4 credits) from January 3rd through March 22nd and Interior Design I (4 credits) from April 1st through June 15th. All appeared on KTCA-TV, Channel 2 on Monday evening from 9:00 to 10:00 P.M. The World of Islam (4 credits) was presented on WCCO-TV, Channel 4 on Tuesdays, Thursdays and Saturdays, from 6:30 to 7:00 A.M. from September 25th through January 12th. Courses are also offered periodically via University Radio Station KUOM.

The *University of Nebraska at Omaha* started its *"TV Classroom"* back in 1952 as a joint venture with station KMTV (Channel 3) in Omaha. This program has continued uninterrupted since then. KYNE-TV (Channel 26) is the educational television station located on the campus, and extensive studio and equipment capability have enabled the University to produce hundreds of programs for the benefit of the students.

Indiana University at South Bend has noteworthy electronic education programs. College credit can be earned at home for Art Appreciation and Music Appreciation courses. The Art Appreciation course has been given in cooperation with WSBT-TV (Channel 22). Fifteen hour-long televised lectures have been delivered on consecutive Sundays from 9:00 to 10:00 A.M. Three hours of college credit could be earned by those who successfully completed the course requirements; the latter included going to the IUSB campus to take three examinations during the fifteen week period.

Indiana University at South Bend also offers a Music Appreciation course in cooperation with WSND-FM. On thirteen consecutive Thursdays, hour-long radio lectures are delivered from 11:00 P.M. to midnight. The program has also been repeated on Sundays from 5:00 to 6:00 P.M. Two or three hours of credit may be earned by taking this course; those who wish three credits are required to write a report at the end of the course.

Electronic education courses are also conducted at Indiana University on closed circuit television of the *Indiana Higher Education Television System* (IHETS). A new and important program offered through IHETS is the three-semester certificate course in *Nursing Home Administration.* The course originates from the Indiana University Medical Center, 1100 W. Michigan St., Indianapolis, Ind. 46202. Students may attend classes at this location or via closed-circuit television at any of the following regional campuses: *Purdue University* at either the Fort Wayne, Hammond, Lafayette or Westville campus; *Indiana State University* at the Evansville or Terre Haute campus; *Indiana University* at the Bloomington, New Albany or South Bend campus; *Ball State University* at Muncie; and *Vincennes University* at Vincennes.

Purdue University (West Lafayette, Ind.) has an extensive program of electronic education. It started broadcasting credit courses on radio station WBAA in the Fall of 1969. Courses in Art Appreciation, Biomedical Engineering, Drugs—Use and Abuse, Economics, Frontiers in the Geosciences, Literature, Marriage and Family Relationships, Philosophy, Psychology, Radio and Television Broadcasting, Sex Education in Schools and Sociology have been offered through this medium.

The *Purdue Television Unit* has produced hundreds of live closed-circuit presentations for many different departments of the university. Pre-recorded tapes have been distributed to and used in many classes. Of special value is the microwave television system with the accompanying talkback system which permits the instructor to hear questions asked by students in the receiving classrooms.

In the Spring of 1973, *Portland Community College* (Portland, Ore.) telecast its first presentation of "Man and Environment." This was the first course broadcast on commercial television by an Oregon community college. The program is one hour in length, consisting of a half-hour documentary and a half-hour panel discussion, on Sunday evenings from 9:30 to 10:30 P.M. for eleven weeks.

"Man and Environment" is presented on open circuit television by Portland C.C. in cooperation with KPTV (Channel 12, Portland, Ore.). It carries three credits in environmental education. Enrollment is open to anyone regardless of prior education. Five quizzes and a final examination are mailed to everyone who is enrolled for credit.

For additional information, write to "Man and Environment," Portland Community College, 12000 S.W. 49th Ave., Portland, Ore. 97219.

Five television courses were offered during the Summer of 1974 by the *University of Tennessee* via Tennessee's five open circuit educational television stations. The courses were telecast throughout the state. Students registered through the University's Center for Extended Learning. The credit they received for these television courses was registered on the University campus from which the class originated.

Three quarter hours credit were granted for the successful completion of each of the following four courses: Education of the Exceptional Child, Human Cultures (Anthropology), Psychology for Law Enforcement, and Women Writers in England and America. The fifth course, Analytic Geometry and Calculus, carried four quarter hours credit. The television courses encompass the same academic material as the comparable on-campus classes. The students must take the required examinations at the specified times and places.

If you would like details about these college television courses, write to any one or more of the following: 1) Dean of Continuing Education, University of Tennessee at Chattanooga, Chattanooga, Tenn. 37401; 2) Director, Center for Extended Learning, Division of Continuing Education, Communications and University Extension Building, University of Tennessee, Knoxville, Tenn. 37916; 3) Director, Educational Development and Research, University of Tennessee at Martin, Martin, Tenn. 38237; and 4) Director, Public Service Activities, University of Tennessee at Nashville, 323 McLemore St., Nashville, Tenn. 37203.

"America and Her Critics," produced by *Stockton State College* (Pomona, N.J.), was the first statewide television course in the history of New Jersey. It was telecast during the Fall and Spring of the 1973-74 academic year on Tuesdays and Thursdays at 12:30 P.M. and repeated again at 7:00 P.M. Channels 23 (WNJS), 50 (WNJN), 52 (WNJT) and 58 (WNJB) carried the course.

The telecasts were successful and the TV course proved attractive to many persons who were eager to earn college credit but unable to travel to a college campus. Students could earn four credits for successfully carrying out the requirements for completion of this course.

In the Fall of 1974, "America and Her Critics" was telecast to the greater New York metropolitan area on Channel 13 (WNET), one of the largest public television stations. This TV course ran for twenty-six consecutive weeks at 8:00 A.M. and again at 3:00 P.M. In view of the success of their first course, Stockton has scheduled new future programs.

Enrollment forms for those who would like to take this course and further details may be obtained from the Department of Television Instruction, Stockton State College, Pomona, N.J. 08240.

Ohio University in Athens, Ohio, has a Telecommunications Center and radio and television are used for miscellaneous classroom and campus purposes. There are three broadcast TV series: 1) Operation Slide Rule (one hour), 2) Understanding Africa (three hours) and 3) The Way Things Are (three hours). The latter is an introductory physical science series which is telecast over WOUB-TV, Athens, and WVIZ-TV, Cleveland. "Slide Rule" and "Africa" are broadcast via closed circuit on campus.

The Center also operates a closed circuit television facility which makes it possible for video tape playbacks from the Radio-TV Communications Building to be received in many different locations on the campus.

Black Hawk College in Moline, Illinois, offers courses in Psychology of Women and Dollar Power through television.

A three credit course in Family Risk Management is presented via Cable TV by *Sangamon State University* (Springfield, Ill.). Thirty half-hour programs are presented to assist viewers in understanding how wise risk and insurance planning can protect them from economic loss. The course covers such subjects as social security and insurance, auto insurance, life insurance, health insurance and protection, homeowners insurance, tort liability and total family risk strategy.

Curriculum of the Air was introduced by *C. W. Post Center of Long Island University* (Greenvale, N.Y.) in September 1974. The Curriculum offers undergraduate courses, for credit or non-credit purposes, over the college's radio station, WCWP, an FM station. For the September 1974 term, two courses were broadcast, one in Government and the other on Shakespeare. The course on Shakespeare was presented on Mondays and Wednesdays and the government course on Tuesdays and Thursdays. Both courses were broadcast at 3:00 P.M. and repeated at 7:00 P.M. Listeners who were enrolled for credit wrote a paper and took a final examination at the conclusion of the series of broadcasts. Detailed information about the Curriculum of the Air may be obtained by contacting the Office of Special Programs, C. W. Post Center, Long Island University, Greenvale, N.Y. 11548.

Central Connecticut State College has a complete television production center. Regularly scheduled undergraduate courses in Art, Mathematics, Psychology and Science are taught via television.

The *Sunrise Semester* television program has been presented by *New York University* (New York, N.Y.) since 1957. It started as a local offering in New York, New Jersey, Connecticut and parts of Pennsylvania. Since the Fall of 1963, Sunrise Semester has been shown on network television. In the greater New York area, it appears on WCBS-TV (Channel 2). Two four-credit courses are offered each semester from 6:30 to 7:00 A.M. Each course is telecast three mornings weekly during the Fall and Spring semesters. African Civilizations and The Meaning of Death were the courses offered during the Fall 1974 semester. The courses may be taken on a non-credit basis or for credit toward the B.A. degree. Persons living in cities (other than New York) where the courses are televised may contact their local colleges to determine whether these colleges wish to grant credit for these courses. Information about Sunrise Semester may be had by writing to the Office of the Associate Dean, Washington Square College, New York University, 5 Washington Square North, New York, N.Y. 10003.

At *Goshen College* in Goshen, Indiana, lectures delivered in many of the courses are directly recorded on tape cassettes. These cassettes are then stored in the college library where they are available for student use. The cassettes are generally available to all students whether or not they are registered in the specific course.

Instruction by Newspaper

Higher education came into the homes of millions of Americans via "*Newspaper University, U.S.A.*" in the Fall of 1973. A potential 50,-000,000 newspaper readers had the opportunity to take a course entitled "America and the Future of Man" through their hometown newspapers.

This national program offers college courses through the medium of more than 250 newspapers throughout the nation. The idea for "courses by newspaper" was originated and developed by Caleb A. Lewis, Director of Media Programs at University Extension, University of California, San Diego. Readers participate in this clever project for college degree credit or for intellectual enrichment with no desire for college credit. There were 188 cooperating institutions of higher education involved in the first course. Each institution is in complete charge of the course in its own area and may require that students attend mid-semester and final "contact" sessions and also pass final examinations or alternative assignments for college credit.

The first course started the week of September 30, 1973 as a 20-lecture/article series. The second "newspaper course" is entitled "In Search of the American Dream" and it started on September 29, 1974. The focus of this course was on the utopian dreams and spirit that helped shape the institutions and destiny of the United States. The course consisted of 18 consecutive weekly lectures/articles. The academic quality of these courses is under the supervision of an Academic Advisory Committee composed of professors on the University of California, San Diego faculty.

Materials for the first course are still available for $12.25 postpaid from America and the Future of Man, 415 North Highway 101, Solana Beach, Calif. 92075. For the second course, participants, in addition to reading the newspaper lectures/articles, are required to use a supplementary Reader and Study Guide. The Reader ($4.50) and Study Guide ($2.50) may be purchased by mail from In Search of the American Dream, P.O. Box 999, Bergenfield, N.J. 07621.

The newspaper courses are funded by the National Endowment for the Humanities, with additional funds provided by the Exxon Education Foundation. Would you like to know if a newspaper in your city and a college in your geographic area are cooperating with this valuable intellectual adventure? If you would, then request further information from: Project Director, Courses by Newspaper, University Extension, University of California, San Diego, P.O. Box 109, La Jolla, Calif. 92037.

Independent Study Projects

Independent study projects are for students who are enterprising, resourceful, self-reliant and well-motivated. Students who engage in independent study generally do so under the supervision of faculty members, but, essentially, they are on their own. In those colleges throughout the nation wherein independent study is permitted, it exists in many different fashions.

At *Houghton College* (Houghton, N.Y.), students may pursue topics of special interest to them by means of independent study. Here, independent study is considered to be a directed course in reading or research, which should in no way duplicate regular existing courses. Students may take this course for one, two or three hours per semester. A maximum of twelve semester hours in independent study is permitted toward graduation. Students in independent study work at their own pace. They choose a faculty member who supervises their projects and with whom they meet only for direction, progress reports and evaluation. Responsibility for learning and completing these projects rests with the students.

A student at *Mercy College* (Dobbs Ferry, N.Y.) who wishes to engage in an independent study project must present a proposal, including a brief description of the project, an outline, a bibliography, an assignment plan and the procedure for evaluating the project. Here, independent study projects are not regular courses, but rather individually developed or group projects. Credits assigned to these projects vary with each project. No more than fifteen credits of independent study are allowed toward a degree.

The *Independent Study Program* at *Bryan College* (Dayton, Tenn.) aims to help fulfill the college's educational objectives, namely, "to encourage students to think critically, to work independently and to express themselves creatively in their search for truth." Participation in this program is voluntary.

Each student who wishes to conduct an independent study project must organize a project committee consisting of at least three faculty members. As the project proceeds, the chairman and/or members of this committee meet with the student at least once weekly for guidance, discussion and evaluation. These are not weekly lecture sessions, but meetings at which the committee members suggest to the student reading materials, experiments, trips, topics to be pursued and other matters of value to the student. Upon completion of the independent study project, the student must submit a typed report of the project and results to the committee.

Students may earn no more than a total of nine credit hours by means of independent study projects. Each department reserves the right to decide how many credits in its major may be earned by independent study.

Furman University (Greenville, S.C.) requires the successful completion of thirty-two courses for graduation. One of these courses must be an independent study project. Such projects have included in-depth library work on a subject not covered in any of the traditional courses, special scientific laboratory research and independent research projects or internships in varied hospitals, industries, government laboratories or other universities.

A highly motivated *Princeton University* (Princeton, N.J.) upperclassperson may participate in the *Independent Concentration Program*. This program is geared to the student who has developed a combination of academic interests which cannot be studied as thoroughly within the existing departmental programs. By means of this independent program, this student can concentrate on a group of related courses and independent work projects which focus on his/her combined interests. At least two faculty members must serve as advisors and support the student's individual independent program.

Cochise College (Douglas, Ariz.) is located adjacent to the Sonora, Mexico, area and most of the students and the population north of the border are of Mexican descent. At Cochise, *"individual studies,"* which is their term for independent study, may be undertaken in many subject areas. Students who demonstrate academic ability in a specific discipline are permitted to work at and solve a problem under the direction of a member of the faculty. Independent work, for from one to four units of credit, may, with approval, be undertaken in such departments as Anthropology, Aviation Technology, Biology, Botany, Business, Chemistry, Drafting Technology, Economics, Geography, Geology, History, Mathematics, Physics, Psychology and Zoology.

North Country Community College (Saranac Lake, N.Y.) has developed a new program with an *Individual Studies Option*. The number of semester hours in required subjects has been reduced and fifteen semester credits have been allotted to the Individual Studies Option. The latter is a project of special interest to the individual student. There are many, varied individual studies projects in which the students can engage independently depending upon their individual interests and vocational goals. For more information about this program, write to: Director, Individual Studies Program, North Country Community College, 20 Winona Ave., Saranac Lake, N.Y. 12983.

At the *University of Notre Dame* (Notre Dame, Ind.) students who, by their senior year, have demonstrated qualities of personal and academic maturity may be elected to be *Collegiate Scholars.* The Scholars are permitted to undertake an extended program of advanced independent study and writing in place of the regular curriculum of the senior year. This program consists of a creative project involving self-disciplined research and writing based on the Scholar's level of achievement and interests. Throughout the year, the Scholar works under the direction of a member of the faculty and attends colloquia at which all the Scholars discuss their projects and benefit from an exchange of comments and criticism.

The *Para-College Program* of *Westmar College* (LeMars, Iowa) is a unique form of independent pursuit and study. A para-college experience is described as "a learning experience which complements an academic program and is encountered outside of Westmar's curriculum." The student must submit a proposal which lucidly states the nature of the project or problem to be investigated, where it will be conducted and techniques and resources which will be used in this "experience."

For every two to four weeks of full-time work experience meeting para-college standards, one credit unit will be granted. No more than three course credits of para-college experience may be allowed toward graduation. Essentially, the para-college experience option permits students to earn credit for engaging in a project outside the classroom (on or off the campus) which preferably has academic relevance. The students must use their intelligence, judgment and understanding to interpret and analyze what they have experienced.

Independent work is a noteworthy aspect of the *Johns Hopkins University* (Baltimore, Md.) undergraduate program. A student may engage in independent study or research under the supervision of an appropriate faculty member and receive academic credit for it. No more than twenty-four independent study credits are accepted toward the baccalaureate degree; a maximum of six credits may be earned in an academic year. If a student receives payment for an independent study project, no credit will be granted for this work.

University College of the *University of Minnesota* in Minneapolis has an independent study program which permits students to design their own projects and investigate subjects generally not covered in traditional courses. These projects are usually interdisciplinary and, in most cases, include off-campus experiences and resources.

Rust College (Holly Springs, Miss.) has *Individual Study Programs* in most of its major fields of concentration. These programs provide the students with opportunities for self-directed experiences, introduction to research and practice in reporting the results of investigations. Students who have demonstrated their ability to do individual study and who have an acceptable academic average may be allowed to do independent study in the form of an Individual Study Project. This project may consist of: 1) reading selected books and preparing book reports about them, 2) writing a literary or journalistic piece, 3) performing in Music, Art or Dramatics or 4) producing a competently written report on a research project. No student may receive more than twelve semester hours of credit for Individual Study and no more than six of these may be earned in one semester.

An extensive program of independent study is available to students at *Finch College* in New York City. Starting in their freshman year, students are allowed to devote as much as one fourth of their work each term to an independent project. The project may be conducted on or off campus and must be sponsored by a faculty member with expertise in the subject of the project.

Students at *Trinity College* in Hartford, Conn., who may not want to participate in the Individualized Degree Program (see Chapter 4), but may want to undertake independent study projects for specific courses, may receive approval from a member of the faculty to enroll for one or two course credits in independent study. This mode of study may involve library, laboratory or field work.

The *Open Semester Program* at Trinity College offers students the opportunity to undertake full-time independent study or an internship in a government agency or private organization. Under this program, the qualified student is allowed to indulge in academically acceptable independent research or study. This semester may be spent on or off campus and generally takes place during the student's sophomore or junior year. The project of an individual student's Open Semester Program is usually allied with that student's educational objective. Thus, there have been recent Open Semester projects in creative writing, dramatics, study of theology in Switzerland, experimental work in environmental psychology, evaluation of the criminal justice system in Hartford, study of the economic development of the Philippines and internships in municipal government, clinical psychology programs, journalism and educational television. Upon the successful completion of an Open Semester Program project at Trinity, the student may receive up to four courses worth of credit toward satisfying the requirements toward the bachelor's degree.

Independent study courses are available in many departments throughout the *University of Arizona* (Tucson, Ariz.). Students study on their own aided by occasional conferences with their teachers. No limitation has been placed on the number of units students may accumulate by means of independent study.

Students at the University of Arizona may take such independent study courses as Aerospace and Mechanical Engineering, Biological Sciences, Educational Psychology, Electrical Engineering, Elementary Education, Finance—Insurance—Real Estate, French, Geography, Geology, German, Government, History, Home Economics, Italian, Journalism, Library Science, Marketing, Mathematics, Metallurgical Engineering, Music, Natural Resources, Recreation, Office Administration, Oriental Studies, Pharmaceutical Sciences, Philosophy, Physical Education for Women, Physics, Portuguese, Psychology, Public Administration, Range Management, Reading, Religious Studies, Secondary Education, Sociology, Spanish, Speech Communications, Systems and Industrial Engineering, and Watershed Management. For detailed information, write to: Director, Independent Study, Division of Continuing Education, University of Arizona, 103 Administration Bldg., Tucson, Ariz. 85721.

After the freshman year, students at *Simpson College* in Indianola, Iowa may request permission to undertake independent study. The subjects of these independent projects may belong to any one of a vast variety of major or other areas as long as they have academic justification and are approved by responsible faculty members.

At *Newton College* (Newton, Mass.), all students except first semester freshmen may take one course of independent study per semester under the direction of a faculty member. This is an individual study course and it may be in the form of a research project or a program of reading in a particular field. The research or reading must be in a subject matter not covered in any of Newton's regular courses. Generally, a maximum of one unit of credit is granted for the successful completion of a course of independent study.

7.
OFF THE CAMPUS
—ON TO THE COMMUNITY

Among the many new developments in the realm of nontraditionality is the concept of "off-campus experiences." There are many varieties of off-campus experiences and, in the main, they are valuable in providing concurrent practical applications of what has been, or is being, learned in the classrooms.

Field Experience

The *Applied Study Experience* (or, the *Applied Study Quarter,* as it is also known) at *Sangamon State University* in Springfield, Illinois, is a full quarter of field experience designed to give the student experiential learning in an off-campus environment. All candidates for the B.A. degree must successfully complete an Applied Study Quarter. Students spend ten to eleven weeks in a work assignment suited to their educational and/or career goals. These assignments may be in business, community service, government, politics, teaching or any other suitable activity.

A proposal endorsing the concept of a general *Field Experience Program* was approved in September 1973 by the College Park Campus Senate of the *University of Maryland* (College Park, Md.). A Field Experience here is defined as "a service-learning experience in which the student earns academic credit for field work and related academic study."

The Field Experience offers students an experiential link between their academic work and the realities of the community beyond the college campus. Students who wish to participate in Field Experience projects must register for the courses entitled Field Experience Assignment (Course 386) and Field Work Analysis (Course 387). In this way, students may incorporate the experience gained in the field work with the knowledge acquired in the classroom. Upon completion of the projects, the students present a report or product representing an integration of practical experience and theoretical analysis.

Students may earn from one to three semester credits for the completion of Course 386 and from one to three semester credits for participation in Course 387. A representative from the sponsoring agency at which the Field Experience assignment takes place and a member of the University of Maryland faculty act as project advisors to the students and offer guidance as needed. Thus, the Field Experience serves as a vehicle for relating curriculum with community and vice versa.

The juniors and seniors at *Elmhurst College* in Elmhurst, Illinois, put their "interim" month of January to good use in a *Field Experience Program*. The purpose of this program is to complement classroom learning with educational and work experience gained through serving for a month on a job related to the student's academic major. The Placement Advisor and department chairman cooperate with each student to obtain a field placement that will provide a meaningful experience. The student receives financial compensation from the employer and course credit from the college.

Elmhurst students have held such Field Experience positions as the following, in accord with their majors: Accounting Trainee, Arboretum Program Assistant, Bank Intern, Biochemical Research Assistant, Chaplain's Assistant, City Management Assistant, Commercial Art Intern, Computer Programmer Trainee, Drama and Art Program Aide, Financial Planning Trainee, Guidance Intern, Hospital Assistant (student with disability), Laboratory Technician, Library Assistant, Newspaper Reporter (Assistant), Personnel Assistant, Pharmacy Trainee, Political Party Worker, Recreation Program Assistant, Retailing Trainee, Social Worker Assistant and Urban Planning Commission Aide.

St. Mary's College (Notre Dame, Indiana) has an interesting *Tucson Program* which gives students the opportunity to spend a semester in an educational and geographic setting very different from the home campus. The Tucson "campus" is approximately twenty minutes northwest of center city Tucson, Arizona. The program aims to provide the students with an educational-social-spiritual experience as an exciting, stimulating alternative to the home campus. Students must have completed their freshman year to be considered for the Tucson Program.

The curriculum at Tucson stresses the unique southwestern areas of study and the benefits from the tremendous resources of the Tucson region. The integrating factor of the program is its spiritual dimension and its spiritual activities to heighten the students' self-understanding and enable them "to grow ever closer to the God of us all." Courses in the Tucson Program include Native-Arts, Jewelry, Weaving, Southwest History, Desert Biology, Socio-Cultural Aspects of the Southwest and Community Studies (The Tucson Region).

At *Mount Saint Mary's College* (Emmitsburg, Md.) selected Sociology, Psychology and Business majors in their junior and senior years are allowed to spend a specified amount of time at supervised work activities related to their academic major programs. This work is done at nearby institutions. Sociology and Psychology majors, for example, may work in orphanages and mental and penal institutions, and with probation and parole officers in neighboring communities.

Keuka College (Keuka Park, N.Y.) has a five-week (mid-November through December) *Field Period* in which Keuka students participate during each of the years they are in residence at the college. The Field Period is a valuable off-campus learning experience. Students may engage in any of the following three types of Field Period experiences: 1) Individual Placement—students become involved in a community service activity or in exploring areas in which their vocational interests may lie; they may be placed in positions in hospitals, libraries, schools, government agencies or social agencies; 2) Group Experience —groups of students attend seminars in varied locations, such as Washington, Canada, Mexico, the United Nations in New York City and a Theater Tour in New York City; and 3) Keuka World Emphasis Service (KWES)—students may work or study in another country after receiving the necessary preparation by the faculty member in charge of this experience.

In the Fall of 1973, the *School of Community Service and Public Affairs* of the *University of Oregon* began to offer bachelor's degree programs in Community Service, Public Affairs (Administration) and Leisure, Environmental and Cultural Services. Supervised field study is an integral part of these programs. Students must spend a minimum of one term, usually two to three terms, in an off-campus practical learning experience. The specific number of terms required varies with each department. Students earn credit for this field study. The formal field instruction consists of three regular courses: 1) Field Supervision (two credits)—gives students the opportunity to visit and observe varied organizations and enables them to decide where they would like to do their field study; 2) Supervised Field Study (twelve credits)—students work under faculty and agency supervision in a community setting at full-time jobs related to their major studies; thus, for example, students in Community Services may serve as group counselors in a community agency, students in Public Affairs may serve as assistants to the City Manager and students in Leisure, Environmental and Cultural Services may serve as tourist facility managers; 3) Theory-Practice Integration (three credits)—classroom concepts are linked with practice in this seminar which accompanies the Supervised Field Study.

Details about this field instruction program may be obtained from the Director, Field Experience, School of Community Service and Public Affairs, University of Oregon, Eugene, Ore. 97403.

The *University of Pennsylvania* (Philadelphia, Pa.) has an Office of External Affairs which conducts an extensive field study program in cooperation with numerous agencies and firms in the Philadelphia metropolitan area. Internship and field study opportunities are available for students in most major departments of study. Internship positions are available in civic and public service agencies for Urban Studies majors. Programs for all students are planned in consultation with the Field Study Committee.

At *North Central College* (Naperville, Ill.), students have many off-campus opportunities gathered together under the title, *IMPACT*. Via IMPACT, a student may: 1) study abroad for a term or an academic year (most often foreign language students participate in this); 2) attend another school in the United States and take courses related to the student's objectives at North Central (Political Science credit may be acquired by those who participate in *The Washington Term* at *American University* in Washington, D.C. and *The United Nations Term* in New York City in cooperation with *Drew University*, Madison, N.J.); and 3) live off campus, perhaps even out of the country, and conduct field research and/or participate in relevant work situations. (More than one discipline may be involved in the research study;

for example, those who enroll in the *Urban Term* can earn credits in Psychology, Education, Religious Studies or other related major subject area.)

The *Undergraduate Research Opportunities Program* (*UROP*) at the *Massachusetts Institute of Technology* (*MIT*) stimulates intellectual commitment and self-direction. Students are encouraged to participate in any one of a wide range of research projects in this program. Although some of these projects are on campus, most of them are off-campus activities. Students who participate in these projects have excellent opportunities for personal and professional growth by working together with and establishing special ties with faculty members, exploring areas and topics otherwise unavailable to them, coming face-to-face with real world problems and situations and establishing a focus for their future careers.

The participating student has a faculty supervisor and an off-campus professional co-supervisor. Collaboration between the student and the cooperating off-campus organization may start at any time during the academic year. Many government agencies, corporate research laboratories, museums, hospitals and miscellaneous non-profit institutions are among the organizations that offer opportunities to UROP students. Students may receive academic credit or remuneration for participation in UROP, but not both.

Opportunities for participation exist in all of the academic departments and range from the Humanities and the Social Sciences to Science and Engineering. The *Director of MIT Undergraduate Research Opportunities* gives complete information about UROP and lists the "Current UROP Off-Campus Contacts."

Princeton University, West College in Princeton, N.J. has a credit-granting *Semester-in-the-City* program. Students who participate in this program live in a selected city and affiliate themselves with a municipal government agency or a private, non-profit organization. The Office of Urban Studies operates this program.

Coker College (Hartsville, S.C.) has incorporated *Field Service* as an integral part of its curriculum. The *Field Service Program* started in February 1972 and since then approximately one out of three students has participated in this program during each quarter term.

Field Service is considered Coker's "classroom in the community." It is a learning experience that enables students to put their skills to use and explore new avenues while trying to arrive at career decisions. Students devote a minimum of eight hours a week to their Field Service commitments. Some extend their field work to sixteen-hour internships and, in some cases, to full-time internships.

In entering upon a Field Service position, the student is making a commitment to a particular field for the purpose of relating study to work. There are many participating community agencies which have varied apprentice positions and internships available to Coker students in accord with their areas of study. Details about this program may be obtained from the Field Service Director, Coker College, Hartsville, S.C. 29550.

Radcliffe College (Cambridge, Mass.) has an off-campus program of social action projects called *Education for Action* or *E4A*. E4A aims to help undergraduates become involved in social change. Students may devise their own projects, with the aid of and direction from E4A, or E4A may assist them in locating an existing project which meets with their personal social involvement interests. Where necessary, students are subsidized to enable them to work on these projects.

E4A has a network of contacts throughout the United States. Students may work on miscellaneous projects in the neighboring Cambridge community or thousands of miles away. One student worked to expand a food cooperative to include the elderly in the community; another worked with the legally indigent to assist them in getting the best possible legal help; and yet others have organized a health agency in a Black community, worked as a medical assistant to Chicanos in New Mexico, aided divorced mothers, investigated the attitudes of Congresspersons in Washington, D.C. on important issues, done abortion counseling and participated in a variety of other projects to be of assistance to their fellow human beings.

If you would like more information about E4A, write to the Director, Education for Action, Radcliffe College, Agassiz House, Cambridge, Mass. 02138.

Lynchburg College (Lynchburg, Va.) has a *Released Semester General Perspectives Program,* which permits students to travel almost anywhere in the world to seek the kind of experiences which they desire and consider relevant to their future. Students who wish to participate in a Released Semester must draw up a general plan of activities with the assistance of a faculty advisor and have it approved by a committee.

At the end of the Released Semester, the students are required to present a well-written 25,000 word diary or essay for deposit in the college library. Twelve hours of credit are awarded for a successful Released Semester. The following semester, these students enroll in a three-hour seminar wherein they share their experiences and discuss their projects and encounters in the many different places where they traveled and lived.

Students at *Brown University* (Providence, R.I.), *Dartmouth College* (Hanover, N.H.), *Hampshire College* (Amherst, Mass.), *Trinity College* (Hartford, Conn.), *Tufts University* (Medford, Mass.) and *Wesleyan University* (Middletown, Conn.) who decide to take a term away from their respective schools to acquire off-campus experiences may be placed on voluntary or paying positions by the Institute for Off-Campus Experience of Boston, Mass., which has agreements for this purpose with these colleges. Students may be placed in business, government and industry, and in political, social service, labor and science agencies in varied geographical locations throughout the United States.

Internships

To give students a view of what it is like in "real life" situations, *Saint Francis College* in Biddeford, Maine, instituted a number of *Internship Programs.* Education—Teacher Preparation students may intern in local schools, Business Administration and Economics students in banks, corporations and similar organizations, Sociology students in welfare or social agencies and Political Science students in City Hall or the State House. These internships not only give students practical experience in the fields they hope to enter, but also often result in job offers to the internees who consequently have jobs waiting for them as soon as they receive their college degrees.

Every student attending *Endicott Junior College* in Beverly, Mass., must participate in the *Internship Project.* The Internship here is a four-week, off-campus assignment in the month of December during the two years in which a student is enrolled at Endicott. This assignment is related to the student's major field of study. At work as an Intern, the students have the opportunity to discover whether or not they made the correct choice of major and to gain experience in their major field. Some organizations at which these students work as Interns compensate the students for their work. Many, however, do not. Endicott does not require that the students be compensated for their work as Interns. The college intends that the four-week work opportunity be a learning experience and an exploration and introduction to the student's intended career rather than a means of earning money while attending college.

Students serve internships in the following academic major programs: Advertising, Art (Ceramics, Commercial Art, Fashion Design, Interior Design), Child Development and Education, Hospitality Administration (Hotel-Motel Management, Restaurant Management, Institutional Management), Photography, Radio-Television, Retailing and Secretarial (Executive, Legal, Medical, Technical) and the following pre-professional majors: Dental Hygiene, Medical Record Librarian, Medical Technologist, Nursing, Occupational Therapy, Physical Education, Physical Therapy, Social Service and Teaching.

If you would like to have details about these Internship Programs, write to: President, Endicott Junior College, Beverly, Mass. 01915.

The *Converse Career Program* of *Converse College* (Spartanburg, S.C.) is a carefully planned opportunity for students to explore the occupational elements within the liberal arts; it is, thus, liberal arts with the addition of practical experience through an internship. The program aims to challenge college women to a life of service and work.

Converse has a traditional four-year baccalaureate degree program. The Career Program bridges the gap between the traditional degree program and the world of practical affairs. There are many types of Career Programs at Converse depending upon the students' major. All include an internship. The internship enables the students to apply and test out what they have learned in their classroom lectures and from their required readings. English majors who are interested in journalism may serve a six-week term as interns on a newspaper in either their junior or senior year. Sociology majors concerned about urban affairs may serve an internship of similar time length in an urban planning office. The locale of the internship varies with the individual major.

Would you like detailed information about the Converse Career Program in your desired major? If so, write to the Vice President for Academic Affairs, Converse College, Spartenburg, S.C. 29301.

Summer internships are a tradition at *Mount Holyoke College* (South Hadley, Mass.). All Mount Holyoke students who so desire may serve summer internships in Washington, D.C., and in international organizations in such places as Bangkok, Geneva, London, Paris, Rome and Vienna. Internships are valuable forms of experiential learning and students in all major departments are encouraged to participate. The internship should be related to the student's major. Thus, a History major may serve an internship in an historical archive and a Theater major may work in a summer theater.

In 1972, the *School of Business Administration* of the *University of Dayton* (Dayton, Ohio) initiated its *Internship Program* for full-time undergraduate students. This is "an off-campus professional development opportunity." Employers in the Dayton area who participate in this program have salaried and non-salaried internships available for the students. The student must serve three and one-half hours per week for each internship credit hour. For details about this program, contact the Internship Coordinator, Office of Special Services, School of Business Administration, University of Dayton, Dayton, Ohio 45409.

Students at *Finch College* in New York City may pursue any one of numerous internships available to them while also participating in regular on-campus courses. The internships may be for the month of January only or they may be for an entire semester. Internships may be arranged in such departments as History and Government, Sociology and Anthropology, English and Comparative Literature and Art History and Art. The degree of professional experience gained is evaluated by the supervising faculty member in conjunction with the professional internship supervisor.

In September 1973, *Adrian College* (Adrian, Mich.) established a sixteen-hour *Internship Program* to enable students to apply their classroom concepts to practical work situations in the outside world, preferably in the immediate vicinity of the college. During the Spring 1974 semester, students in the Art, Biology, Earth Science, English (Language), History, Home Economics, Language, Physical Education, Psychology, Religion and Sociology departments participated in internships.

A senior internship in Psychology for which students may earn up to a maximum of eighteen semester hours credit is available at *Central Wesleyan College* (Central, S.C.) to superior students who show promise of professional development. Placement with supervised training is generally in a community service agency.

College of DuPage, a community college in Glen Ellyn, Illinois, offers some interesting work-study experiences through *Internship Programs.* Some of the fields included in these programs are: Building Construction, Engineering Drafting, Food Services, Graphic Arts, Hotel-Motel Management, Radiological Technology, Secretarial Science and Supermarket Management.

Accounting majors at *Central Connecticut State College* (New Britain, Conn.) may participate in the *Business Administration Intern Program* and benefit from a year-long internship in the work-study program of the Internal Revenue Service.

The term *"apprenticeship"* rather than internship is used at *Harriman College* (Harriman, N.Y.). The final phase of the Secretarial Studies curriculum leading to an associate degree is a six semester hours *Apprenticeship in Secretarial Occupations.* This is a supervised work experience program in local offices. Students who are interested in merchandising careers may participate in a *Store Service Apprenticeship.* This may be taken as a one semester course for three semester hours or for two semesters for six semester hours. It gives students the chance to acquire actual store experience under competent supervision.

In Chapter 8, mention is made of the Great Lakes Colleges Association (GLCA) and its overseas programs. GLCA also sponsors an *Arts Program in New York* and an *Urban Semester in Philadelphia.* Students in all of the GLCA member colleges may participate in the Arts Program and the Urban Semester. (See Chapter 8 for the names and addresses of the member colleges.)

The Arts Program in New York aims to provide the participants with expanded experience and knowledge of all the Arts through daily access to the tremendous cultural resources of New York City. Junior and senior Arts majors are given preference in the selection of this program's participants. However, non-Arts majors and sophomores who have demonstrated their abilities in the Arts are sometimes accepted too. The "arts" here refers to Creative Writing, Dance, Drama, Fine Arts, Journalism and Music.

Most students who participate in the Arts Program accept *apprenticeships* in order to get an intimate and realistic view of the professional standards, procedures, materials and personnel associated with the branch of the Arts in which their major interest lies. The apprenticeships occupy at least twelve hours of a student's time per week.

There are many cooperating sponsors of apprenticeships and they include varied theater and theater groups, dance workshops, art galleries, museums, magazines, music schools, composers, painters, sculptors, filmmakers, photographers, television producers, novelists and poets.

Those who do not wish to become apprentices may undertake independent study projects or some other individually planned study or research project. All of the students meet at a Program Seminar once each week and share and discuss their experiences. Students are encouraged to take advantage of the many cultural resources available to them by attending museum lectures and exhibits, visiting studios and reading to keep up with latest occurrences in the visual and dramatic arts. Students may receive sixteen credit hours for a full semester of participation and ten and two-thirds credit hours for a full quarter of participation.

Details about this program may be obtained from the Campus Representative for the Arts Program at each GLCA member institution or by writing to: Great Lakes Colleges Association, Arts Program in New York, 2182 Broadway, New York, N. Y. 10024.

The GLCA Urban Semester in Philadelphia aims to prepare students to live in an increasingly urbanized society and to stimulate their own personal, social and professional development. Germantown, a multi-racial community in northwestern Philadelphia, is the site of the GLCA program. The major facilities where the students work and learn about urban problems are found in the churches, schools, related agencies and recreational areas in Germantown and in greater Philadelphia.

Hope College is the agent for this program on behalf of the other GLCA member colleges and participants in this program are enrolled at Hope for the semester. Credit for the work done by the students participating in the Urban Semester in Philadelphia is granted through the Department of Interdisciplinary Studies of Hope College. The credit is transferred to the student's home college after the satisfactory completion of this Semester. Further information about this Semester may be obtained from a GLCA member institution and from the Great Lakes Colleges Association, Philadelphia Urban Semester, 59 West Chelten Ave., Philadelphia, Pa. 19144.

Off-Campus Volunteer Services

EB-WELL, the abbreviated version of *"East Boston-Wellesley,"* is a recently developed social service program between the East Boston community and *Wellesley College* (Wellesley, Mass.). Wellesley students and faculty members may volunteer to serve in the East Boston community on jobs specified by the community. The EB-WELL house located in East Boston serves as the coordinating center for these activities. Students who are concerned about urban problems have an excellent opportunity to work and study here; members of the Wellesley faculty give some Sociology courses at this center.

Susquehanna University in Selinsgrove, Pa., is a small, church-related, residential, coeducational college where numerous off-campus volunteer programs enrich the on-campus curriculum. Involvement in these programs is voluntary. There are more than twenty University organized and coordinated volunteer programs through which students are able to contribute to the well-being of the greater regional area. Some students volunteer at the Selinsgrove State School, others at the Day Care Center and yet others at approximately twenty different social agencies in the Central Susquehanna region. These services are of value to the community and educationally rewarding to the student-volunteers.

The *Office of Volunteer Programs* of *Johnson State College* (Johnson, Vt.) was established in 1972 to enable students to use their talents and energies to ease community problems. This Office locates human services projects in neighboring areas and places interested students in these projects. The students are awarded academic credit for their volunteer work. It is possible too for students to work on a volunteer project during the Summer and earn credit for it.

There are about twenty-five different projects now open to students through the Office of Volunteer Programs. The settings of these projects are child development centers, community recreation programs, hospitals, mental health agencies, prisons, schools, tutoring and special education projects. These volunteer projects are for mature, committed students who wish to become involved off campus in relevant educational experiences on a voluntary basis.

All students who hope to earn a baccalaureate degree, including the new Bachelor of General Studies degree, from *Iowa Wesleyan College* (Mount Pleasant, Iowa) must complete a project of volunteer services. This is known as the *Responsible Social Involvement (RSI) Program*. Upon successfully completing an RSI project, the student receives six semester hours of credit. Iowa Wesleyan is probably the only American institution of higher education which requires all of its students to participate in a volunteer service project and grants credit for it. The RSI experience is so meaningful to the students that about one-third of the students modify their career directions as a result of the RSI project in which they participate.

Iowa Wesleyan has incorporated the RSI project into the undergraduate curriculum as a graduation requirement because it believes that responsible service to society is as essential an aspect of education as classroom participation, laboratory work and book reading. The RSI project offers a fine opportunity for students to combine action, idealism and learning. It is equivalent to six weeks of full-time work. Students are free to create their own projects, ideally involving socially valuable services in some area of pressing social needs.

Iowa Wesleyan deserves high praise for requiring this project of all of its students and thereby, hopefully, instilling a sense of social commitment and cooperation in its students. If you would like further information about RSI, contact the Director, The Office for Responsible Social Involvement, Iowa Wesleyan College, Mount Pleasant, Iowa 52641.

Public Libraries

Many libraries throughout the country have for some time held seminars and lectures on subjects of special interest to the adults in their communities. Now, some libraries have begun to cooperate with colleges and universities in their cities and states by making it possible for persons of all ages to obtain college credits through the use of the libraries' facilities.

Western Kentucky University (Bowling Green, Ky.) recently established a system of public library courses as part of their *Extended Campus Program.* During the 1973-74 year, about 600 students were enrolled in public libraries in neighboring counties and cities. The courses, for either college credit or continuing education units, were taught in classrom facilities in the public libraries. Among these courses were English, Psychology, Accounting, Music, Folk Guitar, Home Economics, Family Living and Home Decoration.

Barat College in Lake Forest, Illinois, in a mutual arrangement with the members of the Associated Colleges of the Midwest consortium (see Chapter 8 for the names of the members of ACM), participates in a *Newberry Library Program in the Humanities.* The Newberry Library is one of the great research libraries in the United States. The students in this program conduct research in the Humanities and study a selected topic or historical period through access to Newberry Library's approximately one million volumes and four million manuscripts. Academic credit is granted by Barat College or any of the other ACM member colleges to the students who successfully conclude a research study in this library program.

During the Winter Session program which takes place during the month of January at *Lincoln College* in Lincoln, Illinois, home reading courses, facilitated by public library books, are offered in the fields of Biology, Business Administration, Political Science and Parapsychology. (For more information on this, see Chapter 3.)

St. Clair Shores Public Library in St. Clair Shores, Michigan, functions as a *"College Without Walls"* (CWW) in cooperation with *Macomb County Community College* (Warren, Mich.). The only requirement for participation in CWW is the desire to be involved in a self-study program either for college credit or solely for self-improvement. Essentially, this College Without Walls is a program of individual study for self-enrichment and/or for college credit (via preparation for CLEP).

To enroll in CWW, students visit the St. Clair Shores Public Library for an interview and discussion of the courses available. After arriving at a decision as to which courses they will take, students are issued a CWW library card. Study materials and detailed reading lists are available for each course. There are no fees, no classes to attend, no homework assignments, no teachers and no time limits. Students may study at their own pace. Counseling and independent study services are offered free of charge.

Since one of the aims of the CWW program is to prepare participants for CLEP exams, courses are offered in the subjects for which CLEP exams are available. If you would like more information about this College Without Walls program, contact the St. Clair Shores Public Library, 22500 Eleven Mile Rd., St. Clair Shores, Mich. 48081.

Wheels, Wagons, Water and Wings

Students from time immemorable have used traveling time for studying or learning purposes. On buses and trains, in cars and wagons, students have sat with open books reading their next assignment, doing homework or cramming in some last minute information for an exam. Now, however, there are some standard college classes taking place in varied means of transportation enabling students to get college credits while in the process of traveling.

Berea College in Berea, Kentucky, has a *"Classroom on Wheels Program,"* which is essentially Nursing courses on wheels. Berea offers a four-year Nursing Education program leading to a B.S. degree which makes it possible for a student to earn a college degree while meeting the qualifications for becoming a Professional·Nurse. Junior student nurses, in order to get clinical experience not available in Berea, must travel four mornings per week to nearby hospitals. This involves spending many hours on the road. This travel time is put to good use, for Berea has several passenger vans arranged like miniature classrooms.

In these vans, as the students travel to and from their hospital assignments, they participate in discussions about the clinical procedures at the hospitals. The hospitals at which the students get their training specialize in child care, surgical nursing, tuberculosis and mental health problems.

Classrooms on Wheels are used too by seniors who take the twelve-week Public Health Nursing course. In this course, the students work with the people of the rural areas and also spend some time working at the State Tuberculosis Hospital in London, Kentucky. Classroom learning takes place in the vans as these student nurses travel back and forth between the Berea campus and the hospital and rural areas.

The drivers of the "classrooms on wheels" vans are regular Berea College students and this work is their labor assignment. (See Chapter 10 for a description of "labor assignment.")

Classroom-On-Wheels is also the title of a program of *Adelphi University's School of Business Administration* (Garden City, N.Y.). Credit courses in Business Administration on both the undergraduate and graduate levels are given on the Long Island and Penn Central Railroads.

Three-credit courses in Business Statistics, Corporation Finance, Government Politics and Business, and Taxes for Non-Accounting Majors were available to commuters on the Brewster Line of the Penn Central Railroad in the Spring 1974 term. In the Fall of 1974, commuter-students were offered courses in Microeconomic Analysis, Securities Markets and Introduction to Electronic Data Processing for three credits each. For the convenience of the students, courses are offered in the evening as well as the morning commuting hours. Those who plan to get their baccalaureate degrees should apply to have their business and life experience evaluated for possible college credits.

If they wish, commuter-students may take these Classroom-On-Wheels courses on a non-credit basis. There are also non-credit courses on schedule in conversational French and Spanish, Psychology and Speed Reading.

Details about the Classroom-On-Wheels program may be obtained from the Director, Classroom-On-Wheels, Adelphi University, School of Business Administration, Garden City, N.Y. 11530.

A Portland Community College (Portland, Ore.) teacher offers instruction in basic learning skills to members of neighboring communities and counties in his "classroom in a truck." He drives and teaches in PCC's mobile learning van.

The route of his traveling classroom and the time schedules of places where he parks are publicized in advance. Anyone who wishes to brush up on Math or English, study literature, prepare for the high school equivalency examination or study for the Oregon driver's test are welcome in the van. All of the facilities and learning materials are provided by PCC.

Portland Community College is to be commended too for another use to which it puts a specially designed van. Persons (students and others) with physical disabilities are provided with transportation from their homes to any of the college centers and back again to their homes by means of a specially designed van equipped with an electric lift, tracks and seatbelts. The van is in operation from 6:45 A.M. to 6:00 P.M.

Catonsville Community College (Catonsville, Md.) has an interesting feature on wheels. It has a *Mobile Van* which travels throughout the community, to shopping centers, industries, schools, the Timonium Fair and elsewhere, and is used to explain the nature of the college programs and courses to the citizenry. It also serves as a place for class registration and book sales.

A *Mobile Counseling Unit* is operated by *Penn Valley Community College* (Kansas City, Mo.). This unit tours the urban areas of Kansas City. It aims to find and train the unemployed, especially high school dropouts, and to provide them with information on occupational and educational opportunities open to them.

Try to visualize taking a course on a Mediterranean cruise ship. Delightful thought, isn't it! Well, it can be done. The *Evangel College Travel Seminar* is a Mediterranean cruise course conducted by *Evangel College* (Springfield, Mo.) during the January term. Classes take place aboard ship and field trips are conducted at most of the Mediterranean ports. Students receive three credit hours from the Bible Department. Evangel has invited *Lee College* (Cleveland, Tenn.) students to participate in this cruise course. Would you like details? Then, write to the Office of the Dean of either Evangel College, Springfield, Mo. 65802, or Lee College, Cleveland, Tenn. 37311 for further information.

Wheels, wagons, water—and soon it will be "wings." Yes, the time is probably not far off when you will fly across the country or across the oceans in a jet and, instead of watching a Grade B motion picture, you will take a course in such relevant subjects as the culture, geography, history or language of the region or country to which you are traveling. Jetucation—education in a jet—is surely one of the nontraditional forms of education of the future in this jet age.

8.
THE WORLD IS YOUR CAMPUS —STUDY ABROAD

Increasing numbers of colleges and universities are providing study abroad opportunities to those of their students who wish to partake of these overseas course offerings. There are over 500 study abroad programs operated by American institutions of higher education. Many of these overseas programs are for an academic year or term; others are specifically for the Junior year, the Summer Session, the January Interim or lesser periods of time.

You will also find mention of study abroad programs in several of the other chapters since, as I have already stated, there is a good deal of unavoidable chapter-category overlapping. Here, we will highlight significant study abroad programs. Much that is learned in this non-traditional manner can be put to good use for future career purposes.

Academic Year or Term Abroad Programs

After completing their freshman year, students at *DePauw University* (Greencastle, Ind.) are eligible to participate in an *International Studies* program for a year or a term. In the Eastern Europe Semester, the formal academic period is in Vienna and students choose three of the following courses: History of Contemporary Eastern Europe, Literature of Eastern Europe, Comparative Politics of Eastern Europe and East European Economic Relations.

In the Western Europe Semester, the formal academic program takes place in Freiburg, Germany, and the students choose from such courses as European Literature in the Twentieth Century, Art in Western Europe, Economics of European Integration and Applied German.

DePauw University also serves as an agent college for Africa within the Great Lakes Colleges Association. As a result, DePauw students may participate in African Studies programs at the University of Dakar in Senegal, Fourah Bay College in Sierra Leone, University of Nairobi in Kenya, University of Ibadan in Nigeria, the University of Legon in Ghana and Cuttington College in Liberia.

Students in all of the other member colleges of the Great Lakes Colleges Association may also participate in these programs. The colleges of the GLCA are: *Albion College* (Albion, Mich.), *Antioch College* (Yellow Springs, Ohio), *Denison University* (Granville, Ohio), *Earlham College* (Richmond, Ind.), *Hope College* (Holland, Mich.), *Kalamazoo College* (Kalamazoo, Mich.), *Kenyon College* (Gambier, Ohio), *Oberlin College* (Oberlin, Ohio), *Ohio Wesleyan University* (Delaware, Ohio), *Wabash College* (Crawfordsville, Ind.) and *College of Wooster* (Wooster, Ohio).

For more information about DePauw's international programs, write to: Assistant Dean for International Studies and Off-Campus Programs, International Center, DePauw University, Greencastle, Ind. 46135. If you would like further information about GLCA's overseas programs, write to: Great Lakes Colleges Association, 555 E. William St., Ann Arbor, Mich. 48108.

Ohio Wesleyan University (Delaware, Ohio) has a comprehensive assortment of study abroad programs of its own in addition to the programs in which its students may participate because of Ohio Wesleyan's membership in the Great Lakes Colleges Association.

Students at Ohio Wesleyan may participate in study abroad programs in their sophomore, junior or part of their senior year. The programs are in Europe, Africa, Asia, Latin America and the Middle East. Some are one term in length; others are for a full year. For details about these programs, write to the Off-Campus Study Office, Ohio Wesleyan University, Delaware, Ohio 43015.

Students at *St. Mary's College* (Notre Dame, Ind.), if they desire it, may spend their sophomore year at St. Mary's campus in Rome, Italy; or they may choose a foreign study program through Notre Dame University at Angers, France or Innsbruck, Austria. In Rome, they may take courses in Archaeology, Italian Arts, Italian Language, Italian Literature, Contemporary Italian Problems, and Religion in Life and Culture.

The *Kentucky Committee on International Education* (KCIE) consists of representatives from the state's institutions of higher education who have joined together to coordinate and promote international education programs among public colleges and universities in Kentucky. This is similar to a consortium in that the member colleges and universities have agreed to accept in their foreign study programs students from all of Kentucky's public institutions of higher education in the same manner as their own students.

On this KCIE arrangement, *Eastern Kentucky University* in Richmond makes the following international education opportunities available: 1) a *Study Tour of England and Scotland* for three credits in English Literature; 2) a *Trip to France* for three credits in French; and 3) a *Travel-Study Program in Mexico* for three credits in Spanish. The *University of Kentucky* in Lexington makes the following available: 1) *UK-Universidad de Oriente Cooperative Project* in Venezuela for a variable number of credits in Education; 2) *UK-Federal University of Santa Maria, Brazil,* for a variable number of credits in Education; 3) *UK-Romania Summer Resident Center* for six credits in Social Sciences, Humanities or Communications; 4) *UK Summer School in Mexico* for six credits in Spanish, Social Sciences or the Humanities; and 5) *UK College of Home Economics European Fashion Merchandising Study Tour* for three credits in Home Economics.

Via the same KCIE arrangement, *Murray State University* in Murray, Kentucky, offers the *Murray Program* in Merida, Mexico, for six to nine credits in Latin American Studies, History, Spanish or Education and *Northern Kentucky State College* in Highland Heights offers an *Archaeological Field Program* in Italy. *Western Kentucky University* makes the following foreign study opportunities available: 1) *Western Kentucky in France Program* for up to thirty credits in French Language and Literature, Fine Arts, Humanities, Languages, Social Sciences, Natural Sciences or Engineering and Technology; 2) *London Theatre Study Tour* for three credits in Theater; 3) *American Association of State Colleges and Universities Junior Year in Mexico Program* for up to two semesters of credit in Anthropology, Applied Arts, Art History, Business Administration, Economics, English Language and Literature, French Language and Literature, Geography, Government, History, International Relations, Music, Natural Science, Philosophy, Psychology, Sociology and/or Spanish Language and Literature; and 4) *Holy Land Study Tour* for three credits in Religion.

The *State University of New York at Albany* (Albany, N.Y.) has an extensive assortment of study abroad programs open to its students. In the academic year programs, students register for thirty to thirty-two credits and, in some programs, for a presession of eight or nine additional credits. Current program sites of the academic year programs are Nice, France; Wurzburg, Germany; Jerusalem and Tel Aviv, Israel; Cuernavaca and Guadalajara, Mexico; Nanyang, Singapore; and Madrid, Spain. At each site, the programs involve a wide variety of academic subjects and disciplines.

For details about these and other study abroad programs available to SUNY at Albany students, write to the Office of International Programs, State University of New York at Albany, 1400 Washington Ave., Albany, N.Y. 12203.

Students who attend *Wesleyan College* (Middletown, Conn.) have available to them the following seven Wesleyan-sponsored semester programs of foreign study: 1) *Vassar-Wesleyan Semester in Madrid* to study Spanish; 2) *Wesleyan in Germany* to study German; 3) *Wesleyan in Paris* to study French; 4) *Hebrew Program in Israel* to study Hebrew in Jerusalem; 5) *Latin American Studies* in a Latin American country; 6) *Classical Studies* at the Intercollegiate Center for Classical Studies in Rome; and 7) *Kyoto in Japan* to study Japanese.

Women of *Barat College* (Lake Forest, Ill.) may participate in a number of study abroad programs as a result of Barat's arrangement with the *Associated Colleges of the Midwest* (ACM), a consortium of the following liberal arts colleges: *Beloit College* (Beloit, Wisc.), *Carleton College* (Northfield, Minn.), *Coe College* (Cedar Rapids, Iowa), *Colorado College* (Colorado Springs, Colo.), *Cornell College* (Mount Vernon, Iowa), *Grinnell College* (Grinnell, Iowa), *Knox College* (Galesburg, Ill.), *Lawrence University* (Appleton, Wisc.), *Macalester College* (St. Paul, Minn.), *Monmouth College* (Monmouth, Ill.), *Ripon College* (Ripon, Wisc.) and *St. Olaf College* (Northfield, Minn.)

Those who are interested in Central America may join the *Costa Rican Development Studies* program. San Jose, Costa Rica, is the home base for those who participate in this program of interdisciplinary field research in the Social and Biological Sciences. Japanese culture may be studied by those students who take part in the *East Asian Studies in Japan* program; the students take courses in Waseda University in Tokyo while living in the home of a Japanese family. Those who find Indian culture appealing may join the *India Studies* program which involves study at Deccan College in Poona, India, participation in seminars and independent research.

Barat College or any of the member colleges of the ACM consortium which the student attends awards the student academic credit for participating in any of the programs.

Drake University (Des Moines, Iowa) has a variety of study abroad opportunities for its students. Among the most attractive of these is the *Art in Florence (Italy) Program* during the academic year and on a special basis in the Summer term. This program is staffed by members of the faculty of the College of Fine Arts.

Goshen College, a small Mennonite college in Goshen, Indiana, has a most unusual study abroad program. Goshen requires all of its students to participate in its *Study-Service Trimester Abroad.* There are three other colleges in the United States that require all their students to spend some time studying abroad, namely, *Kalamazoo College* (Kalamazoo, Mich.), *Lake Erie College* (Painesville, Ohio) and *Callison College of University of the Pacific* (Stockton, Calif.). Goshen differs from all of these in that not just *study,* but also *service* is involved in its program.

Most Goshen students participate in the Study-Service Trimester Abroad during one of the trimesters of their sophomore year. These students are sent to a developing nation to spend a period of time at study and field work (service).

The Study-Service Trimester is fourteen weeks in length and it presents the students with the opportunity to become acquainted with the values, goals, ideals and accomplishments of another culture. There are two parts to this Trimester. During the first part, the host country is studied; the students study the country's language and such other subjects as its history, geography, government, economics, literature, art, music, social customs, religions, educational system, agricultural and industrial development and relations with the United States. During the second part, the students are sent to field locations on work or service assignments, where they serve without salary. Generally, the field work service assignment takes place in a government institution or agency operated by the host country; students help at remote rural clinics, assist mission programs, act as nurse aides in hospitals, teach English, serve as apprentices and helpers in government agencies and perform miscellaneous manual labor functions.

During both parts of this Trimester, the students live in the home of a family of the host country. Since the start of this Study-Service Trimester program in 1968, Belize (British Honduras), Costa Rica, El Salvador, Guadeloupe, Haiti, Honduras, Jamaica, Korea and Nicaragua have served as host countries. Poland and Yugoslavia were the 1974 hosts. For details about the SST Program, contact the Provost, Goshen College, Goshen, Ind. 46526.

Junior Year Abroad Programs

Many colleges offer their students the opportunity to spend their junior year in a study program overseas. This is popularly known as the *Junior Year Abroad*. A number of colleges permit their students to apply for admission to approved Junior Year programs sponsored by other institutions of higher education. Thus, students at *Bryn Mawr College* may spend their junior year studying in Paris under programs sponsored by *Sarah Lawrence College* (Bronxville, N.Y.), *Smith College* (Northampton, Mass.) and *Sweet Briar College* (Sweet Briar, Va.).

In most study abroad programs, the students have little, if any, real social or cultural involvement in the host institutions. *The Academic Term (in the Junior Year) Abroad* sponsored by *Lake Erie College* (Painesville, Ohio) differs from most of the other study abroad programs in this and a number of other ways. This program is an English, French, German, Israeli, Italian, Spanish and Swiss cultural, linguistic and academic experience. This experience is designed by staff members of the host institutions especially for Lake Erie students.

Unlike many other study abroad programs, this Academic Term Abroad is available to *all* Lake Erie students in the second term of their Junior year, without additional charge and regardless of the students' areas of academic concentration or economic status. There is a one-term orientation program in which all students take part before they go abroad in the Winter. When they return, the students participate in a one-term re-orientation program in which they analyze and evaluate the experiences they had; this "post-study abroad evaluation program" is of much value to the students.

While abroad, the Lake Erie students generally live with local host families and thus have the opportunity to experience a culture and life style different from their own on a twenty-four-hour-per-day basis. The students keep a journal of their experiences during their stay abroad. Academic credit is granted for the term abroad.

Inquiries about the Academic Term Abroad should be addressed to the Admissions Office, Lake Erie College, Painesville, Ohio 44077.

The Center for International Programs, which is a joint enterprise of *Franklin and Marshall College* (Lancaster, Pa.) and *Beaver College* (Glenside, Pa.), sponsors several study abroad programs. Among these programs are the Junior Year in Great Britain, the Vienna Semester and the Asian (Hong Kong) Semester.

Summer Abroad Programs

"The Classical World" is the title of the Summer Studies in Europe program conducted by *Pace University* (New York, N.Y.) in Rome and Athens from July 1st through August 19, 1974. This program was open not only to Pace students but to students from other colleges and universities and even to graduating high school seniors who had been accepted in a college for the 1974 Fall session.

Two courses were taught at this summer abroad: The Art and Architecture of Greece and Rome, four credits; Civilization of the Ancient World, four credits. They were taught in English by Pace professors. Classes were held in Rome for the first three weeks. Following this, the students were flown to Athens for the final three weeks of instruction. Two long weekends enabled the students to expand their educational experiences and visit other places of interest.

If, in a future Summer, you might like to participate in "The Classical World" or other Pace study abroad program, write for details to the Director, Summer Studies in Europe, Pace University, One Pace Plaza, New York, N.Y. 10038.

In the Summer of 1974, the *University of North Carolina in Greensboro* and *Guilford College* (Greensboro, N.C.) co-sponsored *"Overseas Summer Schools with Travel Abroad."* Each program consisted of six weeks of school and three weeks of individual travel, including two courses for six hours credit.

The courses in the London Summer School were: Form and Idea in the Literature of Drama and Parliament in Contemporary British Politics. In the Paris Summer School, the courses were French Conversation and French Culture and Civilization. The Athens Summer School offered The Golden Age of Athens and The Greek Experience in Classical Tragedy and Contemporary Fiction. The German Summer School offered Cultural and Political Contrasts in the Two German

States and German Conversation. The Summer School in England (University of Reading) offered Social Foundation of Open Education and Psychological Foundation of Open Education. In the Turkish Summer School, the courses were History of the Ottoman Empire and the Republic of Turkey and Business and Society.

For further information about these programs, contact the Office for Overseas Education, either at the University of North Carolina at Greensboro, Greensboro, N.C. 27412 or Guilford College, Greensboro, N.C. 27410.

Milligan College (Milligan College, Tenn.) conducts six-week *Humanities Study Tours* of Europe during the Summer Session. Students participate fully in all the events on the tour and also fulfill reading and writing requirements to receive credit for this study-tour course. A Milligan professor acts as a guide for each tour and also lectures and oversees the reading and writing assignments.

Participants in these tours may earn six hours of credit in Humanities. In some cases, credit may be granted in Art or History instead of Humanities. Completion of one year of the regular Humanities program or its equivalent is a prerequisite for admission to the Milligan College Humanities Study Tours of Europe. For details about these Study Tours, write to the Academic Dean, Milligan College, Milligan College, Tenn. 37682.

Yeshiva University (New York, N.Y.) offers a Summer program of study in Israel. Undergraduates are granted three credits for successful completion of this program.

The Division of Continuing Education of *Trenton State College* (Trenton, N.J.) offers a two-month Summer study abroad program in Italy. Classes in Art, History, Literature and Italian are held in the Stensen Institute in Florence. The courses are taught by Trenton State faculty members in two consecutive three-week sessions. Students may take a maximum of nine credits and a minimum of six credits; all of the courses are for three credits, with the exception of Italian for Beginners which carries four credits.

Students in good standing from other colleges and universities, in addition to Trenton State students, may join this culturally rewarding Summer study program. Those who would like to participate in this program should request details from the Director, Summer Study in Italy, Trenton State College, Trenton, N.J. 08625.

SPAN is the acronym for *Student Project for Amity among Nations.* It started on a small scale in 1947. Now, with headquarters at the *University of Minnesota,* it is a respected, student-led organization consisting of twelve Minnesota institutions of higher education. As of 1974, SPAN had sent more than 1,000 Minnesota students to about sixty-five different countries.

SPAN is an unusual foreign study program. It stresses that its essential purpose is international peace, understanding and friendship. Students who participate are known as SPANners. The SPANners who will be going to the same country the following Summer participate in a preparatory program in which they meet every Saturday morning during the preceding academic year for language sessions and approximately every other Saturday afternoon for culture/seminar/briefing sessions.

In the Summer of 1974, SPANners went to Brazil, Czechoslovakia, Japan and Micronesia. During the 1973-74 academic year, the advisor for each of these four country groups met with the students of each respective group and helped these students to plan the research or other project they were to conduct in their SPAN country. The advisors are faculty members who have lived in the SPAN country of their group and speak the language fluently.

Fortified with a knowledge of the history, way of life, current problems and language of their SPAN country, which they acquired in their preparatory program, the SPANners arrive in their host country in June. They spend a minimum of eight weeks working on their study projects, which may involve interviews, investigations, visits to appropriate institutions and other related activities. Before they return home in September, SPANners often have the time to visit one or more neighboring countries. Upon their return, SPANners share their experiences with school and community groups. During the Fall, they complete their project by writing it up, developing and printing accompanying photographs and doing whatever else is necessary for them to present a completed report to their advisors by the following January. SPANners earn twelve quarter credits or eight semester credits upon successfully completing their projects.

Those who would like to participate in SPAN should complete the application form and give it to the SPAN Campus Representative at their member college. Applicants are chosen on the basis of self-reliance, maturity and scholastic ability. The following are the SPAN participating institutions of higher education: *Augsburg College* (Minneapolis), *Bethel College* (St. Paul), *Carleton College* (Northfield), *College of St. Catherine* (St. Paul), *College of St. Thomas* (St. Paul), *Gustavus Adolphus College* (St. Peter), *Hamline University* (St. Paul), *Macalester College* (St. Paul), *St. Cloud State College* (St. Cloud), *St. Olaf College* (Northfield), *University of Minnesota-Duluth* (Duluth) and *University of Minnesota* (Minneapolis).

If you would like to obtain details about the SPAN program, write to the headquarters office: Minnesota SPAN Association, University of Minnesota, 720 Washington Ave., S.E., Minneapolis, Minn. 55455.

Trinity College in Hartford, Conn., has a Trinity College/Rome Campus arrangement whereby undergraduates who wish to broaden their cultural horizons may spend a Summer and a Fall semester at the Rome Campus. This Campus is located on one of the original seven hills of Rome, overlooking the Tiber. In addition to courses in Italian Language, Literature and Civilization, courses are also offered in the Humanities, History, Studio Arts, Art History, Comparative Literature, Music History, Classical Civilization, Cinema, Philosophy and Sociology. With the exception of courses in Italian Language and Literature, all courses are taught in English.

There are opportunities for side trips in and around Rome and to the Vatican City, Tivoli, Ostia Antica, Tarquinia and Cerveteri, and for excursions to Pompeii, Paestum, Naples, Florence, Assisi and Perugia. There is time for stimulating encounters with Italian students at the University of Rome, for interviews with noted writers and other important figures in Roman life and for attending musical and theatrical events. Credits earned at these Summer and Fall semester programs are added to the students' total credits toward the undergraduate degree.

January Interim Abroad Programs

Macalester College (St. Paul, Minn.) participates in and serves as the headquarters for the Upper Midwest Association for Intercultural Education (UMAIE). This consortium annually provides students from the member colleges with Interim term study abroad opportunities.

UMAIE includes the following ten institutions: *Augustana College* (Rock Island, Ill.), *Bethel College* (St. Paul, Minn.), *Carleton College* (Northfield, Minn.), *College of St. Benedict* (St. Joseph, Minn.), *College of St. Catherine* (St. Paul, Minn.), *Gustavus Adolphus Col-*

lege (St. Peter, Minn.), *Hamline University* (St. Paul, Minn.), *Luther College* (Decorah, Iowa), *Macalester College* (St. Paul, Minn.) and *St. John's University* (Collegeville, Minn.). During the January 1974 Interim term more than 300 students from these colleges studied in eighteen different countries in Africa, Asia, Europe and Latin America, and in Hawaii, the Virgin Islands and Canada.

Study abroad courses carrying three college credits are held during the January term at *Mount Saint Mary's College* (Emmitsburg, Md.). In January 1974, one course took place in London and was entitled Life and Literature. In previous years, courses have been held in Paris and Madrid and may be held there again in the near future.

Students at *St. Joseph's College* in Brooklyn, New York, may participate in a British Culture Workshop and a Field Trip to England during their January Intersession. Since these two Intersession courses are sponsored and conducted by two faculty members, one from the English department and the other from the History department, students who participate may choose to earn credit in either English or History. During the June mini-semester, students may earn credit in Social Science, since that department offers a Field Trip to Puerto Rico. This course is similar to the English trip except that it has the additional distinguishing feature of providing students with the opportunity to stay at the homes of families in the rural areas.

Nine-Day World Campus Program

New York University (New York, N.Y.) has unique nine-day non-credit seminar course-trips which it offers through its School of Continuing Education. This *World Campus Program* gives adult students an unusual opportunity to study with distinguished scholars while living in an exciting cultural center of the world. A week prior to departure, the participants attend a seminar meeting at NYU.

The 1973 seminars abroad were: Archaeology in Mexico, Art in Paris and Theater in London. For the 1974-75 academic year, the following seminars were available: Archaeology and Culture of Egypt, Archaeology in Mexico City/Cuernavaca, Art and Culture of West Africa, Ballet in Moscow/Leningrad, Mayan Archaeology in the Yucatan and Music in Vienna/Salzburg.

If you would like to receive a complete schedule of these seminars with detailed information, write to: World Campus Program, New York University, Two University Place, Room 21, New York, N.Y. 10003.

9.
HOME IS YOUR CAMPUS TOO
—CORRESPONDENCE STUDY

Probably the oldest form of nontraditional education is correspondence study. Many changes have taken place in the realm of correspondence instruction in recent years. Essentially, the use of the mail for the exchange of instructions and completed lessons between the student and the teacher is still the basis of correspondence study. However, to facilitate the learning process, home study by correspondence now also makes use of audio tapes, cassettes, records, telephone conferences and various other audio-visual aids. As time goes on, computers too will be used to an ever greater extent.

There is a growing trend toward the replacement of the terms "home study" and "correspondence study" with the term "independent study." The reason for this change is the desire to give recognition to the student's educational development and emphasis to the process of learning how to learn independently rather than to the geographic location of the learning or to the mail as the medium.

It must be stressed here, however, that students and professors alike must be careful not to confuse the terms "independent study" as used in Chapter 6 and "independent study" as used here. To avoid this possible confusion, it would be best in referring to correspondence study to use the longer term "independent study through correspondence." Most schools are still using the terms "home study" and "correspondence study"; in discussing certain schools in this chapter, I will use the terms employed by each individual school.

A college degree cannot be earned in any accredited college or university in the United States on the basis of credits accumulated solely through correspondence study. The amount of correspondence study credits accepted toward a degree varies with each institution of higher education. You must check with the registrar's office of the institution from which you would ultimately like to receive a degree as to the maximum amount of credits it will accept from correspondence study; the correspondence courses need not have been taken at this same institution.

Let us look at some of these courses and programs that are especially worthy of note.

Colorado Consortium for Independent Study

The *University of Colorado* (Boulder, Colo.), *University of Northern Colorado* (Greeley, Colo.) and *Colorado State University* (Fort Collins, Colo.) have joined together to form the *Colorado Consortium for Independent Study*. Students may earn high school and college credits and even take special certification courses by way of this consortium. This Independent Study is correspondence study which may also involve multi-media learning packages, credit by consultation and/or group study. The multi-media program may include audiotapes, slides, readings and video cassettes.

These Independent Study students are of varied ages and backgrounds. They may be a seventeen-year-old high school student or a seventy-year-old retiree, a prison inmate or a prison guard, a forty-year-old housewife or a thirty-year-old teacher seeking certification credit and a vast variety of other people who wish to learn and gather credits toward a degree while earning a living and/or caring for a family. Most are preparing for entrance or advancement in their first career; others are preparing for their second career. Students may start their studies at any time and proceed at their own speed.

Courses are available in the major areas of Accounting, Anthropology, Biology, Business, Child Development, Economics, Education, English, Fine Arts, Geography, German, History, Humanities, Journalism, Management, Mathematics, Music, Natural Resources, Office Administration, Philosophy, Physical Education and Health, Physics, Political Science, Psychology, Sociology, Spanish and Theater. Certification courses are offered in the Real Estate Certificate Program and in Childhood Education.

Details may be obtained from any of the following: 1) University of Colorado, Division of Continuing Education, Bureau of Independent Study, 970 Aurora Ave., Boulder, Colo. 80302; 2) University of

Northern Colorado, Department of Special Studies and Continuing Education, Greeley, Colo. 80639; 3) Colorado State University, Department of Continuing Education, Fort Collins, Colo. 80521.

Georgia Center for Independent Study

In Chapter 15, there is a write-up of the University of Georgia Center for Continuing Education. This Center also provides independent study programs for *Georgia College* (Milledgeville, Ga.), *Georgia Southern College* (Statesboro, Ga.) and *Valdosta State College* (Valdosta, Ga.) in addition to the *University of Georgia*. Originally, this service was called Home Study and certain courses were known as Correspondence Courses. The Center recently changed the name of this service to Independent Study to stress the extended breadth of this service.

A student may register with the *Georgia Center for Independent Study* at any time of year and take up to a maximum of three courses simultaneously. These courses may be taken for college credit or otherwise. There are courses of instruction in the following subject areas: Accounting, Agriculture, Anthropology, Art History, Banking and Finance, Business Law, Classics, Computer and Information Science, Drugs, Ecology, Economics, Education, English, Entomology, Environmental Health Services, Forestry, French, Geography, German, History, Home Economics, Journalism, Landscape Architecture, Latin, Management, Marketing, Mathematics, Pharmacy, Philosophy, Police Science, Political Science, Psychology, Religion, Sociology, Spanish and Speech.

Western Kentucky University Office of Correspondence Studies

Western Kentucky University (Bowling Green, Ky.) has a comprehensive program of college credit correspondence courses. A maximum of one-fourth of the required credits for a degree or certificate may be earned via correspondence study.

Western Kentucky offers college correspondence courses in the following subject areas: Accounting, Anthropology, Biology, Business Administration, Business Education and Office Management, Economics, Engineering Technology, English, Geography, Government, Health and Safety, History, Journalism, Mathematics, Physical Education and Recreation, Psychology, Sociology and Speech.

If you would like to enroll in any one or more of these courses and want further information, write to: Director, Office of Correspondence Studies, Western Kentucky University, Bowling Green, Ky. 42101.

University of Kansas Extramural Independent Study Center

The *University of Kansas* (Lawrence, Kans.) is another school that uses the term "independent study" for its correspondence courses. The *Extramural Independent Study Center*, a department of the University of Kansas' Division of Continuing Education, offers correspondence instruction for college or high school credit. A maximum of thirty hours of such independent study may be applied by a student toward a baccalaureate degree from the University of Kansas.

Correspondence courses are offered by Kansas in the subject areas of Anthropology, Art History, Astronomy, Business and Accounting, Economics, Education, Engineering, English (including Literature, Poetry and Creative Writing), French, Geography, German, History, Human Development, Italian, Journalism, Latin, Mathematics, Philosophy, Physical Education, Physics, Physiology, Political Science, Psychology, Sociology (including Criminology) and Spanish.

You may take any of these courses regardless of whether you have ever attended college or are presently attending some other college full- or part-time. If you would like an Enrollment Data Blank and further information, write to the Director, Extramural Independent Study Center, University of Kansas, Lawrence, Kans. 66044.

Indiana University Independent Study Division

Indiana University has a comprehensive Independent Study Division which includes credit and non-credit courses. The non-credit courses, however, do carry Continuing Education Units (see Chapter 15 for meaning of C.E.U.s).

The following departments offer correspondence courses for degree credits: African Studies, Anthropology, Business, Classical Studies, Comparative Literature, Computer Science, Economics, Education, English, Fine Arts, Folklore, Forensic Studies, French, Geography, Geology, German, Health-Physical Education and Recreation, History, Home Economics, Journalism, Linguistics, Mathematics, Music, Optics, Pharmacology, Philosophy, Political Science, Psychology, Reading and Study Skills, Sociology and Spanish. For C.E.U.s rather than for degree credits, there are courses in Citizenship, Leisure Time Living on Wheels (Trailerites), Real Estate, Labor Journalism, Securities and Investing and a study of the Comic Book in America.

Would you like more information and perhaps an application for one or more courses in this Division? If so, write to: Independent Study Division, Owen Hall, Indiana University, Bloomington, Ind. 47401.

Community College of Baltimore Home Study Program

A variety of college credit correspondence courses are offered by the *Home Study Program* of the *Community College of Baltimore* (Baltimore, Md.), Division of Continuing Education. Students may begin a course at any time during the year and are given up to one year to complete the course. These courses are available not just to those who can "attend" college only by means of correspondence, but students who are taking traditional studies on campus are also permitted to take part in this Home Study Program.

Among the correspondence courses available through this program are: Accounting, Business Law, Data Processing, Elements of Geography, Economic Geography, History of American Civilization, Law Enforcement, Mathematics, Philosophy, Political Science-American Government, Psychology and Sociology.

Enrollment information and other details may be obtained by writing to the Office of Extended Services, Division of Continuing Education, Community College of Baltimore, Baltimore, Md. 21215.

Eastern Michigan University Independent Study Through Correspondence

The Division of Field Services of *Eastern Michigan University* (Ypsilanti, Mich.) has a program of *Independent Study Through Correspondence*. Students taking courses through this program must be officially admitted to Eastern Michigan as part of the enrollment procedure. Courses are to be completed within one calendar year from the date of enrollment. A maximum of fifteen semester hours of credit from this program may be applied toward the bachelor's degree.

Courses available from Eastern Michigan's Independent Study Through Correspondence include Biology (Genetics), Community Health Problems, Comparative Study of Religion, Earth Science, Economics, Education, Educational Psychology, English Composition, English Grammar, Evolution of American Democracy, Expository

Writing, Greek History, History, Labor Problems, Literature, Modern American and British Poetry, Psychology, Roman History, Rural Sociology, Shakespeare and Sociology.

Details about this program of correspondence courses may be obtained from the Director, Independent Study Through Correspondence, 113 Sherzer Hall, Eastern Michigan University, Ypsilanti, Mich. 48197.

University of Minnesota Department of Independent Study

The *University of Minnesota* offers more than 250 courses through its *Department of Independent Study.* Some of these courses are for the improvement of one's business skills, others for occupational advancement and yet others for enjoyment and cultural enhancement. Most courses can be taken for University credit. There are also courses that meet the requirements toward a variety of University Certificate Programs.

Courses are available in the following subject areas: 1) Business—Accounting, Business Law, Business Studies, Data Processing, Finance, Industrial Relations, Insurance, Production; 2) Humanities—Art, Literature, Music, Philosophy, Recreation, Rhetoric and Theater Arts; 3) Languages—Chinese, Finnish, French, German, Greek, Japanese, Latin, Norwegian, Polish, Russian, Serbo-Croatian, Spanish and Swedish; 4) Sciences—Agriculture, Astronomy, Engineering, Entomology, Forestry, Geology, Horticulture, Mathematics and Physics; and 5) Social Sciences—Anthropology, Economics, Education, Family Studies, Geography, History, Journalism, Political Science, Psychology, Public Health, Social Studies, Social Work and Sociology.

For further information about credits, certificates and application procedures, write to: Department of Independent Study, Continuing Education and Extension, University of Minnesota, 45 Wesbrook Hall, Minneapolis, Minn. 55455.

University of Nevada-Reno, Independent Study Division

College credit and non-credit courses are offered by the *University of Nevada-Reno, Independent Study Division.* A maximum of two courses may be taken concurrently, although one course at a time is recommended. A course should be completed within one year from the date of enrollment. The maximum number of these independent study credits applicable toward a bachelor's degree in the University of Nevada System is fifteen.

Independent study courses through correspondence are offered at the University of Nevada-Reno in the following subject areas: Accounting, Animal Science, Anthropology, Biology, Economics, Education, English, Finance, Foreign Languages (French, German, Italian, Russian, Spanish), Geography, History, Home Economics, Journalism, Management, Managerial Science, Mathematics, Philosophy, Physical Education, Political Science, Psychology, Social Services and Corrections, Sociology and Zoology.

Those who would like further information about this correspondence study program should contact the Director, Independent Study Division, General University Extension, University of Nevada-Reno, Reno, Nevada 89507.

Ohio University, Extension Division
(Independent Study)

College credit may be earned by successfully completing any of a variety of correspondence courses offered by the *Extension Division (Independent Study)* of *Ohio University* (Athens, Ohio). College students, working men and women, housewives and adults from many avenues of life who would like to further their educational aims will find it profitable to pursue courses in this program. Ohio places no maximum on the amount of correspondence credit which can be applied to an Ohio University degree.

There are course offerings in the following departments: Accounting, Aviation, Botany, Business Law, Chemistry, Classical Languages, Economics, Economic Education, Education (Elementary), Education (Secondary), Engineering, Engineering (Chemical), Engineering (Civil), Engineering (Graphics), English, Film, Foreign Literatures in Translation, Geography, Government, Health–Physical Education and Recreation, History, Home Economics, Humanities, Interpersonal Communication, Journalism, Library Science, Marketing, Mathematics, Music, Philosophy, Physical Science, Physics, Psychology, Quantitative Methods, Radio-Television, Sociology and Zoology.

If you would like to receive a bulletin with detailed information and enrollment form, write to: Independent Study, Tupper Hall, Ohio University, Athens, Ohio 45701.

Pennsylvania State University Independent Study
by Correspondence

At *Pennsylvania State University* (University Park, Pa.), *Independent Study by Correspondence* is a service of Continuing Education. A student may enroll in a correspondence course at any time during the year. If correspondence study is carried on concurrently with resident (on campus) work, students must receive concurrent study permission. The various colleges of Penn State set their individual limitations as to the amount of credit a student may earn through correspondence study toward a degree at these respective colleges.

College credit courses through Independent Study by Correspondence are available in the following departments: Accounting, Art History, Biology, Business Law, Civil Engineering, Comparative Literature, Economics, Educational Psychology, Electrical Engineering, Engineering Graphics, Engineering Mechanics, English, Finance, French, Greek, History, Industrial Engineering, Journalism, Law Enforcement, Mathematics, Mechanical Engineering, Meteorology, Nutrition, Philosophy, Political Science, Psychology, Sociology, Spanish and Statistics.

If you would like to receive catalogues with course descriptions and an enrollment application, write to the Pennsylvania State University, Independent Study by Correspondence, 3 Shields Building, University Park, Pa. 16802.

University of Virginia School of Continuing Education
Independent Study Department

At the *University of Virginia* (Charlottesville, Va.), the *School of Continuing Education* has an *Independent Study Department* offering "independent study courses through correspondence." The amount of credit through independent study courses which may be applied toward a University of Virginia degree is determined by the dean of the University school or department from which the student wishes to obtain the degree. The School of Continuing Education of the University of Virginia also awards certificates to students upon their satisfactory completion of one-year and two-year programs of independent study in Arts and Sciences and in Business and Commerce.

The Independent Study Department additionally has a program of Reading Courses. Ten Reading Courses are available in varied subjects for those who wish to conform to a program involving the reading of good books. There are the following Reading Courses: American Art and Artists, American Problems, Arts and Crafts, Colonial Virginia History, English and American Poetry, Famous American Women, Great Books, Interior Decoration, Music in America and Latin America. Enrollment is open to anyone for $3.00 per course. A student-reader is entitled to a certificate after completing four courses, which consist of four books to be read and reported on in each.

Students may enroll for these courses through correspondence at any time of the year. It is suggested that no more than two courses be taken at one time. All students who wish degree or certificate credit are required to take a final examination at the completion of an independent study course.

If you have any questions you would like answered about any of these programs, address your inquiries to: Independent Study Department, School of Continuing Education, University of Virginia, P.O. Box 3697, Charlottesville, Va. 22903.

Indiana State University Independent Study, Division of Continuing Education and Extended Services

The *Division of Continuing Education and Extended Services* of *Indiana State University* (Terre Haute, Ind.) offers correspondence courses for which undergraduate credit may be earned. A maximum of thirty credits earned by way of correspondence study may be applied toward an undergraduate degree at Indiana State.

Students may enroll in these independent study courses at any time and work at their own pace. Each course must be completed by one year from the date of enrollment; however, an extension of six months is granted for acceptable reasons. Depending upon their time, ability and individual needs, students may take one or two courses simultaneously. After a student has been accepted, he is sent a lesson outline indicating all assignments and the text(s) for each course, lesson covers, lesson input envelopes and examination request forms. A supervised final examination is scheduled after the student has completed all the assignments.

Among the degree credit courses offered by Independent Study at Indiana State are: Art, Newspaper Writing, English Grammar, Literature, Short Story, American Novel, Latin, Spanish, Geography, Astronomy, History, College Algebra, Trigonometry, Analytic Geometry,

Statistics, Political Science, Psychology, Sociology, Courtship and Marriage, Social Work, Child Welfare, Theater, Broadcasting, Film Production, Broadcast and Film Writing, Accounting, Business Report Writing, Elementary Education, Tests and Measurements, Secondary Education, Exceptional Children, Personal Health Science, First Aid, and Health—Physical Education and Recreation.

All questions concerning correspondence courses should be addressed to: Independent Study, Division of Continuing Education and Extended Services, Indiana State University, Terre Haute, Ind. 47809.

Roosevelt University Division of Extended Services

Correspondence study is available at *Roosevelt University* (Chicago, Ill.) from the *Division of Extended Services*. This Division permits students to enroll at any time during the academic year and to work at whatever pace their personal circumstances permit. All correspondence courses carry three semester hours of credit and no more than two courses may be taken at any one time. A maximum of thirty semester hours of correspondence study may be accepted toward a Roosevelt University degree.

This Division offers courses in Accounting, Economics, Geography, Geology, History, Literature, Marketing, Physical Science, Political Science, Retail Merchandising, Sales Training, Sociology, Social Personality and Statistics. Details may be obtained from: Coordinator, Division of Extended Services, Roosevelt University, 430 S. Michigan Ave., Chicago, Ill. 60605.

University of Arizona Correspondence Instruction

The *University of Arizona* (Tucson, Ariz.) offers over eighty courses for credit through *Correspondence Instruction*. Among the many course offerings are: Accounting, Aerospace and Mechanical Engineering, Agronomy and Plant Genetics, Algebra, Animal Science, Anthropology, Business Law, Calculus, Criminology, Economics, Educational Psychology, Elementary Education, English, English Literature, Entomology, First Aid, French, Geography, Geology, Government, Health Education, History, Journalism, Mathematics, Oriental Studies, Personnel Management, Philosophy, Psychology, Public Relations, Race Relations and Urban Society, Safety Education and Accident Prevention, Secondary Education, Sociology, Spanish, Statistics and Trigonometry.

Would you like more information? Then, write to: Director, Correspondence Instruction, University of Arizona, 103 Administration Bldg., Tucson, Ariz. 85721.

Marywood College/International Correspondence Schools Program

Marywood College (Scranton, Pa.) and the *International Correspondence Schools* (Scranton, Pa.) have joined together to combine the virtues of an institution of higher education with those of a respected system of independent study. There are seven undergraduate college courses available in this *Marywood/ICS Program* for those who wish to study independently or who cannot attend classes on campus.

The following six courses carry three credits each: Income Tax Procedure, Labor Relations, Management by Objectives, Marketing Management, Modern Management and Personnel Management. Calculus is a four credit course. If you would like to participate in this method of learning by means of specially prepared instructional texts and examinations, apply to the Program Coordinator, Marywood/ICS Program, Marywood College, Scranton, Pa. 18509.

10.
EARNING WHILE LEARNING
—COOPERATIVE EDUCATION

Cooperative education started at the *University of Cincinnati* in 1906. Today, there are more than 300 institutions of higher education with cooperative education programs.

The original purpose of cooperative education at the University of Cincinnati was stated as follows: ". . . if college students could spend a portion of their time working in business and industry, their education would be richer and more meaningful." Present-day programs are meaningful for the employers as well as for the students. "Co-op" students are generally highly motivated, career-oriented young people.

The integration of practical work experience with theoretical classroom studies has proven to be of much benefit to students and employers alike. Although this nontraditional route to careers started many years ago, it has been revised and improved in many ways, and work-study programs can be considered nontraditional even today. Let us here view some especially meaningful work-study programs.

Berea College Labor and Learning Program

The most unique work-study program is the *Berea College* (Berea, Ky.) *Labor and Learning Program*. This program started more than a century ago, way back in 1859. However, it is so different from all other work-study programs that it is certainly unique and nontraditional now in the last quarter of the twentieth century.

Berea College is tuition free, and students must not only meet high academic and personal standards but also have financial needs. The Labor Program is part of the educational program and each student is required to perform some of the labor needed to maintain the college. In this way, the students acquire an appreciation of the worth and dignity of labor, gain some useful skill and develop a sense of responsibility for a particular task. The Labor Program makes it possible to provide an opportunity for higher education for students from Appalachia who have superior mental ability but limited financial resources.

In addition to carrying the usual academic program, each student is expected to work at least ten to fifteen hours per week. Those students who wish may work more than these hours if they have the approval of the academic, labor and financial aid offices. Upon admission, each freshman is given a specific labor assignment at a basic level of work. It is hoped that, with academic advancement, the student will also progress to more skilled and more responsible levels of work.

The students work in ninety different labor departments. Some are involved in helping to meet the college's basic needs for food, cleanliness and care of the buildings. Others do secretarial work in various departments and perform direct educational services such as working as teaching associates, tutors or laboratory technicians; they also perform varied duties in the library, health service department and accounting, admissions, registrar and labor offices. Still others work with the student industries as general laborers, craftsmen and managers, and in community service programs to which Berea is committed.

Berea is most unusual in that its students relate to each other not just as classmates, but also as co-workers. Training, direction and guidance in their assignments are offered to the students by labor supervisors. These labor supervisors are members of the college faculty. Thus, the students have professors and labor supervisors. This combination of labor and learning provides a solid bridge for a smooth transition between campus life and independent self-supporting living after graduation from college.

Would you like to learn more about Berea College and its Labor and Learning Program? Write to the Vice President for Development, Berea College, Berea, Ky. 40403.

Indiana State University Cooperative Professional Practice Program

Indiana State University (ISU) (Terre Haute, Ind.) has an impressive *Cooperative Professional Practice Program.* This program is an unusual five-year plan during which students acquire four years worth of academic education plus approximately one and a half years of valuable practical experience in their field of professional choice. In the main, the freshman year is spent in on-campus academic activities. Co-op rotation may start in the sophomore or junior year, varying with the specific major field areas. In such major field areas as Biology, Chemistry, Geology, Physics, Mathematics and Technology, more academic background is needed before the student may go out on a job and, therefore, the co-op programs in these areas do not begin until the junior year. In those major fields in which interpersonal relationships prevail, and in which early occupational orientation is considered advisable, such as Art, Business, Education, Food Management, Home Economics, Journalism, Marketing, Nutrition, Political Science, Psychology, Radio and Television, Retailing and Sociology, co-op programs begin in the sophomore year. Thereafter, co-op students alternate semesters and Summers between the campus classroom and Professional Practice Assignments off campus. The final semester is always spent on campus.

The off-campus positions held by ISU co-op students are known as *co-opportunities*. These co-opportunities exist in such geographically diverse locations as Xerox Corporation in Rochester, New York, U.S. Office of Education in Washington, D.C., Marshall Field and Co. Department Store in Chicago, Ill., U.S. Army Missile Command in Huntsville, Ala., Woods Hole Oceanographic Institute in Woods Hole, Mass., and Chrysler Corporation in St. Louis, Mo.

In 1973, ISU made a valuable addition to its Cooperative Professional Practice Program by initiating a *Parallel Program*. In the standard co-op program, the student spends forty hours per week at work in his off-campus position, which may be many hundreds of miles away from the college campus. The "parallel co-op" student is on campus for a minimum of twelve academic hours per week and spends about twenty hours per week in a career-related position within commuting distance of the campus. Thus, acceptable part-time employment with its many advantages to the student and the employer is now under the aegis of the Cooperative Professional Practice Program.

Starting with the Fall 1973 semester, additional emphasis has also been given to *Co-op Sponsorship*. Sponsorship is an agreement between a high school student and an employer in which the student agrees to attend a college that offers a co-op program and to "co-op" with that employer. This agreement facilitates the transition from high school to college and the student need not "shop around" later for a co-opportunity. Sponsored co-op students generally start their off-campus work experience in their second semester at ISU rather than in their second or third years as the other co-op students do.

If you would like to have more details about this program, contact the Director, Cooperative Professional Practice Program, Indiana State University, 310 Hulman Center, Terre Haute, Ind. 47809.

Trenton State College Center for Cooperative Education

The *School of Arts and Sciences of Trenton State College* (Trenton, N.J.) offers a cooperative education program on an elective basis through its *Center for Cooperative Education*. Co-op here is based on an individualized student-oriented learning contract. Students alternate periods of work with periods of study on campus. On their work assignments, students are employed by cooperative employers and receive academic credit for the learning which they derive from their cooperative education experience.

Upon successful completion of the terms of their learning contract, co-op students may earn six credits for each co-op experience. In most work assignments, the co-op students are paid by the cooperative employers; in some assignments, the students receive valuable educational benefits but no remuneration.

The Art, Biology, Criminal Justice, Political Science, Social Welfare, and Speech, Communication and Theater departments participate in the Center for Cooperative Education's program. For details about this co-op program, contact the Director, Center for Cooperative Education, 203 Green Hall, School of Arts and Sciences, Trenton State College, Trenton, N.J. 08625.

Tuskegee Institute Pre-Cooperative and Cooperative Education Programs

All students at *Tuskegee Institute* (Tuskegee Institute, Ala.) may participate in the *Cooperative Education Program*. Among the many students who may avail themselves of the opportunity to combine off-campus work experience with their on-campus studies are those who are majoring in Architecture, Biology, Building Technology, Business, Chemistry, Economics, Education, Electrical Engineering, Electronics Technology, English, Food Administration, Forestry, Mathematics,

Mechanical Engineering, Nursing, Physics, Political Science and Veterinary Medicine.

Tuskegee also offers a unique *Pre-Cooperative Education Program* which is designed to encourage disadvantaged students to go to college and obtain a bachelor's degree. High school graduates who are accepted for this program are placed in positions as *Pre-Cooperative Trainees* with cooperating employers during the Summer period prior to their starting at college. The pre-cooperative employment period ends when the Fall term starts. Students who have successfully completed their pre-cooperative period are given financial assistance for tuition, fees and books for their freshman year. Trainees, after completing their freshman year, are eligible to participate in the Cooperative Education Program.

"Pre co-op" trainees may work toward a bachelor's degree in many major academic areas. Included among the latter are Accounting, Biology, Business, Chemistry, Engineering, Industrial Technology, Mathematics and Physics. For more details about Tuskegee's Pre-Cooperative Education Program or Cooperative Education Program, write to: Director, Cooperative Education Program, Tuskegee Institute, Tuskegee Institute, Ala. 36088.

Springfield Technical Community College Cooperative Education Program

Springfield Technical Community College (Springfield, Mass.) has a *Cooperative Education Program* in the following major career areas: Automotive Technology, Bio-Medical Instrumentation, Business Administration, Civil Engineering, Data Processing, Electronics, Environmental Technology, Graphic Arts, Landscape Technology, Machine and Tool Design, Mechanical Technology and Secretarial Science.

Students who participate in the Cooperative Education Program have the opportunity to apply what they have learned in the classroom to a related off-campus work situation, be paid for this work and receive college credit for this work experience. The co-op assignments are directly related to each student's major field of study. Thus, students are able, through these work situations, to test their suitability for and interest in the careers for which they are preparing.

Since Springfield Tech is a community college, it is a two-year institution. Students, therefore, go out on co-op assignments twice.

These assignments extend the time it takes to acquire the associate degree by six months or a year. However, the time is well spent since the students are earning money to defray their college expenses and are acquiring experience that will make it easier to gain employment after graduation.

Inquiries about this program should be sent to the Director, Cooperative Education Program, Springfield Technical Community College, One Armory Square, Springfield, Mass. 01105.

Catonsville Community College Office of Cooperative Education

Coöperative education at *Catonsville Community College* in Catonsvills, Md., consists of a two-semester internship which gives students the opportunity to engage in full-time paid employment in industry, business or other center of work experience consistent with their career objectives. Each semester's "co-op internship" consists of a forty-hour week for about four months.

The cooperative internship work period is known as a "professional internship" and co-op students alternate semesters of on-campus study with off-campus professional internships. The co-op intern period starts generally in the students' second year. The co-op students are under the supervision of college and company coordinators during the work period. They receive the same wages as regular employees doing the same level of work at their place of employment.

Cooperative work-study arrangements are available in the following career programs at Catonsville: Air Traffic Management, Air Transportation Services (Airline Stewardess, Ground Personnel and Pilot Training), Applied Art and Design, Architectural and Engineering Design Technology, Business Accounting, Chemical Technology, Correctional Services, Data Processing Technology, Electronics Technology (Communication Electronics, Digital Electrics and Biomedical Equipment Technology), Engineering, Fire Service Technology, Marketing Management (Advertising, Retailing and Supermarket Management), Medical Laboratory Technology, Mental Health Associate, Mortuary Science, Nursing (R.N.), Police Administration, Quality Control, Recreation Leadership, Secretarial (Executive, Legal and Medical) and Traffic and Transportation Management.

Detailed information about cooperative education at Catonsville may be had by contacting the Office of Cooperative Education, Room

204, Mansion-Administration Building, Catonsville Community College, 800 S. Rolling Rd., Catonsville, Md. 21228.

Miscellaneous Cooperative Education Programs

The *Cooperative Education Program* at *Cochise College* in Douglas, Arizona, consists of an arrangement between the employer, the students and the college whereby the student works part-time (and, in some instances, full-time) on a job related to the student's career interests. The co-op student receives on-the-job instruction from the employer and on-the-job visitation from a member of the college staff who observes the student's progress and behavior on the job. The student receives college credit after successfully completing a prescribed number of hours at this work. Cooperative education opportunities are available at Cochise in such career areas as: Business and Office, Construction, Fine Arts and Humanities, Manufacturing, Marketing, Police Science, Public Service, Social Work and Teacher-Aide.

Students who have completed their sophomore year at *Central Connecticut State College* (New Britain, Conn.) are offered the opportunity to incorporate meaningful employment experiences into their bachelor's degree curriculum via the *Cooperative Education Program*. Instead of four additional semesters at college (two as juniors and two as seniors), those who enter this program must complete three more full-time semesters which alternate with two six-month periods of full-time employment. Thus, their total time from college entrance to graduation is four and one-half years. Each student is paid by the employer on the basis of the job and responsibilities involved. The employer evaluates the student-employee's performance at the end of each work period.

At *Loras College* in Dubuque, Iowa, the Departments of Psychology, Accounting—Business, Education, Engineering and Political Science have had students enrolled in *Cooperative Education Projects*. Such projects may be either on a full-time basis for a semester or three credits per semester.

The *School of Engineering* of the *Louisiana Polytechnic Institute* (Ruston, La.) has set up a *Cooperative Education Program* for its Civil Engineering students in conjunction with the State of Louisiana

Department of Highways. To be considered for this program, students must have satisfactorily completed one year of Engineering study. After they are accepted, the co-op students work one semester or Summer, then return to college for one semester and thus continue to alternate between employment with the State Department of Highways and college until their graduation from Louisiana Poltech.

The *Cooperative Education Program* at *New Mexico State University* has been in existence since 1929. Participation is on a voluntary basis. Co-op students in the *College of Engineering* and the *College of Business Administration and Economics* may be given academic credit for "work-phase experience," as it is called here. There are different types of work-phase/school-phase schedules depending upon the specific participating employers. There are now more than 125 such employers. Students who are considering entry into the co-op program are encouraged to discuss this with their professors, returning co-op students, employer representatives and potential participating employers. This will aid them in choosing the employers from whom they believe they will receive the most valuable work experience for their future optimum career development.

At *Notre Dame College* in South Euclid, Ohio, through the *Cooperative Education Program,* students may receive credit for paid or volunteer work experience related to their major fields of concentration. This work experience is designed to enhance the possibilities for employment after graduation. Generally, students must be in their sophomore year to be eligible for participation in the Cooperative Education Program. One college credit may be earned for a minimum of forty-five clock hours of cooperative work-education. A maximum of six credits may be applied toward the requirements for the baccalaureate degree.

Drexel University in Philadelphia, Pa., has been offering *Cooperative Education Programs* to its students for over fifty years. The standard undergraduate curriculum combines campus study and related work experience. Academic credit was not awarded for work experience until recently, but credit is now awarded for the experiential learning acquired from a cooperative work assignment.

At the *California Polytechnic State University* (San Luis Obispo, Calif.), the *School of Engineering and Technology* has *Cooperative Programs* available to those students who desire them. Cal Poly co-op students can gain practical experience by working in government installations or industry. They usually work every other quarter, alternating periods of work and study, and thus receive experience in their future profession in addition to remuneration during their work periods.

A score of years ago, *Antioch College* (Yellow Springs, Ohio) was well known for its *work-study program*. Now, it is more popular for its University Without Walls program and for being the headquarters of the Union for Experimenting Colleges and Universities, which are covered in Chapter 13.

11.

A DEGREE BY ANY OTHER NAME —IS NOT THE SAME

The Bachelor of Arts (B.A.) and the Bachelor of Science (B.S.) degrees have long been the traditional bachelor's degrees. In recent years, new baccalaureates have been appearing in our institutions of higher education. These nontraditional baccalaureates are not necessarily the same in quality, acceptance value, prestige or other features as the traditional ones.

If you simply want to acquire a four-year college degree, then it may not matter whether you earn a B.A. or a B.G.S. or B.L.S. or any other bachelor's degree. If, however, you want to continue on to graduate school or to a professional school, you may discover that some of the nontraditional degrees are not acceptable for admission to such schools. Some nontraditional degrees are acceptable for such purposes; others are not. You should, therefore, ask yourself what is your purpose in seeking a bachelor's degree and then investigate to determine whether the specific bachelor's degree you may earn will suit your purpose.

Let us look at some of the noteworthy nontraditional baccalaureates.

Bachelor of Applied Science

Millions of students, after their high school graduation, continue on to vocational and technical schools. After successfully completing the programs at these schools, they receive certificates or associate degrees. With the passage of time, many of these students yearn to attend a four-year college to receive a baccalaureate degree. This degree, they often believe, will help them advance in managerial and other positions of added responsibility. Unfortunately, however, they generally find that the four-year colleges will not give them credit for their vocational or technical training and that they, therefore, do not meet the requirements for admission to these colleges.

These students should be pleased to learn about the new *Bachelor of Applied Science* degree offered by *Westmar College* (LeMars, Iowa). Westmar aims to build on the specialization each student brings to the college. Among the vocational-technical programs considered for transfer toward the B.A.S. degree are: Data Process Analyst, Electronic Technician, Mechanical Drafting and Design, Police Science, Nursing (Associate Degree Level), Accounting, Floriculture, Industrial Marketing and Mechanical Technology. If you have completed some other vocational-technical program, do not hesitate to ask Westmar to evaluate your past training for present credit toward the Bachelor of Applied Science degree.

Westmar grants graduates of approved vocational-technical schools credits for the training they acquired in these schools and then specifies the additional courses they must complete at Westmar to qualify for the B.A.S. degree. If you would like to know more about this new degree, contact the Coordinator, Bachelor of Applied Science, Westmar College, Le Mars, Iowa 51031.

Bachelor of Career Studies

The College of Racine (Racine, Wisc.) offers a unique, nontraditional baccalaureate for junior college and "voc-tech" students. This is the *Bachelor of Career Studies (B.C.S.)* degree.

The program leading to this degree consists of three components. Component Number I is *Vocational Proficiency.* This recognizes the need for income-producing skills and consists of the associate degree (or the equivalent) training in a technical or vocational field at an accredited institution. Component Number II (Life Studies) recognizes the importance of liberal arts and consists of the interdisciplinary studies taken at the College of Racine. Component Number III is *Vocational Mobility;* this allows junior college graduates to choose a major or a supplementary career program at Racine to give them the flexibility needed to move from one occupation to another should they so desire.

Details about this baccalaureate program may be obtained from the Director of Admissions, c/o Bachelor of Career Studies Program, The College of Racine, 5915 Erie St., Racine, Wisc. 53402.

Bachelor of Creative Arts

The *University of North Carolina at Charlotte* initiated an unusual program in 1972 known as the *Bachelor of Creative Arts (BCA)* program. This is not an art program. It is an educational program that starts by utilizing a student's central interest in the arts and leads out toward a broader education. Thus, the program goes from the specific to the general. The options for BCA students are Art, Music and Theater.

There is neither a core curriculum nor formal classes scheduled in the BCA program. However, students may make a request to audit a class outside the Creative Arts Department. BCA students do not accrue credit hours per se. They proceed at their own rate of speed on projects with the guidance of their advisors. Students must complete a minimum of eight semesters of work (or its equivalent), the last two of which must be completed in residence in the BCA program. Candidates for the degree must present a portfolio, manuscript or performance for appraisal.

If you have any questions you would like to have answered about this degree, send your inquiries to the Chairman, Department of Creative Arts, University of North Carolina at Charlotte, UNCC Station, Charlotte, N.C. 28223.

Bachelor of General Studies

The *Bachelor of General Studies* degree program was approved for the *College Park Campus* of the *University of Maryland* in June 1972. This degree does not call for any concentration in a specific department or discipline. Students in this program are allowed to obtain this degree in as broad a set of disciplines as are offered at the College Park campus.

Motivation and direction are the students' responsibility, although the advice and guidance of faculty members are available to them. This B.G.S. degree program does not satisfy graduate school admission requirements or professional employment requirements. Those who nonetheless believe it will suit their purposes for entry into positions where a bachelor's degree is needed and, therefore, would like to obtain details about this program, should write to the Office of the Dean for Undergraduate Studies, University of Maryland, College Park Campus, College Park, Md. 20742.

The Bachelor of General Studies degree was offered by the *University of Nebraska at Omaha (UNO) College of Continuing Studies* for the first time in 1951 as a degree especially for adults. This was a very innovative step at that time. Since then, over 13,000 persons have been awarded this degree by the University of Nebraska at Omaha. The program leading to the Bachelor of General Studies is flexible. The adult student is permitted to build a program based on personal needs and desires. Knowledge gained from self-education and from life-work eperiences is also translated into college credit toward this degree.

A unique feature of this degree program is the *Academic Amnesty Policy.* Under this policy, adults who demonstrate academic maturity and competence are forgiven any "D" and "F" grades they may have received at UNO or other college or university when they were younger. The mature adult is in this manner given a "second chance." Would you like further information about this degree? If you would, write to the Office of the Dean, College of Continuing Studies, University of Nebraska at Omaha, Omaha, Nebr. 68101.

The *College of Arts and Sciences* of the *University of Dayton* (Dayton, Ohio) offers the Bachelor of General Studies degree too. Students who want maximum flexibility in planning their program of studies will find this degree attractive since there are no specific departmental requirements. They can design their programs as they wish on the basis of their individual objectives. For details about this degree, contact the Associate Dean for Humanities, College of Arts and Sciences, University of Dayton, Dayton, Ohio 45409.

In addition to the traditional degrees, the *University of Michigan–Flint* also offers a General Studies degree for those students who wish to develop individualized programs that meet their own specific interests. The program of this Bachelor of General Studies (B.G.S.) degree varies with the individual needs of each student who matriculates for this degree. Would you like to know more about this B.G.S.? If you would, then get in touch with the Assistant Dean of Special Projects, University of Michigan-Flint, 1321 E. Court St., Flint, Mich. 48503.

Iowa Wesleyan College (Mount Pleasant, Iowa) has a new and unusual Bachelor of General Studies degree program. This is a two-year plan that should be very appealing to those over twenty-four. Persons beyond the age of twenty-four may have their life experiences evaluated and converted into the equivalent of two years of college level credit. They then have the opportunity to earn the new Bachelor of General Studies degree in two years.

The requirements for this degree consist of: A) A Planning Seminar which meets three hours one night per week for fourteen weeks; B) Thirty semester hours credit from junior and senior level courses in a Major Area of Concentration; C) Thirty semester hours credit from junior and senior level General Education Supporting Courses; and D) Six semester hours credit for participating in the Responsible Social Involvement (RSI) Project. (See Chapter 7 for more information about this project.)

If you would like details about this new plan, write to the Director, BGS Degree Program, Department of Continuing Education, Iowa Wesleyan College, Mt. Pleasant, Iowa 52641.

The *College of Continuing Education, Roosevelt University* (Chicago, Ill.) also awards a Bachelor of General Studies degree (see Chapter 15).

Bachelor of Independent Studies

The *University of South Florida* (Tampa, Fla.) recently began "the second chance university," namely, the *Bachelor of Independent Studies (BIS) Adult Degree Program.* This is an external degree program based on an interdisciplinary liberal arts curriculum. Applicants for this degree should be twenty-five years of age or older and have high school diplomas (or the equivalent).

The BIS degree program has no such traditional features as classes, courses, semesters or letter-grades. Most of the BIS students' work is done off campus in the form of independent study (this is the reason for the title, Bachelor of *Independent Studies*) and directed reading. Independent study and a short-term seminar are required for each of these study areas: the Humanities, the Natural Sciences, the Social Sciences and Inter-area Studies.

If you have any questions about the Bachelor of Independent Studies degree and, perhaps, would like an application form, address your inquiries and requests to: Director, BIS Adult Degree Program, University of South Florida, Tampa, Fla. 33620.

Bachelor of Individualized Studies

A nontraditional degree known as the *Bachelor of Individualized Studies* is offered by *Central Michigan University's Institute for Personal and Career Development.* See Chapter 14 for information about this degree.

Bachelor of Liberal Studies

The *College of Liberal Studies* (originally the College of Continuing Education) of the *University of Oklahoma* (Norman, Okla.) offers a *Bachelor of Liberal Studies (B.L.S.)* degree program designed particularly for adult students. Most students in this program are between the ages of thirty and sixty-five. Since this program was started in 1961, the oldest person to be awarded the B.L.S. degree was eighty-three years of age.

This program is developed around the theme "Man in the Twentieth Century" using the "central learnings—central problems" approach. The students select the sequence in which they enroll in the three broad areas of knowledge, namely, the Humanities (Fine Arts, Intellectual History, Literature, Philosophy and Religion), the Natural Sciences (Biological Sciences, Earth Sciences and Physical Sciences) and the Social Sciences (Anthropology, Economics, Geography, History, Political Science, Psychology and Sociology).

After completing studies in these three areas, students enroll in the fourth and final area, the *Inter-Area*. (This fourth area and the preceding three broad areas are similar to the four study areas in the University of South Florida's Bachelor of Independent Studies degree program.) The Inter-Area stresses the interrelationship of all knowledge by integrating the first three areas. Each area is equivalent to one year of college study. However, the flexibility of the B.L.S. program permits students to proceed at their own pace in accord with their abilities, interests, motivation and the amount of time they are able to devote to their studies. Thus, some have completed the B.L.S. degree requirements in two years, whereas others have taken five to six years. The periods of study may also be shortened for those who have had acceptable life experiences.

The B.L.S. degree program combines guided independent study with intensive residential seminars of three and four weeks duration.

During the periods of independent study, students work closely with a faculty advisor; they have a different faculty advisor for each area of study. The faculty advisors assign readings from basic book lists and supervise the students by means of interviews and mail and telephone communications. The students aim to achieve the "central learnings" which will aid them in applying knowledge to the solution of the "central problems" of man in the twentieth century.

The Bachelor of Liberal Studies degree satisfies the requirements for admission toward professional studies at the Graduate College at the University of Oklahoma. If you would like additional information about this degree program for adult students, contact the College of Liberal Studies, University of Oklahoma, 1700 Asp Avenue, Norman, Okla. 73069.

Bachelor of Professional Studies; Bachelor of Technology

The *Campus-Free Degree Program* of the *Center for Community Education* of *Elizabethtown College* (Elizabethtown, Pa.) awards the following nontraditional degrees: *Bachelor of Liberal Studies, Bachelor of Professional Studies* and *Bachelor of Technology*. See Chapter 13 for details about the latter.

Bachelor of University Studies

Mature adults can enroll in the *College of University Studies of North Dakota State University* (Fargo, N.D.) and work toward the *Bachelor of University Studies*. See Chapter 14 for more information.

Associate in Applied Science

Not only nontraditional baccalaureate degrees are being introduced in our nation's institutions of higher education, but also nontraditional associate degrees. In addition to the traditional Associate in Arts and Associate in Science degrees, other associate degrees have been appearing.

Middlesex County College in Edison, N.J., is offering four new two-year education programs leading to the *Associate in Applied Science* degree. These programs are designed to train students to become paraprofessionals and lead to careers as Early Childhood Assistant, Special Educational Assistant, Library-Media Assistant or Teacher Assistant. All four programs have a common core freshman year. The students specialize in their second, and final, year. If you would like more information about these programs plus an application for admission, write to the Admissions Office, Middlesex County College, Edison, N.J. 08817.

Associate in Liberal Studies

The *Associate in Liberal Studies (A.L.S.)* degree is a nontraditional degree offered by *Black Hawk College* in Moline, Ill. The students, in cooperation with an academic counselor, choose courses which meet their specific needs. Contracts are then drawn up, including these courses and whatever else must be completed to fulfill the requirements for the A.L.S. degree. There are no limitations to the amount of time during which the requirements for this degree must be completed. This degree has been found to be especially attractive to students above the age of twenty-five. Details about this degree may be obtained by writing to the Dean of Liberal Studies, Black Hawk College, 6600 Thirty-fourth Ave., Moline, Ill. 61265.

In Chapter 5 on nontraditional courses, studies and other related offerings, there is mention too of other nontraditional degrees. However, since the major emphasis of these degrees is on nontraditional courses and studies, I have decided to include them in that chapter rather than this one.

12.

THE CONSORTIUM
—INTERINSTITUTIONAL COOPERATION

One of the newest of the nontraditional educational innovations and one of the best—and perhaps even *the* best—is the consortium.

Every educational institution, no matter how large and how well endowed, has some limitations. No institution can have limitless resources. As a consequence, the *consortium* was born. The consortium in higher education is a young idea, but it has been growing rather rapidly. Via the consortium, a number of institutions band together to provide their students with a wider selection of course offerings and miscellaneous educational features and facilities than each could provide individually.

The concept of the consortium is an excellent one for interinstitutional cooperation cannot help but be of benefit to the students. In addition to the "exchange" of students, consortium members also hold meetings and conferences among their department chairpersons and other faculty members to bring about curriculum changes, the interchange of staff members and overall improvement of educational and other conditions on their campuses.

Some young consortia exist in name only and have not as yet been activated. Others are in planning stages. Many corsortia are fully functioning and students are reaping many benefits from them. These should be of much interest to you, for you may wish to enroll at one particular college and additionally to take one or two or more specific courses at another college (or colleges). You could do this if these colleges are members of the same consortium.

Let us look at some of the varied forms of consortia especially worthy of note.

The Twelve College Exchange Program

The Twelve College Exchange Program is a fully functioning, highly successful consortium composed of the following institutions: *Amherst College* (Amherst, Mass.), *Bowdoin College* (Brunswick, Maine), *Connecticut College* (New London, Conn.), *Dartmouth College* (Hanover, N.H.), *Mount Holyoke College* (South Hadley, Mass.), *Smith College* (Northampton, Mass.), *Trinity College* (Hartford, Conn.), *Vassar College* (Poughkeepsie, N.Y.), *Wellesley College* (Wellesley, Mass.), *Wesleyan University* (Middletown, Conn.), *Wheaton College* (Norton, Mass.) and *Williams College* (Williamstown, Mass.).

This consortium was started in 1969. Students may live away from their home college and attend a member college for either one semester or a full year. Approximately 2,000 students annually participate in this "exchange." Each student's home college major advisor must approve the program of courses which the student will take at the member college.

Worcester Consortium for Higher Education

The colleges which belong to the *Worcester Consortium for Higher Education* not only permit students from the member colleges to cross-register at any other member colleges for one or more courses, but there are also opportunities for all of the students to participate in the member colleges' special social and cultural activities.

The members of this consortium are: *Anna Maria College* (Paxton, Mass.), *Assumption College* (Worcester, Mass.), *Becker Junior College* (Worcester, Mass.), *Clark University* (Worcester, Mass.), *College of the Holy Cross* (Worcester, Mass.), *Leicester Junior College* (Leicester, Mass.), *Quinsigamond Community College* (Worcester, Mass.), *Worcester Junior College* (Worcester, Mass.), *Worcester Polytechnic Institute* (Worcester, Mass.), *Worcester State College* (Worcester, Mass.) and the *University of Massachusetts Medical School (Worcester, Mass.)*. Eight of these are private and three are public institutions.

Consortium for Continuing Higher Education in Northern Virginia

A most unique consortium is the *Consortium for Continuing Higher Education in Northern Virginia,* which is the only consortium for part-time students. In Virginia, as elsewhere throughout the nation, there is a growing interest in part-time study. This consortium was established in July 1972 for the purpose of making it easier for part-time students to earn college degrees.

The four members of this consortium, all state-supported institutions, are: *George Mason University* (Fairfax, Va.), *Northern Virginia Community College* (Springfield, Va.), *University of Virginia School of Continuing Education's Regional Center* (Falls Church, Va.) and *Virginia Polytechnic Institute and State University* (Reston, Va.).

Most of the evening session, part-time students are adults. Some are completing their studies for the baccalaureate degrees, studies which were interrupted for varied reasons when they were younger, or are studying toward their graduate degrees. Others are taking courses to help them advance on their jobs or for purely cultural reasons. The consortium permits these students to take courses at any of the four cooperating institutions with a reduction of red tape in the processes of admission, registration and transfer of credits. It also allows them great flexibility in planning their degree programs.

The consortium publishes a *Consortium Guide to College and University Courses for Adults,* which lists the offerings of its member institutions. If you would like a copy of this guide or any other information, write to the Consortium for Continuing Higher Education in Northern Virginia, 4210 Roberts Rd., Fairfax, Va. 22030.

Hudson-Mohawk Association of Colleges and Universities

The Hudson-Mohawk Association of Colleges and Universities consists of nine institutions of higher education within the greater four-county Capital District of New York State. The institutions are: *College of Saint Rose* (Albany, N.Y.), *Rensselaer Polytechnic Institute* (Troy, N.Y.), *Russell Sage College* (Troy, N.Y.), *Siena College* (Loudonville, N.Y.), *Skidmore College* (Saratoga Springs, N.Y.), *Union College* (Schenectady, N.Y.) and three specialized schools, *Albany College of Pharmacy, Albany Law School* and *Albany Medical College,* all of Albany, N.Y.

Students at member colleges have cross-registration rights in several programs. They may also participate in a series of "Consortium Night" courses. There are a number of "cluster catalogs" listing all of the course offerings in specific fields in member colleges. The students derive much benefit too from the interinstitutional cooperation of the Placement Officers.

Five-College Cross Registration Program

College of St. Catherine, College of St. Thomas, Hamline University and *Macalester College,* all in St. Paul, Minn., and *Augsbury College* in Minneapolis, Minn., are participants in a *Five-College Cross Registration Program.* Full-time degree-seeking students are permitted to take one course per term tuition free at any one of the other four member institutions if they have received approval from their home institution to take the course. A joint class schedule for the Fall and Spring terms lists all the courses offered by the five cooperating colleges. Interinstitutional cooperation enables the students to profit from this rich range of courses and curricula.

Spring Term Consortium

Hanover College of Hanover, Ind., recently formed a *Spring Term Consortium* with the following colleges: *Alma College* (Alma, Mich.), *Indiana Central College* (Indianapolis, Ind.), *Thomas More College* (Covington, Ky.), *Northland College* (Ashland, Wisc.), *Wartburg College* (Waverly, Iowa), *Westminster College* (Fulton, Mo.) and *William Woods College* (Fulton, Mo.). As a result, the students at these colleges have available to them additional on-campus offerings plus off-campus experiences throughout the United States and the world.

The consortium arrangement makes it possible for the students at these eight colleges to take courses in Painting and Photography in Taos, New Mexico; Canadian Studies in Ottawa, Canada; Greek Mythology in Greece; Contemporary Drama in London; Creative Art Practicum in Northern Italy; French Conversation and Literature in Paris; Contemporary Art in New York City; and Political Science Field Study in Washington, D.C.

Colleges of Mid-America

Unlike most other consortia, the *Colleges of Mid-America* consortium has as one of its most prominent interinstitutional features a cooperative career, counseling and placement service.

The participating colleges of this consortium are: *Briar Cliff College* (Sioux City, Iowa), *Buena Vista College* (Storm Lake, Iowa), *Dakota Wesleyan University* (Mitchell, S. Dak.), *Dordt College* (Sioux Center,

Iowa), *Huron College* (Huron, S. Dak.), *Mount Marty College* (Yankton, S. Dak.), *Northwestern College* (Orange City, Iowa), *Sioux Falls College* (Sioux Falls, S. Dak.), *Westmar College* (LeMars, Iowa) and *Yankton College* (Yankton, S. Dak.).

For more information about this feature, write to: Director, Career and Placement Services, Colleges of Mid-America, Inc., Insurance Exchange Building, Suite 415, Sioux City, Iowa 51101.

Associated Colleges of the Mid-Hudson Area

Bard College (Annandale-on-Hudson, N.Y.), *Bennett College* (Milbrook, N.Y.), *Dutchess Community College* (Poughkeepsie, N.Y.), *Marist College* (Poughkeepsie, N.Y.), *Mount Saint Mary College* (Newburgh, N.Y.), *State University at New Paltz* (New Paltz, N.Y.), *State University of New York College at Purchase* (Purchase, N.Y.), *Ulster County Community College* (Stone Ridge, N.Y.) and *Vassar College* (Poughkeepsie, N.Y.) are banded together in the consortium entitled, the *Associated Colleges of the Mid-Hudson Area*. For the mutual benefit of their students, these colleges in the mid-Hudson area of New York State cooperate administratively, educationally and socially.

Cross-registration permits students to take courses at any of the member colleges and receive credit for these courses. The Inter-Library Loan Services make the libraries of the member colleges available to all of the students. There is also interinstitutional cooperation in extra-curricular activities.

Mountain State Association

Another consortium that includes inter-library cooperation is the *Mountain State Association*. This consortium is made up of *Alderson-Broaddus College* (Philippi, West Va.), *Davis and Elkins College* (Elkins, West Va.), *Salem College* (Salem, West Va.) and *West Virginia Wesleyan College* (Buckhannon, West Va.). Students may cross-register among the member colleges. Additionally, the libraries cooperate to offer students and faculty members loan plan service on a 24-hour per day basis.

Tri-College Cooperative Arrangements

Marymount Manhattan College in New York City, *Wilmington College* in New Castle, Delaware, and *Marymount College* in Boca Raton,

Florida, have a Tri-College arrangement. The three colleges cooperated in a *Tri-College Inter-Session* in January 1974 to enable their students to partake of fascinating learning opportunities in any one of the three locations.

At Marymount Manhattan College, the oldest and largest of these three institutions, where the most popular majors are Psychology, Sociology, Urban Studies and Communication Arts, there were such three credit couse offerings as Museum Art, Fine Arts, The Dancer's World and Psychology of the Urban Woman. There was also a three credit Fine Arts Seminar in Europe including visits to the theater, opera and ballet in London and Paris, and tours of the Louvre, British Museum, Versailles, Chartres and Canterbury. At Wilmington College, students could have earned three credits for each course by successfully completing courses in Art, Urban Sociology or Business Administration. Marymount College in Boca Raton similarly offered three credit courses in Art, Musical Comedy Production, Pre-School and Elementary Education and Natural Sciences ("The Everglades: Its Ecology" and "The Ocean: Its Character, Life and Force").

Cooperation between Wilmington College and Marymount College permits students in these colleges to attend school in the North or South while studying toward a bachelor's degree with major in Communication Arts, Behavioral Science, Criminal Justice, History—Government, Accounting, Business Management, Aviation Management, Hotel-Motel and Restaurant Management or Fashion Merchandising, or toward an associate degree in General Studies, Art, Pre-School Education, Theater Arts, Real Estate or Secretarial Science.

For details about present Tri-College programs, write to: Director of Continuing Education, Marymount Manhattan College, 221 East 71st St., New York, N.Y. 10021; Director of Admissions, Wilmington College, New Castle, Del 19720; and/or Director of Admissions, Marymount College and Wilmington College Extension Center, Boca Raton, Fla. 33432.

Another example of interinstitutional cooperation is the *Dubuque Tri-College Cooperative Effort*. The three schools involved are *Clarke College, Loras College* and the *University of Dubuque*, all in Dubuque. There is free transportation from any one of these campuses to the others. As a result of the schools' joint calendars and cross-registration, it is possible for students who are enrolled at either Clarke, Loras or Dubuque to take simultaneously courses at their home college and at either one of the other two. Thus, greater academic opportunities are open to them than would otherwise be possible.

The *Tri-College University* is an interinstitutional cooperative arrangement involving *North Dakota State University* (Fargo, N.D.), *Concordia College* (Moorhead, Minn.) and *Moorhead State College* (Moorhead, Minn.). Students pay their regular home school tuition and then may enroll in courses in either of the other two schools. Bus transportation connecting the three campuses is available to the students.

The *Three-College Plan for Cooperation* allows for interinstitutional cooperation among three small colleges, *Bryn Mawr College* (Bryn Mawr, Pa.), *Haverford College* (Haverford College, Pa.) and *Swarthmore College* (Swarthmore, Pa.). The resources of each of these colleges are augmented by their participation in this consortium. Students at all three colleges are permitted to take courses for credit at the other schools without the payment of additional fees. The colleges share certain facilities and students may use the libraries of all three colleges.

Coordinate Campus

A unique effort in interinstitutional cooperation is the *Coordinate Campus* of *St. Joseph's College* (Brooklyn, N.Y.) and *C. W. Post Center of Long Island University* (Greenvale, N.Y.). The Coordinate Campus is located in Brentwood, New York. It is a cooperative effort by two liberal arts institutions to offer extended educational opportunities at the upper-division and master's level for residents of Suffolk County, New York.

The programs of the Coordinate Campus are designed to blend with those of neighboring two-year colleges. These colleges offer associate degree programs which may readily feed into the Coordinate Campus' upper division (junior and senior levels) undergraduate degree programs. The Coordinate Campus has upper division undergraduate level programs with major areas of study in Child Study (Elementary Education), Human Relations and Business Administration, and areas of concentration in English, History and Criminal Justice. There is a special three-year cooperative bachelor's/master's degree program in Criminal Justice which enables students to pursue both degrees simultaneously.

For further information and full course descriptions, write to St.

Joseph's College/C. W. Post, Coordinate Campus, Brentwood, N.Y. 11717.

Miscellaneous Arrangements of Interinstitutional Cooperation

Some consortia have no special name, but interinstitutional cooperation exists nonetheless. *Marygrove College* of Detroit, Michigan, has a working arrangement of faculty and student exchange with the *University of Detroit, Mercy College* (Detroit, Mich.) and *Madonna College* (Livonia, Mich.). This forms a cluster of Catholic colleges in the greater Detroit area. A minibus system provides transportation to students and faculty members travelling from one member college to another.

A college may have an exchange agreement with one other institution instead of becoming a participant in a consortium which may have many members. *Johns Hopkins University* in Baltimore, Md. has an exchange agreement with *Goucher College* in nearby Towson, Md. Johns Hopkins sophomores, juniors or seniors may enroll in one course each semester at Goucher if that course is not offered at Johns Hopkins. A similar agreement exists between Johns Hopkins and the *Maryland Institute of Art*.

During the 1973-74 year, Johns Hopkins also started a limited exchange program with *Towson State College* (Towson), *Morgan State College* (Baltimore), *Loyola College* (Baltimore) and *College of Notre Dame of Maryland* (Baltimore).

Wellesley College (Wellesley, Mass.) and the *Massachusetts Institute of Technology* (Cambridge, Mass.) have a cross-registration program for their undergraduate students. This exchange program extends and diversifies the curricula and courses available to students of both Wellesley and MIT. Cross-registered students have at their disposal free bus transportation between the two institutions.

An unusual exchange program between *Springfield Technical Community College* (Springfield, Mass.) and the *University of Massachusetts* (Amherst, Mass.) should be of great benefit to the students involved. This program is called *Tech Ed* and is designed for technically oriented STCC and UMass students who would like to teach in their particular skill area and become teachers of vocational education at the secondary school and post-secondary levels. Students at these two institutions may take advantage of STCC's curricula (approximately fifty career programs) in the technology and allied health fields and UMass' education and elective courses. Thus, they could have a four-year program leading to a baccalaureate degree and including both STCC's technical training and UMass' teacher training.

Two institutions may sometimes agree to cooperate in a one-way program of benefit to the students in one of the institutions. *Cooper Union* in New York City consists of two schools, the *School of Art and Architecture,* with curricula leading to the *Bachelor of Fine Arts* and *Bachelor of Architecture,* and the *School of Engineering and Science,* which confers the *Bachelor of Engineering* and the *Bachelor of Science.* Although Cooper Union also has a Division of Humanities and Social Science in which undergraduates must take at least one course each semester, there are limitations to the elective courses which this Division can offer to the students. Therefore, Cooper Union recently formed an agreement with nearby *New York University* whereby Cooper Union students may fulfill certain elective requirements by taking courses at NYU. Cooper Union students have already attended NYU classes for electives in such subject areas as Chinese, Education, Genetics and Russian Literature.

Central Wesleyan College (Central, S.C.) has an interinstitutional arrangement with *Clemson University* (Clemson, S.C.) whereby Central Wesleyan students may take special courses at Clemson. This arrangement gives Central Wesleyan students access to a greater selection of specialized courses.

Ripon College (Ripon, Wisc.) has a *Ripon-Skidmore Exchange Program* whereby Ripon students may attend *Skidmore College* (Saratoga Springs, N.Y.) for a semester or a full academic year and receive full credit for courses taken there and vice versa.

Many consortia are in the process of being formed. One that was recently established is the *West Suburban Intercollegiate Council* (WSIC) which includes *North Central College* (Naperville, Ill.), *Aurora College* (Aurora, Ill.), *Illinois Benedictine College* (Lisle, Ill.) and *George Williams College* (Downers Grove, Ill.). Some interesting innovative ideas should be forthcoming from WSIC.

You will find consortia included in other chapters of this book too, where a major feature of these consortia is the subject of the respective chapter, such as the *Colorado Consortium for Independent Study* in Chapter 9 on the subject of independent study through correspondence. The chapter that follows discusses external degrees and includes information about the *East Central College Consortium* and the *Consortium External Degree*.

13.
THE WALLS COME CRUMBLING DOWN

Colleges and universities have long been known for their cloistered campuses and the ivied walls that fenced them in from the rest of the world. In recent years, many of the walls have come crumbling down—some slowly, some rapidly—and institutions of higher education have been offering self-reliant students the advantages of attractive alternate approaches to undergraduate degrees.

We have already discussed several means whereby the walls have given way—off-campus experiences, study abroad, independent study through correspondence, work-study programs, television courses and other individual methods. However, the walls, in these cases, have cracked and crumbled, but they are still there.

There is a concept in which the walls have truly vanished. This is the recent nontraditional development known as "university without walls."

University Without Walls

The *Union for Experimenting Colleges and Universities* (UECU) is a consortium of institutions of higher education seeking to stimulate nontraditional alternatives on the campuses throughout the country. In 1969, the staff of UECE proposed that the members of this consortium put into action the concept of the *University Without Walls* (UWW). The UECU-UWW came into being in September 1971 when twenty member institutions admitted their first UWW students. By 1974, UECU had thirty participating member colleges and universities; collectively, there were thousands of students at these UECU-UWW units and hundreds of graduates.

The UECU-UWW units conform to a basic pattern, but each college and university has its own unique features. Varied, related "university without walls" programs have been developed at a number of colleges and universities throughout the country that are not members of the Union of Experimenting Colleges and Universities. Essentially, UWW is an individualized program of study in which the world is the students' campus. It is a program that leads to the Bachelor of Arts or Bachelor of Science degree in a vast variety of subject areas, but it is not a structured program with traditional degree requirements. The student does not take "courses" in the usual sense of that word. Instead the student and college advisor together design an academic program based on the student's specific needs, interests and goals.

Students assume responsibility for their progress in fulfilling the objectives of their programs and eventually must demonstrate the knowledge and competency required for the bachelor's degree. Graduation does not depend upon credit hours or grades as in traditional programs, but instead depends upon these demonstrable competencies.

The participating members of UECU include: *Antioch College* (Yellow Springs, Ohio), *Antioch College/Philadelphia* (Philadelphia, Pa.), *Antioch College/West* (San Francisco, Calif.), *Bard College* (Annandale-on-Hudson, N.Y.), *Chicago State University* (Chicago, Ill.), *College of Racine* (Racine, Wisc.), *Florida International University* (Miami, Fla.), *Franconia College* (Franconia, N.H.), *Friends World College* (Westbury, N.Y.), *Goddard College* (Plainfield, Vt.), *Hofstra University* (Hempstead, N.Y.), *Howard University* (Washington, D.C.), *Kirkland College* (Clinton, N.Y.), *Loretto Heights College* (Denver, Colo.), *Morgan State College* (Baltimore, Md.), *New York University* (New York, N.Y.), *Northeastern Illinois University* (Chicago, Ill.), *Pitzer College* (Claremont, Calif.), *Roger Williams College* (Bristol, R.I.), *Shaw University* (Raleigh, N.C.), *Skidmore College* (Saratoga Springs, N.Y.), *Staten Island Community College* (Staten Island, N.Y.), *Stephens College* (Columbia, Mo.), *University of Alabama, New College* (University, Ala.), *University of Massachusetts* (Amherst, Mass.), *University of Minnesota* (Minneapolis, Minn.), *University of the Pacific* (Stockton, Calif.), *University of Redlands, Johnston College* (Redlands, Calif.), *University of So. Carolina* (Columbia, S.C.), *University of Wisconsin at Green Bay* (Green Bay, Wisc.), *Webster College* (St. Louis, Mo.) and *Westminster College* (Fulton, Mo.).

For specific detailed information about any of these programs, write to the Director, University Without Walls Program to one or more of the preceding colleges or universities of your choice. If you would like more overall information about UECU-UWW, write to: Dr. Samuel Baskin, President, Union for Experimenting Colleges and Universities, c/o Antioch College, Yellow Springs, Ohio 45387.

Bard College UWW

At *Bard College* (Annandale-on-Hudson, N.Y.), the UWW program is designed for the serious adult (twenty-three years of age or older) students who were unable to complete their education in a resident college program. The program here is limited to those who have finished at least two years of college studies at another institution.

The *Bard UWW* program is known too as an *Independent Studies Program* because the UWW student at Bard is involved in a good deal of self-directed independent study. These students also participate in tutorials, internships and regular college courses. A full-time program includes three five-credit study units per six-month semester. In their senior year, Bard UWW students must demonstrate competence in their field of concentration by completing a *Major Project* in this field. Students may earn the bachelor's degree in from one to three years depending upon the amount of college study completed prior to entrance into Bard's UWW program and the amount of UWW units the students take each semester.

Further information about this UWW program may be obtained from the Project Coordinator, University Without Walls, Bard College, Box 63, Annandale-on-Hudson, N. Y. 12504.

NYU's Experiment in Individualized Instruction

New York University in New York City refers to its University Without Walls program as an *Experiment in Individualized Instruction*. UWW is considered to be a process in which mature, self-directed students aid in planning their own education. This the students do with the help of careful individual advisement from advisors who are assigned to them on their entry into UWW. These advisors help the students to plan programs consistent with their goals.

UWW students need not choose any majors. Field experiences, internships, independent study, travel and a minimal amount of conventional classes are integrated into coherent undergraduate programs.

Individual programs are tailored to each student's personal needs and interests. According to their interests and desires, students may attend most NYU undergraduate courses as well as courses offered by any of the members of the Union for Experimenting Colleges and Universities.

To earn the Bachelor of Arts degree in the NYU-UWW program, students must successfully complete 120 credits distributed as follows: a) Classwork—although there are no required courses, UWW students must complete forty classroom credits in courses of their choice; b) Independent Study—forty credits in independent study projects must be completed under the supervision of a UWW advisor; c) Internships—forty credits in internships involving work-related experiences in the student's field of interest are required; and d) Life Experience—a maximum of thirty life experience credits may be granted and these may be substituted for an equivalent amount of independent study or internship credits. UWW students must also master the books listed as essential on the UWW *Humanities: Basic Bibliography* and pass a two-hour oral examination before they are awarded the UWW B.A. degree.

The UWW program is not suited for all students. Students must work well in flexible settings and be willing to experiment. If you think you are one of these students and want more details about this program at NYU, write to the Director, University Without Walls, New York University, Samuel Rubin International Residence Hall, 35 Fifth Ave., New York, N.Y. 10003.

University of Northern Colorado Center for Special and Advanced Programs

There are a number of institutions of higher education throughout the United States that do not belong to the Union for Experimenting College and Universities, but that nonetheless do have programs consistent with the concept of "University Without Walls."

In association with the *Center for Special and Advanced Programs* (CSAP), the *University of Northern Colorado* (UNC) provides adult students with the opportunity to enroll in accredited undergraduate and graduate degree programs via the "University Without Walls" concept. The programs are designed to make it possible for students to partake of higher education with as little interference with their full-time positions as possible. UNC/CSAP offers courses at military installations, government and corporation facilities and other settings throughout the nation. There are no campus residence requirements.

UNC/CSAP serves a variety of adult students, including military personnel, government agency sponsored staff and independent students. These students embark on programs relevant to their career objectives. Specially designed programs via UNC/CSAP allow for flexibility and there are no fixed time commitments in any of these programs as there are in traditional curricula. Candidates for admission are not judged on the basis of national test scores or scholastic averages but on their ability to benefit from these programs. They should have successfully completed two years of undergraduate work or the equivalent. Credit may be granted for adult work experience.

The UNC/CSAP confers the Bachelor of Arts in Social Science with concentration in Public Administration, Sociology or Urban and Regional Planning and the Bachelor of Science in Business Administration. Details about curricula, programs, courses and admissions may be obtained from: Academic Director, Center for Special and Advanced Programs, University of Northern Colorado, Greeley, Colo. 80639.

UNC/CSAP has three other offices and, if it is more convenient for you, you may want to visit or write to any one of these offices. They are located at the following addresses: 1) 2000 "L" St. N.W., Suite 805, Washington, D.C. 20036; 2) 11451 Tribuna Ave., San Diego, Calif. 92131; and 3) 2450 N.E. 201st St., No. Miami Beach, Fla. 33160.

The External Degree

The *external degree* is a recent addition to nontraditionality in higher education. There are many varieties of external degrees and no one single definition of this degree seems to exist. However, what could be said is that the term "external degree" applies to degrees granted on the basis of all or most of the credits or competencies having been accumulated or acquired "externally" beyond the college campus rather than "internally" on the college campus in traditional classrooms or laboratories.

In the main, credits accumulated toward external degrees are earned through such means as correspondence study, CLEP and other examinations, radio and television courses, newspaper courses, study abroad and life experiences. External degrees are also granted by some states and institutions to persons who have acquired certain competencies as indicated by their passing comprehensive examinations. The external degree programs are as yet small operations, but they possess a great deal of growth potential.

Actually, the external degree could also be called the "non-campus degree" or "nonresidential degree." Within this classification come not only the degrees granted by the "University Without Walls" programs, but also the degrees granted by the external degree programs of a number of colleges and universities (some of which are included in the following pages) and the degrees granted by the state-sponsored, noncampus colleges (Community College of Vermont, Empire State College, Thomas A. Edison College, Minnesota Metropolitan State College), the American versions of the British Open University and the state external degree programs such as the New York State External Degree Programs, all of which are discussed later on in this chapter.

Consortium External Degree Program

A *Consortium External Degree Program* has been designed by the *East Central College Consortium* to enable adults to acquire a college degree without becoming residents at the campus of a member college.

The following colleges are members of the East Central College Consortium: *Bethany College* (Bethany, West Va.), *Heidelberg College* (Tiffin, Ohio), *Hiram College* (Hiram, Ohio), *Marietta College* (Marietta, Ohio), *Mount Union College* (Alliance, Ohio), *Muskingum College* (New Concord, Ohio) and *Westminster College* (New Wilmington, Pa.). The degree may be earned from the Consortium itself or from any of the member colleges.

Participation in this program is restricted to those who live within reasonable driving time of one of the member colleges because this program stresses the importance of student-faculty contact on as frequent a basis as each student may require. The emphasis on independent study makes it possible for students to start the program at almost any time during the year.

Nontraditional study courses developed by professors from the member colleges are at the heart of the Consortium External Degree Program. These courses combine the older techniques, such as syllabi and reading lists, with the newer technological media, such as audio and video tape cassettes. All of the member colleges operate educational radio stations and Marietta College operates a cable television station which provides the immediate area with educational programs.

For details about the Consortium External Degree Program, write to the Director of the Program at any one of the member colleges or to the Chairman, East Central College Consortium, c/o Hiram College, Hiram, Ohio 44234.

Campus-Free Degree Program

Elizabethtown College (Elizabethtown, Pa.) established its Center for Community Education in 1973. The Campus-Free Division of this Center has a *Campus-Free Degree Program* which is comparable to the external degree programs of other institutions of higher education. Much, however, is yet in the stage of development.

The students' total life experiences are evaluated for degree credits. Degree candidates may be granted six semester hours credit for each year of full time work in the area of the candidates' chosen major field. Two semester hours of credit may be granted for each year of full time work in an area other than in the major field. The total credit granted for work experience cannot exceed one-half of the total credits required for the degree which the candidate is seeking.

The remainder of the credits may be earned in one or a combination of such ways as traditional courses in colleges or universities, traditional courses in professional or technical schools, standardized examinations such as CLEP, examinations prepared by the Center for Community Education, correspondence courses, independent study, seminars, workshops, military or government agency courses and other possible academic work approved by Elizabethtown College.

The Center for Community Education grants the following baccalaureate degrees: 1) the liberal arts degree, the Bachelor of Liberal Studies (B.L.S.), with a major in the student's area of concentration; 2) the professional degree, the Bachelor of Professional Studies (B.P.S.), with a major in one of the sciences or professions; 3) the Bachelor of Business Administration (B.B.A.), where there is a concentration in business administration; and 4) the Bachelor of Technology (B.T.), with a major in a specific technology.

If you would like to have details about the Campus-Free Degree Program, contact the Director, Center for Community Education, Elizabethtown College, Elizabethtown, Pa. 17022.

Florida International University External Degree Program

The *School of Independent Studies of Florida International University* was authorized by the Florida Board of Regents to offer the *External*

Degree Program (EDP) and the program went into operation in September 1972. This is a self-directed, off-campus program for residents of the state of Florida. All of the educational resources of the state are available to students in this program. No classroom instruction or residence on any campus is required, although students who so desire may enroll and attend regular classroom sessions if they are unable to master a specific subject solely through independent study.

The EDP applicant's background is assessed and academic credit may be granted for previous traditional and nontraditional education, work and other life experiences. There is no minimum or maximum to the number of such credits the student may be awarded. To be accepted, a student must have completed two years of college studies or their equivalent through other combined experiences.

An educational contract plan is designed for each individual student on the basis of the credits thus awarded and the credits that need to be earned in order to enable the student to be granted a degree. Depending upon the nature of what yet remains to be done by the student, this contract may involve self-directed projects, reading lists and other self-study devices. The length of time from acceptance into the External Degree Program and the conferring of a degree varies according to the credits needed and the pace at which the individual student proceeds.

Degree programs offered in the EDP are: 1) Bachelor of Arts in: Humanities (English, Fine Arts, History, Modern Languages, Philosophy), Liberal Studies, Social Sciences (Economics, Urban Politics, Urban Sociology); 2) Bachelor of Science in: Environmental Studies, Health Science, Social Work, Urban Justice; and 3) Bachelor of Business Administration.

If you would like details about this program, write to: School of Independent Studies' External Degree Program, Florida International University, Tamiami Trail, Miami, Fla. 33144.

California State College, Sonoma, External Degree Program

The Office of Instructional Services and Continuing Education of the *California State College, Sonoma* (Rohnert Park, Calif.) recently introduced an *External Degree Program* leading to the Bachelor of Arts in Criminal Justice Administration. Candidates for admission to this program must have completed two years of college or the equivalent at an accredited institution.

The program aims to enable those who cannot attend classes on campus nonetheless to be able to earn their B.A. in the field of Criminal Justice Administration. Classes are held in convenient off-campus locations and students generally take two courses two nights weekly each semester. If you would like to obtain further information about this EDP, contact the Program Coordinator, External Degree Program, California State College, Sonoma, 1801 East Cotati Ave., Rohnert Park, Calif. 94928.

California State College, Bakersfield, External Degree Program

In 1972, *California State College, Bakersfield* established an *External Degree Program* leading to a B.S. degree in Business Administration for residents of Eastern Kern County. Cal. State Bakersfield has been joined by *Cerro Caso Community College* and *China Lake Naval Weapons Center* in this program.

A minimum of sixty semester credits is required of those who seek admission as degree candidates. These candidates must also be in good standing at the last college they attended. Class attendance at the Bakersfield campus is not required. Courses are given in the classrooms at the China Lake training center and will be given in the new Cerro Caso facility at a future date.

For details about this program, write to the Office of Continuing Education, California State College, Bakersfield, 9001 Stockdale Highway, Bakersfield, Calif. 93309.

California State University, Chico, External Degree Programs

California State University, Chico has designed a Regional Campus Project to establish *External Degree Programs* in Northeastern California. This project is conducted in cooperation with the community colleges at four separate sites in the Northeastern region. These colleges are: *College of the Siskiyous* (Weed, Calif.), *Lassen College* (Susanville, Calif), *Shasta College* (Redding, Calif.) and *Yuba College* (Marysville, Calif.).

Students in these External Degree Programs complete their first two years of college studies at any one of the aforementioned community colleges. They then enter Chico State University upper division as transfer students. However, they need not commute to the Chico campus. Instead they can complete their last two years of undergraduate college studies on their community college campus by taking courses during evening hours and/or on weekends. This enables persons who work or are otherwise occupied during the daytime hours to participate in the External Degree Programs and receive their baccalaureate degrees from Chico.

The degrees available through Chico's External Degree Programs are: B.A. in American Studies; B.S. in Business Administration; B.A. in Child Development; B.A. in Public Administration; B.A. in Social Sciences; and B.A. in Social Welfare.

Any inquiries you may have in regard to these programs should be addressed to: Dean for Continuing Education, Regional Campus Project, External Degree Programs, California State University, Chico, Calif. 95926.

Newark State College External Degree Program

An *External Degree Program* is being developed by *Newark State College* at Union, N.J. It is fashioned in such manner as to permit students to complete their degree requirements with a minimum amount of time spent on campus. The program's major emphasis is on nontraditional courses, but it has the same degree requirements and academic standards as the college's traditional programs.

This External Degree Program was initiated during the 1974-75 academic year. It is expected to be fully operational by the 1978-79 year. If you would like to get in at the beginning and want further information, write to the Director, Non-traditional Studies, Newark State College, Union, N.J. 07083.

Community College of Vermont

In 1970, the state of Vermont established the *Community College of Vermont* (CCV) to make it possible for more citizens of that state to continue their education. CCV has no campus. Instead of a traditional campus, the college uses existing schools, offices, club halls and other community buildings for classroom purposes. CCV has no full time, permanent faculty. In its place are local talent and skilled professionals recruited from the community and neighboring areas.

Courses are developed in response to student interest and community needs. The students work together with members of the faculty to design individualized courses and programs of study. Upon the completion of a program of study, a student may be awarded a certificate or an external associate degree based essentially upon the skills and abilities acquired by this student. External degrees and certificates are awarded in the areas of Administrative Services, General Studies and Human Services.

The age range of CCV students is from sixteen to over seventy. Most students are between twenty-five and forty-four years of age. Nearly two-thirds of the students are employed. More than half are CCV students because they wish to improve or learn new occupational skills.

Would you like to know how much tuition you would be required to pay at CCV? Well, here is something most nontraditional! Your tuition fees are . . . whatever you would like them to be! Yes, at CCV, tuition is voluntary. Students are asked to pay whatever they believe they can afford to pay for the courses they are taking.

CCV has estimated that an average voluntary tuition payment of $30.00 per course from each student will provide sufficient money to support the college's academic activities. It is hoped that students will be as generous as they can be. They may send whatever amounts they can directly to the Montpelier National Bank in bank-by-mail envelopes; all payments are anonymous.

Would you like additional information about CCV and its non-campus educational activities? Then, write to the Community College of Vermont, Central Office, 18 Langdon St., P. O. Box 81, Montpelier, Vt. 05602.

Empire State College

New York State established *Empire State College* (ESC) in 1971 as a nonresidential college designed to give students the opportunity to earn college degrees without attending traditional classes or being attached to a specific campus. ESC is a four-year specialized College of Liberal Arts and Sciences of the State University of New York geared essentially to mature adults who are unable to comply with the demands of a traditional, rigid, on-campus classroom schedule.

ESC has a Coordinating Center and Central Administration Building in Saratoga Springs, N.Y. Its faculty is located in five Learning Centers. These Learning Centers are located in Albany, Rochester, Saratoga Springs, New York City and Old Westbury (Long Island). More such centers are planned and will be opened as the need arises. The faculty members are known as Mentors and students meet with their Mentors at these Learning Centers.

Candidates for admission must have a high school diploma or its equivalent. Admission takes place at any time of year, since there is no academic calendar and the students work independently. ESC offers the Associate in Arts, Associate in Science, Bachelor of Arts and Bachelor of Science degrees.

Each ESC student and Mentor draws up a plan of study, known as a Learning Contract. This describes a series of educational activities. Contracts may be from one to several months' duration. The student and Mentor may choose from many alternatives. Depending upon the individual student's program of study, interests, abilities and goals, the contract may call for the use of tutorials, extensive readings, tape cassettes, television courses, museum visits, correspondence courses, field work, study-travel in this country or abroad and/or varied other forms of independent study and research. Some students may even decide to take one or more special on-campus classroom or laboratory courses at one of the institutions of the State University of New York.

Students and their Mentors meet periodically. They evaluate the progress that has been made on the Learning Contracts and then chart the direction of future study. Later contracts are generally longer and more detailed than the initial contracts.

The *Labor College* is the Labor Division, and an integral part, of Empire State College. The program in this division combines professional courses in industrial and labor relations with independent study, group workshops and tutorials in the liberal arts. Three degrees are available from the Labor College, namely, the Associate in Science in Industrial and Labor Relations, the Associate in Arts with an optional concentration in Labor Studies and the Bachelor of Arts with an optional concentration in Labor Studies. If you would like to know more about these degree programs, write to the Labor Division, Empire State College, 56 Lexington Ave., New York, N.Y. 10010.

Would you like to obtain further information about ESC? Then, write to the Vice President for Academic Affairs, Empire State College, 2 Union Ave., Saratoga Springs, N.Y. 12866.

Thomas A. Edison College

Thomas A. Edison College, the State of New Jersey's non-campus college, is also known as *The New Jersey State College for External Degrees.* It officially enrolled its first student in November 1972. The New Jersey Board of Higher Education has empowered it to confer associate and baccalaureate degrees.

Edison College is innovative in many ways. In place of a resident faculty, it has a staff consisting of a small number of administrators and support personnel. There are no prerequisites for admission. Requirements for a degree can be satisfied entirely by transfer credit and examination. Essentially, the mission of Edison College is to give to those who, for varied reasons, were unable to complete their formal education the opportunity at the present time to demonstrate the knowledge and accomplishments they have achieved and, where equivalent and appropriate, to be granted college credits and degrees for the latter.

Anyone may enroll in Edison College regardless of age, residence or educational background. As of July 1974, for an enrollment fee of $35.00 an applicant receives a complete evaluation of all prior educational experiences. On the basis of this evaluation, the college awards the applicant credits as justified by this individual assessment. The applicant's previously earned college credit, formal military service school training, passing of proficiency or equivalency examinations and individual assessment are then matched against Edison College's requirements for any of the degrees it offers. The applicant then becomes a candidate for the degree and is told how many more credits are needed to earn the degree.

Students are counselled as to the best means whereby they may complete the degree requirements and the various options open to them are explained. If you would like an enrollment form and further details, write to: The Registrar, Thomas A. Edison College, 1750 N. Olden Ave., Trenton, N.J. 08638.

Minnesota Metropolitan State College

The non-campus, State-sponsored college of Minnesota is the *Minnesota Metropolitan State College* (MMSC). Just as Thomas A. Edison College differs very much from Empire State College, so does MMSC differ very much from both Edison and ESC.

The relationship of MMSC with its students is based on the conviction that the students must accept responsibility for and have authority over their own education. With this tenet, MMSC combines competency-based education. The five areas of competency are: Basic Learning and Communication, Personal Development and Social Awareness, Civic, Recreational and Vocational. The students at MMSC develop study units in relation to the areas of competency which are most appropriate to their personal and educational goals.

An MMSC education is community-focused, and the entire community is considered to be MMSC's campus. MMSC's goal is to teach students that "to live is to learn." The full-time faculty members advise students and aim to teach them how to develop the ability for life-long learning.

This experimental college is very young and faces many developmental challenges. If you would like further information about MMSC or have any questions about it, address your requests and inquiries to: Coordinating Center, Minnesota Metropolitan State College, LL90 Metro Square, Seventh and Robert, St. Paul, Minn. 55101.

American Versions of the British Open University

In the Fall of 1970, the Maryland Board of Regents designated *University College* of the *University of Maryland* as a separate administrative unit. University College is dedicated to the task of providing persons twenty-one years of age and over with continuing education opportunities to stimulate their intellect, promote their careers and develop their sense of responsibility to their communities. Its courses generally take place in the late afternoon and evening. University College offers degree and non-degree programs, on and off campus, throughout Maryland, the District of Columbia and twenty-two foreign countries on four continents. It has significant Afro-American Studies and Urban Studies programs.

University College of the University of Maryland was chosen to be one of the American institutions of higher education to test the material and teaching concepts of the British Open University. The Open University was established in England in 1969 to make available to adults educational opportunities which, in traditional forms, were not available to them when they were younger. Its aim was to form an interdisciplinary, cohesive degree program using multi-media learning approaches that would be of benefit to active adults.

University College Open University (UCOU) offers the following thirty-six week Foundation Courses: 1) The Humanities, 2) Social Science, 3) Natural Science, 4) Mathematics and 5) Technology. Each of these UCOU courses includes texts designed to allow for student assessment and feedback, reference books and weekly films and tapes. A tutor is assigned to each student and this tutor is available by phone or at regular weekly scheduled sessions at learning centers. For details about UCOU and any of University College's programs, write to the

Office of the Dean, University College, Center of Adult Education, University of Maryland, College Park, Md. 20742.

Salem State College (Salem, Mass.) started a new program modeled after the British Open University's Foundation Course in the Humanities during the academic year 1972-73. *Salem State Open College* (SSOC) has a program which is interdisciplinary in nature and embraces the disciplines of Art, History, Literature, Music and Philosophy. It is open to students of all ages.

SSOC now offers the two Humanities courses: Foundations Course in Humanities and The Age of Revolutions. Each of these courses carries six credits for the first semester and nine credits for the second semester. These courses are SSOC's new alternative in continuing education. Learning occurs outside the classroom through the study of audio tapes with slide-tape programs, printed material, television viewing and discussion.

For an application for enrollment in these courses or for details about them, write to the Division of Continuing Education, Salem State College, Salem, Mass. 01970.

The *University of Houston* is another American institution of higher education that is offering an *Open University Program.* Houston's Open University is available to regularly enrolled students at the University of Houston and to "special students." The "special student" must be at least twenty-five years of age and not have taken the Scholastic Aptitude Test (SAT). This independent study program uses a wide range of multi-media material, including closed circuit television, radio programs and self-study texts. Lectures on KUHT-TV (Channel 8) weekly, home study and weekly tutorial sessions are features of this Open University which make it possible for students to learn on their own without being required to spend many hours on campus in the classroom.

Houston's Open University offers the Humanities Foundation Course and the Science Foundation Course. Thus, this program covers the relationships between science, technology, culture and society. If you have any questions about this program, send your inquiries to: Director, Open University Program, Room 110 Ezekiel Cullen Building, University of Houston, Houston, Texas 77004.

New York State Regents External Degrees Program

The *New York State Education Department* grants credits and degrees through the *College Proficiency Examination Program* (CPEP).

Candidates for degrees awarded by this *External Degrees Program* take College Proficiency Examinations in specific subjects. Upon passing these tests and thus demonstrating that they have acquired knowledge of the subject matter, whether through life-work experience, correspondence study or any other means, the candidates are granted equivalent credits.

It is possible to earn an associate or baccalaureate degree by passing a series of these proficiency examinations and demonstrating the total knowledge required for these degrees. There are Regents External Degrees of Bachelor of Science in Business Administration, Associate in Arts and Associate in Applied Science in Nursing. On Friday, September 20, 1974, the State University of New York conducted a graduation ceremony at which eleven persons became the first graduates to be awarded the baccalaureate degree under this two-year-old Regents External Degrees Program.

Would you like to learn how you could receive college credits and degrees for what you know? Then, request detailed information from: College Proficiency Examination and Regents External Degrees Programs, New York State Education Department, 1924 Twin Towers, Albany, N.Y. 12210.

The external degree programs are very significant aspects of non-traditionality in higher education. External degrees satisfy an important need for those who desire college degrees to improve their career levels, to pursue advanced areas of knowledge which they could not do without the degrees and to comply with a variety of personal and practical reasons. These external degree programs enable them to earn associate and baccalaureate degrees without traveling along the traditional college routes.

However, I would like to add here that as a result of the survey I conducted I cannot help but conclude that although these are "external" programs, for them to become more accepted and more effective, they must be integrated to a greater extent than at present into the over-all internal structure of the colleges and universities. In this way, the "external" students will have a greater sense of belonging to a specific institution of higher education or state university system, while still having the advantages of not having to attend campus classes on a regular basis. The external degrees would then also rise in prestige.

14.
COLLEGES—NEW AND UNIQUE

Colleges may be categorized as: A) Standard four-year bachelor's degree granting colleges; B) Community and junior level, two-year associate degree granting colleges; C) Middle colleges, which combine the junior and senior years of high school and the freshman and sophomore years of college and grant two-year associate degrees; and D) Senior colleges, which consist of the junior and senior years of college and grant four-year bachelor's degrees.

In recent years, new and unique, nontraditional colleges have been arising in all of these categories on the higher education scene. Let us pay a "visit" to some truly nontraditional and noteworthy ones.

A. STANDARD FOUR-YEAR BACHELOR'S DEGREE GRANTING COLLEGES

Grand Valley State Colleges

Fascinating, innovative adventures in higher education are taking place in Allendale, Michigan. Using the "cluster college" concept, *Grand Valley State Colleges* as a unit offers students the unique opportunity to enroll in any one of four unusual small undergraduate institutions and concurrently also to take courses at any of the other members of the "cluster."

The four undergraduate academic units known collectively as Grand Valley State Colleges are the *College of Arts and Sciences, Thomas Jefferson College, William James College* and *College IV.* Each college has its own special educational philosophy, faculty, admissions standards and grading systems.

Grand Valley State College opened its doors to 226 students in September 1963 as a four-year state supported, liberal arts, basically traditional coeducational college. In January 1973, after other units had been added to form the "cluster," the name Grand Valley State College was changed to Grand Valley State Colleges and the original Grand Valley State College became the *College of Arts and Sciences (CAS)*. As the college developed from 1963 to the time of its name change in 1973, its offerings grew into a wide range and variety of courses, curricula and programs leading to the Bachelor of Arts and Bachelor of Science degrees.

CAS now also includes the School of Business and Economics, the School of Health Sciences, and the School of Public Service. Major programs in Biopsychology, Health Sciences, Medical Audiovisual Technology, Medical Technology, Nursing and Preprofessional (Medical, Dental, Veterinary) Studies are offered by the School of Health Sciences. The School of Public Service offers major programs in Public Service, Criminal Justice and Community Affairs.

Thomas Jefferson College (TJC) is a smaller, four year liberal arts college which opened in September 1968 as the School of General Studies. The name was changed to Thomas Jefferson College in 1969. TJC is a most unusual experimenting college with a freely structured program stressing interdisciplinary, multidisciplinary and transdisciplinary approaches in learning. Graduates are awarded the Bachelor of Philosophy (B.Ph.) degree.

Emphasis at TJC is placed on preparing students to cope creatively and productively with our rapidly changing world rather than on preparing them to enter specific vocations. TJC aims to develop the creative capacities of its students.

Guided by members of the faculty who serve as tutors, students design their own curricula. There are essentially six modes of study available to students at TJC: Exams, Seminars, Special Studies, Group Special Studies, Seasonal Seminars and Independent Projects. Students who wish to plan their course of study on a long range basis may enter the *Contractual Degree Program (CDP)*. To do so, the student must organize a CDP Committee consisting of at least three TJC faculty members who must approve all contracts and any changes made in these contracts.

Off-campus studies at TJC generally entail a full-time commitment of at least one term's duration. There are four forms of such off-campus studies: 1) The Independent Project, which gives the student the opportunity to live and learn in a different setting either here or abroad; 2) The Acadamic Exchange Project, which enables the student to study in another college or university for a specified period of time; 3) The Intensive Research Project, which gives a student the opportunity to pursue a special interest at another locale which may have greater facilities for such a project; and 4) The Off-Campus Special Study, a five-credit special study supervised by a professional member of a nearby community. (Although TJC does not emphasize preparation for vocations, this Special Study is a way by which students could test out possible vocational areas.)

To help TJC students get the fullest benefit from the many travel and study abroad opportunities available to them, special one-term "mini" courses are offered in languages for travelers. These courses emphasize understanding, speaking and acquiring a repertoire of basic expressions in these languages. Among the languages offered are Arabic, Japanese, Portuguese and Serbo-Croatian.

William James College (WJC), the third of the Grand Valley cluster of colleges, opened in the Fall of 1971. Unlike TJC, WJC emphasizes programs with clearly defined professional goals. It offers students career-oriented curricula leading to the Bachelor of Science degree. WJC is person-centered, fostering intellectual and personal growth; future-oriented, linking its programs and activities with humanity's projected needs; and career-directed, enabling students to enter personally satisfying and socially useful professions or to continue on to graduate study.

Traditional majors have been replaced with concentration programs at WJC. These programs are composed by the students on the basis of their individual aims, interests and purposes in life and work. With assistance from their advisors, these students design their programs by putting together a group of courses, independent studies and internships. Concentration programs are offered in Administration and Information Management, Arts and Media, Environmental Studies and Social Relations.

Administration and Information Management involve the Personnel, Finance and Data Processing fields. Arts and Media include Journalism, Radio, TV, Film and Design. Environmental Studies focus on Ecology, Pollution Monitoring and Environmental Planning. The Social Relations program is known as the "people business," namely, Social Work, Mental Health, Urban Affairs, Politics and Community Organization.

All WJC students must take the Synoptic Program. This more or less fills in the gaps of what might be missing in their other programs and gives the students an overview to help them live more meaningful lives. Essentially, the goal of WJC is to make it possible for its graduates "to lead personally meaningful lives of action."

The fourth "cluster" college of Grand Valley State Colleges, aptly called *College IV*, opened in September 1973. College IV emphasizes preparation for specific employment opportunities. It offers not only the B.A. and B.S. degree programs, but also varieties of programs leading to certificates according to the interests of the students, and encourages the creation of innovative programs.

Instead of attending traditional classes or lectures, College IV students choose from a collection of learning packages called "modules." These pre-packaged, self-instructional learning modules enable the students to work at their own speed. Each learning module includes a statement of the goal to be achieved as a result of its study, a study guide to the materials necessary to achieve this goal and a practice self-test to be administered by the student. Essentially, instruction in College IV involves one student working with one faculty member. Thus, when students are confident that they have mastered the material in the module, they contact their faculty members, who schedule a mastery test. After passing this test, indicating that the module has been mastered, the student goes on to the next module.

There are many opportunities for independent study, problem-centered projects and advanced research at College IV. Since this college is so young, the curriculum offerings will be expanding rapidly within the next few years. Areas of study are now available in: Accounting, Anthropology, Art, Astronomy, Biology, Business, Chemistry, Communication (Oral and Written), Computer Programming, Economics, English, Geography, Geology, History, Mathematics, Meteorology, Philosophy, Physics, Psychology, Sociology and Statistics.

There are many exciting happenings in education taking place at the Grand Valley State Colleges. If adventure is what you seek, write for more details about these schools to the Admissions Office, Grand Valley State Colleges, College Landing, Allendale, Mich. 49401, or contact the Director of Admissions at the specific college of your interest— College of Arts and Sciences, Thomas Jefferson College, William James College or College IV—all at Allendale, Mich. 49401.

New College

New College in Sarasota, Florida, was chartered in October 1960. It started with the dynamic idea of offering flexibility, individualism and broad freedom of action to enable each student to play a major role in the construction of his/her own academic program. As you read in Chapter 4, there are colleges that make it possible for students who so desire to design their own individualized degree programs. However, here, at New College, all students have individualized programs.

In September 1974, New College was a small, private, coeducational liberal arts college with a student body of about 550. In October 1974, New College became a public institution, a division of the University of South Florida. New College places great stress on independent study. There are strong demands on the students for self-discipline and high standards of performance. The students at New College are academically unusually well qualified and often have ranked in the top five per cent of their high school classes. New College seeks to promote each student's sense of self-direction in order to maximize his/her academic and personal development. Admission preference is given to those applicants who have demonstrated responsibility, creativity and talent.

There are three academic divisions in New College: Natural Sciences, Social Sciences and Humanities. Students specializing in the Natural Sciences may choose from among the following study areas: a) Mathematics, which includes Computer Programming among its special areas; b) Biology, including such special study areas as Animal Behavior, Ecology, Evolution, Field Botany, Genetics, Marine Biology and Microbiology; c) Chemistry, including Biochemistry; d) Physics, including Electromagnetism; and e) Experimental Psychology, including Cognitive Processes, Perception and Statistics.

Those specializing in the Social Sciences may select from among the following study areas: a) Social Psychology, b) History, c) Political Science, d) Sociology, e) Anthropology and f) Economics. In the Humanities division, students may specialize in: a) Art History, b) Fine Arts (including Ceramics, Creative Drawing, Graphics, Life Drawing, Painting, Sculpture), c) Music, d) Literature (including Drama, Fiction Studies, Poetry, Creative Writing), e) Languages (French, German, Russian, Spanish, Latin, Greek), f) Classics, g) Philosophy and h) Religion (including Buddhism and Hinduism).

The New College academic year consists of three ten-week terms plus a special four-week period before the Christmas vacation for the purposes of independent study. The Bachelor of Arts degree is granted to graduates regardless of the divisions and study areas in which they specialized. It normally takes nine academic terms and four independent study projects to earn this degree. Students may do this in three or four years.

Those who wish to graduate in three years must work for nine consecutive terms and complete two independent study projects during the Summers in addition to the regularly scheduled independent study periods. Students who plan to graduate in four years may take academic leave ("four-year option") for a period equivalent to three terms after their first year in residence at the college. For all, a minimum of five terms of on-campus study is required. This allows for no more than four off-campus terms. The final term must be on campus.

Off-campus study is an important aspect of the educational process at this nontraditional college. Opportunities for cross-cultural study, research and service internships and study at other colleges are provided to the students by the Off-Campus Study Office. A vast variety of domestic and foreign field study opportunities are available. Students may even suggest their own programs of activities for one or more off-campus study terms.

Before the start of each term, each student joins with a faculty member to plan that term's program of activities. The student then signs an Educational Contract describing this program. The contract must be successfully fulfilled by the end of the term, and nine such contracts generally must be completed for graduation from New College.

Would you like to attend a college that challenges you to higher levels of creativity and stimulates you on toward greater responsibility for yourself, a college where many traditional "props" such as grades, required class attendance and dormitory parietals are gone? Then, write for a catalogue and further details to: Admissions Office, New College, University of South Florida, Sarasota, Fla. 33578.

College at Purchase

Another new college with an air of excitement and challenge about it is the *College at Purchase* (Purchase, N.Y.) of the State University of New York. The College at Purchase opened in September 1971. It consists of the College of Letters and Science and the School of the Arts. The College at Purchase is experimental and innovative in a number of ways.

One of its prominent innovative features is its academic calendar. The college year is on a semester basis. However, each semester consists of a long term (twelve weeks) followed by a short term (four weeks). The Fall semester long term is from mid-September through mid-December and the short term consists of the four weeks of January; the Spring semester long term runs from February through April and the short term is in the month of May.

Unlike the traditional colleges, which are organized in the form of departments, College at Purchase is organized on a divisional basis. The College of Letters and Science offers the Bachelor of Arts degree and has divisions of Humanities, Social Sciences and Natural Sciences. The School of the Arts has Dance, Music, Theater Arts (including Film and Television) and Visual Arts divisions. This School offers a Certificate of Accomplishment to the student who satisfactorily completes professional training in a chosen art. Some students may terminate their schooling after receiving this Certificate; others, who continue on to complete the baccalaureate requirements, may receive the Bachelor of Fine Arts degree.

Students are encouraged to assume responsibility in designing their academic programs. They devote much more time to independent study, individual research projects, intensive course work, extended reading periods, field study, small seminars and tutorials than is customary in most colleges.

The nontraditional curriculum of the College of Letters and Science consists of three distinct but related phases in each of which there is a close relationship between the student and the advisor. There is an integrated freshman year, followed by a relatively unstructured middle period, usually two years in length, and a concentrated, but individualized, senior or "baccalaureate" year. Opportunities for acceleration exist in each phase. In the School of the Arts, there is an intensely professional curriculum. In addition to intensive study in the student's chosen division, the student also enrolls in courses in the related arts and in one or more courses in the College of Letters and Science. The entire atmosphere at College at Purchase is designed to encourage creativity and integrate thought and action, artists and scholars and older and younger into a genuine community.

Would you like more detailed information and a catalogue? If so, then, request these from the Director of Admissions, State University of New York, College at Purchase, Purchase, N.Y. 10577.

Stockton State College

Stockton State College in Pomona, New Jersey opened its doors as a public, undergraduate college in September 1971. In its brief existence, it has already initiated numerous innovative and experimental programs.

Stockton emphasizes the importance of developing within students the ability to plan and manage their learning experiences. Since there are no course requirements, students are responsible for planning their own college programs. This they do with the aid of their Preceptors. Each student is assigned to a Preceptor and a Preceptorial Group at the time of admission.

This college has five academic, cross-disciplinary divisions, each known as a "Faculty." There are the Faculty of Arts and Humanities, Faculty of Management Sciences, Faculty of Natural Science and Mathematics, Faculty of Social and Behavior Sciences and Faculty of Health Professions. Students select their degree programs and desired fields of concentration, according to their individual interests, from among the offerings of these divisions.

There is a comprehensive Urban Studies program. The Byzantine Studies program and "The Italian-American Experience" course are unique recent additions that should be of special interest to many students.

In addition to on-campus classes and seminars, off-campus educational experiences, such as internships, research projects and field studies, play central roles in Stockton's degree program concentrations. Independent study and international study are similarly significant features of most students' programs.

Stockton has an agreement with the National Aviation Facilities Experimental Center to allow students to serve, without compensation, as cooperative interns at NAFEC. Stockton students also act as Washington interns in varied capacities on Capitol Hill and in federal agencies. Cooperative internships, with remuneration, have also been available for Accounting, Administrative Studies, Economics, Political Science, Psychology, Sociology and Urban Studies students in several New Jersey counties and cities.

An unusual off-campus experience is the Wilderness Pursuit Program. This is an adventuresome approach to outdoor environmental education. Year-round, this offers a broad range of challenging experiences among which are backpacking, canoeing, cross country skiing, mountaineering, skin diving and spelunking. All students may participate in this program.

Stockton has a rather rare college calendar. Instead of 5-5 or the newer 4-1-4, Stockton has a 3-2-3 academic calendar. The numerals represent the number of months and courses in each term. Thus, the Fall term and Spring term are three months each. The Winter term is two months long and offers the students unusual opportunities for a variety of off-campus experiences. There are Fall and Spring Preceptorial terms of one week each, and a Summer term which allows students to take courses and special programs of less than eight weeks' duration.

If you would like to receive details about these programs, write to the Office of Academic Affairs, Stockton State College, Pomona, N.J. 08240.

Institute for Personal and Career Development, Central Michigan University

Central Michigan University (Mount Pleasant, Mich.) created the *Institute for Personal and Career Development* in order to extend educational opportunities beyond the University's physical campus to all who desired and could benefit from this education but whose jobs or personal circumstances prevent them from doing so by way of traditional means. The Institute employs many innovative methods and learning styles to bring courses to students wherever they are available to take them.

Academic credit toward their degrees may be earned by Institute students through such innovative approaches as structured independent study courses, specially-designed directed reading courses, internships and work-study programs, correspondence study, credit for training experiences from related on-the-job instruction and special schools, and self-study from learning packages consisting of programmed instruction, cassettes, video tapes, film strips and other instructional devices.

As a nontraditional version of higher education, the Institute for Personal and Career Development provides an individualized approach to counseling, teaching and career planning. Compressed and "mini" courses are used extensively to enable students to blend these courses into their job schedules and their personal commitments. Work and life experiences are evaluated and students may be granted a varying amount of academic credit for these experiences in accordance with the major area of study and degree program in which each individual student is matriculated.

Students at the Institute may work toward the standard Bachelor of Arts or Bachelor of Science degrees or toward the nontraditional Bachelor of Individualized Studies. The latter allows for a flexible curriculum. Students working toward the Bachelor of Individualized Studies (B.I.S.) degree design their own individualized plans of study and, since they are not required to have a departmental major, they create their own subject concentrations which are generally of an interdisciplinary nature.

Would you like to know more about this Institute? If you would, then write to: Academic Administrator, Central Michigan University, Institute for Personal and Career Development, Mount Pleasant, Mich. 48859.

College of University Studies, North Dakota State University

In the Spring of 1972, *North Dakota State University* (Fargo, N.D.) was authorized to establish a seventh college. In contrast to its six existing traditional colleges, this seventh one was to be nontraditional. Thus, the *College of University Studies* came into being.

The College of University Studies aims to meet the needs of individual students of all ages, whether they be recent high school graduates, mature adults or senior citizens. It is designed to serve students whose needs could not be adequately met by the existing institutions of NDSU, and to help them plan the best possible educational program for their individual needs. The average student age is about twenty-eight and, in most cases, the education of these students was interrupted for a period of time.

At the College of University Studies, a student can earn a new four-year degree called a Bachelor of University Studies (B.U.S.) degree. Life-work experience credit may be granted toward this degree. Students may also receive credit for instruction received in a recognized trade or technical school, junior college, business school, school of nursing or military service school. Advancement is possible too by earning credit by examination. The College of University Studies gives students the opportunity to work toward a college degree at their own pace, on their terms and in accordance with their personal educational goals.

If you have any questions about this college, send your inquiries to the Dean, College of University Studies, North Dakota State University, Fargo, N.D. 58102.

Johnston College, University of Redlands

Johnston College of the *University of Redlands* (Redlands, Calif.) is considered "a nontraditional alternative" in its entirety. It was incorporated in 1969 as an experimenting college. Self-motivation and accountability are stressed in the individualized programs. A solid core of on-campus courses is integrated with related field work. Contracts of study are negotiated between the students and their professors.

The concept of the contract is at the heart of the Johnston curriculum. Johnston is a small and flexible institution that aims to help students discover for themselves the methods by which they can learn most effectively. The students assume responsibility for their continued growth and the contract is the route by which they do this. Every educational experience at Johnston is organized around a contract which stipulates the quantity, level of difficulty and extent of work involved.

Generally, students select a major area of concentration during their second year at Johnston. They then draw up a *graduation contract.* Some students may decide to specialize in a recognized academic discipline; others choose an interdisciplinary approach; and others yet seek to find new ways of defining academic disciplines and/or major fields. The entire contracting process aims not only to design a plan for graduation, but to point toward possible directions for life long learning.

Johnston provides the students with many opportunities for experiential learning. There is a multitude of off-campus programs. For those who desire it, there is a cooperative education program. A Community Insight program enables students to live with families from cultures other than their own and to undertake projects in community development; this is referred to as "a crosscultural homestay experience." The college is on a 4-1-4 calendar and this Community Insight experience may take place during the January Interim or at any other time of year and in any part of the world.

For further details about this college, write to the Office of the Chancellor, Johnston College, University of Redlands, Redlands, Calif. 92373.

B. COMMUNITY AND JUNIOR LEVEL, TWO-YEAR ASSOCIATE DEGREE GRANTING COLLEGES

The community and junior colleges are two-year colleges that offer the freshman and sophomore years of undergraduate college studies. The public community junior college movement began at the start of the 1900s. It was not until the 1950s, however, that the two-year community colleges began to proliferate and have a tremendous impact on postsecondary school education in the United States. Today, there are over 900 public and over 200 private junior level colleges throughout the nation. Many of the two-year community colleges have a wide range of nontraditional features. Many of them are included throughout this book. A community college that, in its entirety, is noteworthy as new and unique, is *Alpha One* of the *College of DuPage*.

Alpha One, College of DuPage

Alpha One is a small, experimental college which operates within the confines of *College of DuPage*, a community college in Glen Ellyn, Illinois. Student centeredness rather than subject centeredness is stressed. Teaching takes place in a faculty-student relationship resembling that of counselor-student. Individual and independent multidisciplinary programs are available often, including field trips and other off-campus experiences.

Three comprehensive packages of study are offered by Alpha One, namely, 1) Natural History—Biological Focus, in which the student may combine any of the following options: Aesthetics, Animal Behavior, Anthropology, Biology, English, Geology, History, Literature, Photography and Politics; 2) Perspectives on Man—Anthropology Focus, in which any of the following options may be combined: Anthropology, English Composition, History, Literature and Physical Environment; and 3) Science of Human Consciousness—Philosophical Focus, in which any of the following may be combined: English Composition, Literature, Physical Education (Yoga), Philosophy and Psychology.

If you have any questions about Alpha One or would like to have more details, write to: Dean, Alpha One, College of DuPage, Glen Ellyn, Ill. 60137.

C. MIDDLE COLLEGES

Another recent newcomer to the field of education is the middle college. The middle college contains the junior and senior years of high school and the freshman and sophomore years of college. Upon successful completion of these four years, the student is awarded an associate degree and can then, if so desired, continue on to senior college.

Simon's Rock

Simon's Rock (Great Barrington, Mass.), known as "The Early College," is a unique institution of higher education that opened in 1966. It is a liberal arts middle college for young men and women who have successfully completed college preparatory courses through the tenth grade. The philosophy behind Simon's Rock is the belief that many young people are ready to enter a college setting at the age of sixteen.

The calendar at Simon's Rock consists of two (a Fall and a Spring) thirteen-week semesters with a five-week Winter Term between the semesters. During the Winter Term, students have the opportunity to choose from a variety of projects on which they may work independently or in cooperation with members of the faculty.

Most students at Simon's Rock complete their program of studies with the associate (A.A.) degree. In July 1972, it was decided to extend the curriculum beyond the middle college level and a plan for a B.A. degree option was adopted. Candidates for the B.A. degree must choose an interdisciplinary major from among the following: 1) American Studies, 2) Arts and Aesthetics, 3) English Studies, 4) Environmental Studies, 5) Intercultural Studies and 6) Pre-Medical Studies.

The *Extended Campus Program* (ECP) is a program designed to enable students to test the knowledge they acquired in their classrooms against the reality of the off-campus world. A student who wishes to participate in ECP draws up a contract specifying the nature of the proposd off-campus projects, the goals of the project and the anticipated number of credits to be earned upon the successful completion of this project. This is done in consultation with the ECP Director who will decide whether the project merits the student's time and efforts. While on the project, the student's work is observed by the ECP Director and a field supervisor.

Would you like to know more about this unusual college? If so, contact the Director of Academic Affairs, Simon's Rock, Great Barrington, Mass. 01230.

The Middle College, United States International University

The *Middle College* of the *United States International University (USIU)* (San Diego, Calif.) may be attended in Colorado, Hawaii, England and Mexico and at the San Diego Campus. The Middle College of USIU is innovative not only in that it combines the last two years of high school and the first two years of college, but also in the fact that the students have the opportunity to participate in the design and structure of their classes.

The students plan their programs of studies on the basis of their individual interests and needs. A contract is used here too. However, here the contract is utilized as the chief means for individualizing instruction. It stresses the mutual responsibility and commitment of both the student and the instructor and specifies the goals to be accomplished. The students determine their own rate of progress and proceed at their own speed.

USIU emphasizes "areas of human concern and leadership where people work with people," and this same emphasis permeates the Middle College. The Associate in Arts degree is awarded to students who successfully complete the Middle College program. Qualified students may accelerate their programs in a number of ways and complete the requirements for the degree in less than four years.

If you would like further details, write to the Director of Admissions, Middle College, United States International University, 8655 Pomerado Road, San Diego, Calif. 92131.

D. SENIOR COLLEGES

Senior colleges are a recent addition to the college scene. They offer the junior and senior years of undergraduate studies. Graduates of junior-community colleges who wish to continue on for their baccalaureate degrees and who do not wish to enter any of the standard traditional or nontraditional four-year colleges will find the senior colleges very attractive. Let us look at some noteworthy new and innovative senior colleges.

Governors State University

Governors State University (GSU), Park Forest South, Illinois, opened in September 1971 as an innovative, experimental senior division university. It offers the junior and senior undergraduate years leading to the B.A. degree and graduate programs leading to the master's degree.

The GSU academic calendar consists of six eight-week sessions. Four sessions constitute a normal academic year. Students decide which four sessions they would like to attend, or they may attend all six and complete the requirements for their B.A. degree in less than the normal four years.

During each session, the students concentrate on a limited number of learning modules. The learning module is a course and yet it is more than a course. It is an individualized learning experience involving direct teacher-to-student contact. It may last a few days, a few weeks or an entire year depending upon the nature of the learning that is to be achieved. It is an interdisciplinary, self-paced learning mechanism and could include the use of various media, discussion groups, independent studies, on-the-job experiences and/or community research projects. The number of credit units a student receives upon completion of a learning module varies with the nature and size of the module.

GSU includes four colleges offering Bachelor of Arts and Master of Arts programs: College of Business and Public Service, College of Cultural Studies, College of Environmental and Applied Sciences and College of Human Learning and Development.

At the College of Business and Public Service, students may enroll for the Bachelor of Arts in Business and Public Service in any of the following areas: Business Administration, Business Education or Public Service.

An innovative feature of the College of Cultural Studies in the Interdisciplinary Studies Context (ISC). This College offers four ISCs leading to the degree of Bachelor of Arts in Cultural Studies, namely, Popular Culture, Ethnic Studies, Area Studies, and Language and the Human Condition. The Popular Culture ISC promotes an understanding of the nature and diversity of contemporary man by way of a comparative analysis of the relationships among the products of popular culture, classical culture, elite and non-elite culture and counterculture. The two components of the Ethnic Studies ISC are Black Studies and Latino Studies. The Area Studies ISC is a multidisciplinary approach to the study of a geographic area with unique linguistic, cultural, historic and political traits such as Africa, South East Asia and Latin America. The Language and the Human Condition ISC considers the comparative ways various disciplines look at languages and the consequences of these perspectives.

At the College of Environmental and Applied Sciences, students may enter programs leading to the Bachelor of Arts in Environmental and Applied Science with areas of emphasis in Interdisciplinary Science and Environmental Technology, Health Science Practice, Health Science Education, Health Science Administration, Elementary Science Teaching and Secondary Science Teaching.

The College of Human Learning and Development presents Bachelor of Arts degree programs with emphasis in Urban Teacher Education, Human Services, Behavioral Studies and Communication Science.

For more information about the many innovative programs being offered by GSU write to the Office of Admissions and Records, Governors State University, Park Forest South, Illinois 60466.

Sangamon State University

Sangamon State University in Springfield, Illinois, is another senior division university in Illinois. It opened in September 1970 as a liberal arts, public affairs university not just to train students for public service, but also essentially to foster an active understanding of contemporary social, environmental, technological and ethical problems. It is required of all students that they spend some time in the study of public issues.

In addition to the standard liberal arts majors offered at Sangamon, there are also four "University Programs." These are multidisciplinary majors based on important contemporary issues. These Programs are: Communication in a Technological Society, Environments and People, Justice and the Social Order and Work/Culture/Society. Sangamon also permits students who have cross-disciplinary interests or special career goals requiring an interdisciplinary approach not found in existing programs to draw up their own Individual Option Program.

If you would like more information about Sangamon's programs, write to the Office of Admissions and Records, Sangamon State University, Springfield, Ill. 62703.

Concordia Senior College

Concordia Senior College, Fort Wayne, Indiana, is another one of the limited number of senior colleges in our nation. Students are encouraged to develop their own independent study projects and they engage in these projects during the interim term as well as the entire academic year. Foreign study tours are also part of the interim term program.

Florida International University

The Tamiami campus of the *Florida International University,* which is part of the State University System of Florida, opened in the Fall of 1972. Florida International is another senior level institution. Varied nontraditional college degree routes, such as work-study programs, credit for life experience and independent study, exist in many different divisions and departments throughout this university. The major nontraditional program of Florida International University is its External Degree Program, which is discussed in Chapter 13.

School for New Learning, DePaul University

A new, unique, urban-oriented college is the *School for New Learning* (SNL) of *DePaul University* in Chicago. SNL is a nontraditional senior college for adults; it is designed specifically for students twenty-four years of age and older. It was created in the Fall of 1972 to stress that education is a lifelong activity. To help the adult students, classes are held at unusual times, including Saturdays and Sundays.

Individualized curricula and contract learning are featured at SNL. Credit is granted for the adult students' acceptable life experience. It is the responsibility of these students to design their own programs, incorporating the life experience credit awarded to them. Although emphasis is placed on achieving competence rather than accumulating credit, one of the goals of SNL students is to acquire a bachelor's degree. A second goal is to achieve a learning certificate and a third is for continuing education and/or self-renewal.

The first step along the way to the B.A. degree is admission to the Discovery Workshop. Counseling and self-evaluation in intensive small group experiences in the Workshop help these adult learners to develop self-confidence and define their own educational goals; two quarter hours credit are earned for attendance at the Workshop. Each student working with a Committee negotiates an individual educational plan (or contract). To fulfill the contract, the student participates in varied learning experiences which include traditional courses, independent study, field work, internships, seminars, group learning forums and miscellaneous educational alternatives. All candidates for the B.A. degree must complete a field work project and produce a "major piece of work." Students work at their own pace.

Prior to being awarded the B.A. degree from SNL, students must demonstrate competence in the following five areas of expertise: 1) *Vocational/Career*. Students have the option of acquiring meaningful work skills and must specialize in any one of the following areas: a) Developing and Managing Occupations; b) Social Service and Health Care; or c) Professional Preparation (professional, pre-professional and paraprofessional training). 2) *Communications/ Interpersonal.* Involves the understanding of verbal and non-verbal communication with emphasis on the effect of human relations on communications. 3) *Community of Man.* Basic social sciences, especially the nature of man and his relationship to the metropolitan environment are covered. 4) *Quality of Life.* This area considers self-renewal through the arts, leisure activities, the humanities and philosophical or spiritual concerns. 5) *Lifelong Learning.* Abilities to set personal educational goals and create independent learning situations are stressed here.

Students whose goal is to obtain a learning certificate rather than a bachelor's degree must show competence in only one of the aforementioned five competency areas.

SNL is truly an adventure in learning. Would you like a catalogue and details? Then, write to: Dean, School for New Learning, DePaul University, 23 E. Jackson Blvd., Chicago, Ill. 60604.

E. "SKILL-CREDIT CERTIFICATE PROGRAM" COLLEGE

Center for Occupational Education, Andrews University

A unique institution of higher education is the *Center for Occupational Education,* a division of *Andrews University* (Berrien Springs, Mich.). This Center emphasizes the development of skills to meet with the current employment needs and is for students who do not want to enroll in a standard four-year college program.

The skill-credit programs offered by this Center aim to prepare students for a career. The programs are, in the main, one year in length, with the exception of those which require an internship and, therefore, take longer. However, there are programs which run for only one quarter and there is one program, Aviation Maintenance Technician, which takes thirty months to complete. The school calendar consists of four quarters: the Autumn, Winter, Spring and Summer Terms.

Students who successfully complete a prescribed concentration, consisting of core courses, concentration classes, laboratory, and an internship if required and receive faculty recommendation, are awarded a certificate from Andrews University Center for Occupational Education indicating the skills in which they have become proficient. All students take the following core courses in their respective concentrations: Practical Mathematics, Reading Improvement, Communications, Succeeding in the World of Work, Christian Witnessing (Andrews University is sponsored by the Seventh-day Adventist Church) and Introduction to Business.

The area of concentrations are: Agriculture (Dairy, Farm Crops and Horticulture); Auto Mechanics; Aviation (Flight Training-Pilot and Aviation Maintenance Technician); Carpentry; Clerical Training; Computer Training (Key Punch-Verifier Operator, Computer Operator, Computer Programmer and Systems Analyst); Cosmetology; Electrician; Masonry; Occupational Food Preparation; Plumbing; Printing—Graphic Communications; Radiator Repair; Sign Painting; Upholstering; and Welding.

After receiving their certificates from the Center for Occupational Education, some graduates of these skill-credit programs may decide to enroll at Andrews for a college degree. The programs they completed at the Center are then evaluated for possible college credit. The amount of credit granted is determined on an individual basis depending upon the courses completed by each student and the student's performance in these courses.

Are you interested in obtaining details about these skill-credit programs? If you are, contact the Admissions Office, Center for Occupational Education, Andrews University, Berrien Springs, Mich. 49104.

15.

THE THREE "L"s—LIFE LONG LEARNING

Once upon a time—not so very long ago—the word "education" brought forth thoughts of the "3 Rs." Today, instead, we have the "3 Ls." The emphasis has shifted from "Reading, Writing and 'Rithmetic" to "Life Long Learning."

The world is undergoing many changes. Occupations too are changing. Each of us will have several careers during our working lifetimes. To keep abreast of these changes and to make wholesome adjustments to them, we must continue learning. We must continue our education, formally and informally.

Life has become like a treadmill; if we stand still, we go backward. To go forward, to make progress, our education must continue as a life long process.

Continuing education is essential for career advancement, career changes, entry into post-retirement careers, cultural enrichment and the general enjoyment of life. As a result, increasing numbers of colleges and universities throughout the country have been establishing varied versions of continuing education departments. Many employees are required by their employers, their professions, their unions or other organizations to continue their education, and they may do so through a continuing education program of an approved institution of higher education. Unfortunately, until recently, it was difficult to prove that someone had been present and had participated in a course in a continuing education program.

In July 1968, members of over thirty organizations met in Washington, D.C., at a National Planning Conference for the Continuing Education Unit. Among the participating organizations were the Adult

Education Association of the U.S.A., American Association of Junior Colleges, American Association of State Colleges and Universities, American Council on Education, AFL-CIO, American Medical Association, Association of University Evening Colleges, National Home Study Council, National Society of Professional Engineers, National University Extension Association, U.S. Armed Forces Institute, U.S. Civil Service Commission, U.S. Department of Defense and U.S. Office of Education.

The purpose of this Conference was to establish a "Continuing Education Unit" (CEU), a uniform unit of measurement for non-credit continuing education programs. One unit represents ten hours of non-credit instruction in a continuing education program and decimal units represent less than ten hours.

Georgia Center for Continuing Education

The *University of Georgia Center for Continuing Education* in Athens started to award CEUs in July 1972. Students are now able to obtain transcripts of their participation in non-credit continuing education activities at the Georgia Center for Continuing Education.

The Georgia Center for Continuing Education is housed in an ultra-modern five-story building on the Athens campus. It offers a vast variety of learning opportunities to adults from all walks of life, from all of the fifty states and many foreign countries. Cultural and vocational subjects are taught year-round by means of conferences, short courses, extension services and educational television.

Audio-visual aids, including microphones, films, movie and slide projectors, charts, graphs, posters and other illustrative aids, are used. The majority of conference rooms utilize closed-circuit television; programs emanate from the University of Georgia's television studios located in the Center and from remote off-campus locations. "Docu-Drama," dramatic stage presentations highlighting significant issues, are sometimes used to involve the audience personally and emotionally in these issues and to stimulate discussion.

For details about learning opportunities at this Center, write to the Director, Georgia Center for Continuing Education, University of Georgia, Athens, Ga. 30601.

Marygrove College Division of Continuing Education

The *Division of Continuing Education* of *Marygrove College* in Detroit, Mich., offers Continuing Education Units for many of its Career

Development and other courses. Courses are open to all adult students.

In the Spring 1974 term, the following were among the course offerings: Advanced Typewriting (2 CEUs); Intermediate Typewriting (2 CEUs); Business Communications (2 CEUs); Child Care Assistant (5 CEUs); Real Estate Sales Licensing Preparation (2 CEUs); Recreation as Therapy (2 CEUs); Shorthand—Refresher Course (5 CEUs); Workshop for Pre-School Teachers and Teacher Aides (3 CEUs); A Review of Respiratory (Inhalation) Therapy (5 CEUs); Beginning EKG Technology (5 CEUs); Advanced EKG Technology (5 CEUs); Emergency (and Ambulance) Technology (5 CEUs); Mechanical Ventilation of the Critically Ill Patient (5 CEUs); Medical Office Assistant (2 CEUs); Medical Records Clerk (4 CEUs); Medical Terminology (3 CEUs); Nurse Aide (5 CEUs); Ward Secretary (5 CEUs); Effective Speaking (2 CEUs); Rapid Reading (3 CEUs); Reading and Learning Skills (3 CEUs); Securities and Investing (2 CEUs); and The Art of Creative Listening (2 CEUs).

For registration information and details about these courses, contact the Division of Continuing Education, Marygrove College, 8425 W. McNichols Rd., Detroit, Mich. 48221.

Chadron State College Adult and Continuing Education Department

Students of the *Adult and Continuing Education Department of Chadron State College* (Chadron, Nebr.) may also earn Continuing Education Units upon successfully completing their courses. Chadron's ACE Department has a large program of courses available to all regardless of age, sex or previous educational background.

Courses are offered in the general areas of Vocational Education, Personal Development and Adult Basic Education. The *Vocational Education Program* helps students to improve their opportunity for gainful employment. Courses are available in the fields of Health Care, Business and Office Professions, Data Processing, Distribution of Goods, Building Trades and Consumer Related Occupations.

The *Personal Development* courses are designed for the student's self-improvement, enjoyment and personal benefit. There are courses ranging from Cake Decorating to Woodworking, and from Dog Training to Rug Making. Well-motivated, ambitious persons with some knowledge of business can use the knowledge gained from these courses for self-employment.

The *Adult Basic Education Program* aims to help socially and/or economically deprived persons to improve their standard of living. To assist them in acquiring the skills needed to obtain employment previously denied to them, these persons are offered courses in Basic Reading, Writing, Speaking and Arithmetic. Included in this program is a course in Family Management to help the family make better use of its resources.

For detailed information about these programs and courses, write to the Director, Adult and Continuing Education Department, Chadron State College, Chadron, Nebr. 69237.

Western Kentucky University Continuing Education Courses

Western Kentucky University in Bowling Green is another institution of higher education that has approved the Continuing Education Unit as a credit measure. Students may earn regular college credit for completing some of Western Kentucky's continuing education courses and CEUs for other courses. However, this program is still relatively limited.

Fordham University at Lincoln Center, Liberal Arts College Evening Session

EXCEL is an acronym for *Experiment in College Education for Leadership*. This is a program of the *Evening Session* of the *Liberal Arts College of Fordham University at Lincoln Center* in New York City. It was introduced in 1970 to help mature adults in their quest for higher education. In this program, the adult's experience and maturity contribute to the learning process. In accepting students for EXCEL, emphasis is placed on present aptitude and desire for higher education rather than on any previous school records.

EXCEL facilitates the mature adult's pursuit of a bachelor's degree through evening study at Fordham. Students in this program may receive academic credit for acceptable life experience. If you would like further information about this program, write to the Director, EXCEL Program, Evening Session, Liberal Arts College, Fordham University at Lincoln Center, New York, N.Y. 10023.

State University College at Brockport Office of Continuing Education

The Bachelor of Arts in Liberal Studies is the adult degree program of the *Office of Continuing Education* of the *State University College at Brockport*. This is for persons twenty-two years of age or older who wish to earn a college degree without having to attend evening—or day—classes for a number of years. This Bachelor of Arts degree program differs from many other B.A. degree programs in that it is flexible, innovative and designed for adults. Students in this program may be granted credit for relevant *liberal arts* experience and knowledge obtained informally through adult life-work experiences.

This program starts with a series of Comprehensive Examinations followed by the Enrollment Seminar during which the students plan their academic programs. Candidates for this B.A. must satisfactorily complete three-fourths of their program of studies in the following three study areas (i.e., one-fourth of the work must be satisfactorily completed in each of the three study areas): the Social Science Area, the Natural Science Area and the Humanities Area. There are three parts to each study area: the Period of Individual Study, the Area Seminar and the Area Project.

The students have a variety of choices as to the methods and location of conducting and completing their individual studies. Thus, they may choose from any one or a combination of the following: 1) Area reading lists, 2) Discipline reading programs, 3) Transfer credit from previous college work, 4) Travel-study programs, 5) Credit television courses, 6) Correspondence study courses, 7) Classroom courses and 8) Proficiency examinations.

The fourth and final area of study in the Bachelor of Arts in Liberal Studies degree program is the Integrating Area. Here the students should develop an awareness of the interrelatedness of the various disciplines and areas. The final degree project is the last requirement of this degree program.

If you have passed your twenty-second birthday and would like to apply for admission to this adult degree program, write to the Director, Bachelor of Arts in Liberal Studies Program, State University College at Brockport, Brockport, N.Y. 14420.

Johns Hopkins University Evening College Division of Special Programs and Projects

The *Division of Special Programs and Projects* of the *Evening College of Johns Hopkins University* (Baltimore, Md.) offers a series of informal non-credit courses aimed at persons who desire continued intellectual stimulation. Although Johns Hopkins does not use the term "continuing education" per se, a person who has attended and participated in a number of these informal programs for a specified period of time may be awarded a Certificate of Continuing Study.

Among the unique informal courses offered are: Book Collecting and Collections, which considers book collections as a scholarly resource and source of pleasure; Literature and the Feminine Mystique, which explores women in nineteenth and twentieth century literature; Editorial Cartooning, which surveys this art with a view to its present state and future prospects; and Three Centuries of the Symphony, which examines the great works of symphonic literature.

Details about these informal and other special programs may be obtained by writing to: Director, Special Programs and Projects, Evening College, Johns Hopkins University, Baltimore, Md. 21218.

New York University School of Continuing Education

The *School of Continuing Education of New York University* in New York City offers *Certificate Programs in Foreign Languages*. Many of these languages could surely be classed as nontraditional courses. Thus, in the Fall 1974 semester, reading and conversation courses, both regular and intensive, were held in the following languages: Arabic, Chinese, Czech, Danish, Dutch, Finnish, French, German, Greek (modern), Greek (classical), Hebrew, Hindi, Icelandic, Italian, Japanese, Latin, Norwegian, Persian, Polish, Portuguese, Russian, Serbo-Croatian, Spanish, Swahili, Swedish, Turkish, Ukranian, Vietnamese and Yiddish.

For further information about these courses and the Certificates of Proficiency write to the Foreign Language Program, New York University, School of Continuing Education, Three Washington Square North, New York, N.Y. 10003.

Roosevelt University College of Continuing Education

Continuing education has reached an elevated degree-granting status at *Roosevelt University* in Chicago. In 1963, Roosevelt established a Division of Continuing Education to offer undergraduate programs to adults over twenty-five years of age. The level of this Division was raised in 1970 when it became the *College of Continuing Education*. This college offers a unique program for adults leading to a Bachelor of General Studies (B.G.S.) degree. The student must complete prescribed blocks of study, rather than accumulate a specified number of credits to earn this degree.

Roosevelt's College of Continuing Education accepts any adult twenty-five years of age or older who has a high school or equivalency diploma and passes Roosevelt University's entrance examination. The student must satisfactorily complete the following requirements in order to receive the B.G.S. degree: the Pro-seminar, the Area of Concentration, the Senior Seminars and the Internship.

The *Pro-seminar* is a six-semester hour course designed to renew the reading, writing and class discussion skills of adults who are returning to school.

The *Area of Concentration* is similar to a major or minor, except that generally the concentrations are cross-disciplinary. Concentrations are presently available in the following "areas": Anthropology, Art, Business Institutions, Computer Sciences, Education, Engineering Science, History, Human Services, Interior Design, Jewish Studies, Labor Education, Languages, Literature, Medical Technology, Music, Philosophy, Physics, Physics Technology, Political and Economic Institutions, Public Administration, Radiological Technology, Urban Problems and Youth Services.

The *Senior Seminars* are three six-semester hour courses: 1) Man and His Social Environment, 2) Man and His Physical Environment and 3) Man and His Cultural Environment.

The *Internship* is designed to give B.G.S. students the opportunity to become involved in the community and to give thought to the meaning and quality of this involvement. There is an Internship in Community Service and an Internship in Urban Experience.

Would you like to learn more about this program? Then, write to: Dean, College of Continuing Education, Roosevelt University, 430 S. Michigan Ave., Chicago, Ill. 60605.

Notre Dame College of Ohio Continuing Education

Notre Dame College (South Euclid, Ohio) has three "styles" of continuing education: enrichment courses, two-year degree programs and four-year degree programs. A high school diploma or its equivalency is required. The enrichment courses are available in the late afternoon and evening and on Saturdays; there are liberal arts courses in twenty-two fields from among which students may make their choice.

Two-year degree programs are available in eight career-oriented programs, namely, Biotechnology, Business, Catechetics, Chemical Technology, Computer Technology, Criminal Justice, Design—Merchandising and Early Childhood Education. Four-year degree programs are available in the following fields of concentration: Art, Biology, Business, Catechetics, Chemistry, Classical Languages, Communications, Design—Merchandising, Dietetics, English, French, German, Health and Physical Education, Home Economics, Mathematics, Medical Technology, Psychology, Social Sciences, Sociology, Spanish, Speech and Drama and Theology.

For a brochure and more information about these continuing education courses and programs, write to the Director of Admissions, Notre Dame College of Ohio, 4545 College Road, South Euclid (Cleveland), Ohio 44121.

College of Steubenville's Egan Institute of Continuing Studies

At the *College of Steubenville* (Steubenville, Ohio), the *Egan Institute of Continuing Studies* conducts a *Personal Enrichment Program.* This program is for persons eighteen years of age and over who would like to attend college purely out of intellectual curiosity, but who cannot invest a great deal of money in their education and do not wish to be involved with tests, grades, credits or degrees. For one-third of the regular tuition charge, these persons can attend the College of Steubenville as auditors.

Most of the course offerings are available to auditors. They can reserve a seat in the courses which interest them and listen to the professors' lectures and class discussions. They take no tests and receive no college credit. It is not necessary for an auditor to have a high school diploma.

To obtain a list of the courses open to auditors, write to the Associate Dean for Humanities, The College of Steubenville, Steubenville, Ohio 43952.

University of New Hampshire Division of Continuing Education

In 1973, the *Division of Continuing Education* of the *University of New Hampshire* (Durham, N.H.) established a variety of experimental two-year programs leading to the Associate in Arts degree. Programs have been developed with the following options: Accounting and Management Information Systems, Bank Credit Management, Health Care Administration, Insurance, Law Enforcement, Real Estate, Retail Merchandising and Secretarial Studies.

These two-year programs are designed to prepare students for careers which call for some post-secondary school education, but for which the B.A. degree is unnecessary. Students who so desire may, at some future date, continue on toward a four-year degree without much, if any, loss of credit.

Would you like details about these programs? If so, then write to the Office of the Provost, University of New Hampshire, Durham, N.H. 03824.

Cape Cod Community College Department of Continuing Education

The *Department of Continuing Education* of the *Cape Cod Community College* (West Barnstable, Mass.) offers students the opportunity to obtain a certificate in a specialized vocational and/or technical program. At present, there are curricula in three such programs, namely, Law Enforcement, Teacher Aide and Library Aide.

As Community Service Activities, the Department of Continuing Education presents such stimulating non-credit courses as Astrology, Consumerism, Introductory Wine Testing, Interior Decorating, Landscape Design, Oceanography, Photography for the Amateur, and Trade Skills Supervisory and Foreman Techniques.

To obtain further information about Cape Cod's programs and courses, write to the Director, Community Services, Cape Cod Community College, West Barnstable, Mass. 02668.

Many colleges and universities throughout the country are offering continuing education courses for men and women of all ages for general cultural and intellectual enrichment purposes. However, many of these courses could also be used for career entry and career advancement purposes, much depending upon the individual student's abilities, ambition, imagination and motivation. The following are such courses which I believe are worthy of note:

Colorado Mountain College Continuing Education Division

The *Continuing Education Division* of *Colorado Mountain College, East Campus,* a community college in Leadville, Colo., offers credit and non-credit courses to members of the community regardless of age or educational background. In the category of Recreation and Hobby Classes, there are: Flower Arrangement, Wood Carving, Guitar, Tennis, Karate and Fly Tying and Fishing. Wives and husbands who enjoy volleyball and who would like to have a weekly evening of recreation and fun could enroll in Volleyball for Couples. To help students learn to sew for fun or profit, there are courses in Clothing Construction and Teenage Sewing. There are also a Drapery Workshop, an Upholstery Workshop and a Clothing Alterations Workshop.

Southeastern Massachusetts University Division of Continuing Studies

The *Division of Continuing Studies of Southeastern Massachusetts University* (North Dartmouth, Mass.) offers a number of nontraditional courses, including Astrology, Horsemastery (basic techniques of riding, training and showing a horse), Images of Women in Literature, Literature of the Black People, Parapsychology, Portuguese and Vegetable Gardening.

Indiana University Division of Continuing Education

Have you been longing to act? The *Division of Continuing Education of Indiana University at South Bend,* in co-sponsorship with the South Bend Civic Theatre, offers *Theatre Workshops* for all ages. There is a course in Creative Dramatics for children of ages six through eight, Beginning Acting and Advanced Acting courses for young people of ages nine through eighteen and Beginning Acting for Adults.

Georgia State University Division of Special Studies

At *Georgia State University* (Atlanta, Ga.), the *Division of Special Studies* has been offering a Continuing Education program of noncredit courses to the general public since 1963. The courses are in three categories: academic, career and cultural. For those who seek academic reinforcement, there are courses in Biology, Chemistry, English, Mathematics, Physics, Speech and Speed Reading. In the career category, Professional Certificate programs are available in Accounting, Secretarial Science and Data Processing (a course in Systems Analysis is part of this program). The cultural enrichment offerings include many courses, among which are Modern Drama, Guitar, Music, Art History, Interior Decorating, Photography and Twentieth Century American Novel.

William Rainey Harper College Continuing Education Division

The *Continuing Education Division* of *William Rainey Harper College* (Palatine, Ill.) lets you "go shopping" for your education. It offers courses, credit and non-credit, at many different locations. A unique location is the Woodfield Shopping Center. After gathering up groceries and "goodies," shoppers can then "shop" for educational "goodies." Non-credit courses are offered during the morning, afternoon and evening hours. Among these courses are: Weaving, Creative Stitchery, Floral Arranging, Social Poise and Appearance, Astrology, Genealogy, Yoga and Bridge.

Springfield College Evening College

The *Evening College* of *Springfield College* (Springfield, Mass.) offers to its adult students such rare courses as American Indian Literature, Care and Protection of Art Objects, Career Development for the Urban Poor, Problems and Solutions in Community Tensions, Relaxation and Square Dance.

Middlesex County College Division of Continuing Education

A stimulating group of unusual courses known as *Mini-courses* is offered by the Office of Community Services of the *Division of Continuing Education* of *Middlesex County College* (Edison, N.J.). These non-credit courses are designed to satisfy the interests of the public. They range in length from four to ten weeks and are available to everyone regardless of educational background. There are no requirements, grades or examinations. Among the Mini-course offerings in 1974 were: Astrological Dynamics, Baker Workshop, Business and Industrial Problems, Career Opportunities in Photography, Comedy Workshop, Custom Picture Framing, Energy Crisis, Health and Human Sexuality, Home Gardening, Italian Cuisine and Culture, Italian for Tourists, Karate Workshop, Lip Reading, Natural Health Food Cooking, Reincarnation—Belief in the After Life, Rock Music Lecture Series, Silk Screening, Starting Your Own Business, Transcendental Meditation, Vacation Planning, Wine Making at Home and Wrestling Clinic.

Harford Community College Evening Session

Some people are fascinated by puppets. Are you? *Harford Community College* in Bel Air, Md., offers a non-credit Puppetry Workshop in the Evening Session for the general public. This workshop is both educational and entertaining. It is concerned with the art of puppetry as a creative approach to teaching emotionally disturbed, handicapped and disadvantaged children. The only limits to what you can do with the puppets in this workshop are your own imagination.

Bradley University's College of Continuing Education

Bradley University's College of Continuing Education (Peoria, Ill.) offers some unusual, nontraditional courses for cultural improvement and recreation. American Antiques and Collectibles consists of six informal classes dealing with identification of antiques, bottles, primitives and barn antiques, flea marketry, historic homes and books and magazines in this subject area. There are also courses on Antique Clocks, The Art of Making Wine, Beginning Chess, Beginning Chinese, Beginning Handwriting Analysis, Listening and Woodworking for the Home Craftsman.

Indiana University at Fort Wayne Office of Continuing Education and Special University Programs

In the brochures published by the *Office of Continuing Education and Special University Programs* of *Indiana University at Fort Wayne* (Fort Wayne, Ind.), you will find descriptions of such unusual courses (non-credit) as Creative Candle Craft, Self-Development for the Non-Married, Creative Weaving, Creative Sketching for Beginners, Women in French Literature, Macedonian Folk Dancing, What Would You Do If—You Became a Widow?, Techniques of Football Officiating and Cross-Country Skiing Seminar.

Indiana University at South Bend Division of Continuing Education

The *Division of Continuing Education* of *Indiana University at South Bend* offers such rather rare non-credit courses as Book Binding, Window and Interior Merchandise Display, Production and Inventory Control, Investing in the Stock Market, Gemology, Home Remodeling and Repair and Techniques of Genealogical Research.

Adelphi University Division of Continuing Education

The *Division of Continuing Education* of *Adelphi University* (Garden City, N.Y.) has an interesting selection of non-credit courses in its *Skills and Careers Program.* In 1974, courses were available in Careers Exploration, Ceramics, Interior Design, Karate, Multicrafts, Pre-Retirement Workshop, Skin and Scuba Diving, Speech Improvement for the

Foreign Born, Three Dimensional Design and Writing "Who-Done-It" Fiction.

Stockton State College Continuing Education

A *Jazz Workshop* is a ten-week non-credit offering of *Continuing Education, Stockton State College* (Pomona, N.J.). Through the use of lectures, demonstrations and student participation, this workshop aims to stimulate and revive an interest in jazz. Students who complete the course are awarded a Certificate of Completion.

Southampton College Continuing Education Courses

Southampton College, a center of *Long Island University,* in Southampton, N.Y., offers a series of delightful, non-credit, continuing education courses for persons who are intellectually curious. Among these courses are: Beginning Folk Guitar, Jazz—What Is It and How to Listen, Local Bird Watching, Marine Field Biology, Needlepoint, Sailing, Seminar in Great Literature and Yoga.

Plymouth State College Division of Continuing Education

Would you like to learn about White Water Canoeing, Sailing, Skiing, Open and Covered Boat Handling, River Safety, Kayak Building, River Conservation, Mountaineering, Fire Fighting, Map and Compass Work, First Aid Instructions and Rescue and Self-rescue Techniques? *Plymouth State College* of the *University of New Hampshire* (Plymouth, N.H.) offers these courses through its *Division of Continuing Education.*

Elizabeth Seton College Community Education Program

At *Elizabeth Seton College* in Yonkers, N.Y., continuing education courses which aim to meet the needs of young people and adults are offered through their *Community Education Program.* Among the offerings are the following three credit courses which can be applied toward an associate or bachelor's degree: Abnormal Psychology, Acting, Business Law, Children's Literature, Creative Arts for Children, Music Literature: Bach to Rock, Philosophy of Love, Principles and Materials of Interior Design, Principles of Accounting, Principles of Marketing, Religion in the Secular World, Selected Readings from

Hispanic Culture and Literature, Shakespeare, Twentieth Century Literature and Voice Development.

Gonzaga University Continuing Education Department

Gonzaga University (Spokane, Wash.) in seeking new ways to serve the adult community through its *Continuing Education Department* is promoting a series of nontraditional courses. Among these courses are: Basic Law Principles, Life: Who Decides?, Literary Criticism of Best Sellers, New Math for Parents and Watergate and the Constitution.

Genesee Community College Continuing Education Courses

Genesee Community College (Batavia, N.Y.) offers a program of *continuing education non-credit courses* to help students acquire new skills, develop new hobbies, update their talents, pursue old interests and develop new ones and have fun! Among the varied interesting offerings are such courses as Stained Glass Techniques, Rainy Day Puppetry Workshop, Home Nursing Care, Modern Dance Exercise, Value Clarification Workshop, Advanced Sewing and Tailoring, Figure and Portrait Drawing and Painting, Creative Problem Solving in Management and Pottery.

Many courses and other offerings in continuing education departments are designed specifically for women. Recent educational developments for women are discussed in the following chapter.

16.
FOCUS ON WOMEN

In Chapter 5, you read about such newcomers to the college curriculum as Black Studies, Puerto Rican Studies, American Indian Studies and Chicago Studies. One of the most prominent of the newcomers is *Womens' Studies.*

Not only are increasing numbers of college-age women attending institutions of higher education, but additionally, due in large part to the Women's Liberation Movement, there has been a steady stream of older women returning to school. Some of the latter have never attended college and are starting from scratch, whereas others have had a year or more of college training before they became housewives and now wish to complete their college education and receive the baccalaureate degree.

Colleges and universities throughout the nation are making many efforts to meet the special needs of these women, the college-age as well as the older women. Some of the older women are showing preference for courses given in the afternoons or evenings through the Continuing Education Divisions; others are attending day session classes together with the younger women.

The focus is definitely on females as they search for self-fulfillment, college degrees and first or second careers. Let us look in on some especially positive programs for women students.

PORTAL (Cedar Crest College, Allentown, Pa.)

Cedar Crest College (Allentown, Pa.), a liberal arts college for women, has an attractive program for adult women who wish to start or renew their college studies by means of a flexible program that is incorporated into the college's regular curriculum. This program is called PORTAL, an acronym for *Program Of Return To Advanced Learning*.

The women receive assistance in viewing their needs realistically and in attaining their personal goals through optimum use of the college's facilities. There are no time restrictions for earning a degree and requirements for graduation are flexible. Details about this program may be obtained from the PORTAL Coordinator, Admissions Office, Cedar Crest College, Allentown, Pa. 18104.

Span Plan

Purdue University (West Lafayette, Ind.) has a unique program for women called the *Span Plan*. It gets its name from the belief that women should make educational and vocational plans for their total life-span. The Freshman Conference Program is a major focus of the Span Plan. This group conference program aims to help women students become keenly aware of the importance of long-range educational planning. The Student Wife Grant Program of the Span Plan each semester encourages young wives of students to apply for a grant to enable them to enroll for one academic credit course. The third aspect of the Span Plan is the Counseling of Mature Women, designed to assist the older undergraduate woman who is starting or resuming her college education.

If you have any inquiries about this Plan, address them to the Director, Span Plan, Office of the Dean of Women, Purdue University, West Lafayette, Ind. 47907.

Center for Continuing Studies for Women
(Newton College, Newton, Mass.)

The *Center for Continuing Studies for Women* at *Newton College* (Newton, Mass.) offers women from "18 to 80" the opportunity to begin or resume their education on either a full- or part-time basis. Self-designed programs leading to a B.A. or B.S. degree are available to mature women.

A unique career-oriented program offered by Newton is the Women in Political and Governmental Careers program. This is designed to encourage and prepare women to explore the job possibilities in the world of government and politics. It also seeks to stimulate women who have experience as political volunteers to seek elective and appointive office at local, state and national levels. The program consists of three trimesters: 1) a series of intensive weekly seminars for ten weeks during the Fall; 2) a four-month (sixteen hours weekly, December through March) internship in the office of a state legislator or in a government agency; and 3) seminars starting again in April, which include group evaluation of internship experiences and presentation of written case studies on selected urban problems.

Women who are high school graduates may take this unusual study-internship program for college credit if they desire it. For details about this program, write to: Director, Center for Continuing Studies, Newton College, 885 Centre St., Newton, Mass. 02159.

Women's Programs (University of Minnesota, Minneapolis, Minn.)

Women's Programs is a department of the *Continuing Education and Extension Division* of the *University of Minnesota*. There are no entrance requirements for admission to courses in this department. Women of all ages, homemakers or career-minded, single or married, college educated or with minimal formal education—all are welcome. And, *men are welcome* too—there is no discrimination here!

Life-long learning is the aim of Women's Programs. Some courses are non-credit; others carry degree credits. Some who attend these courses are planning for college degrees; others are seeking new friendships, new interests, improved skills, mental stimulation, increased self-confidence and, in totality, a better, more fulfilling life. A wide range of subject matter is covered in the short and yearlong Sunday night seminars, courses, skills workshops and special events.

The University has a Women's Center which serves as an information center and advocate for women students in regard to their curricular and extracurricular activities on campus. The Center helps students seeking new fields for the employment of women and also maintains a resource library.

For detailed information, write to: Director, Women's Programs, 200 Wesbrook Hall, University of Minnesota, Minneapolis, Minn. 55455.

Women: Careers and College (Middlesex County College, Edison, N.J.)

Women: Careers and College is the title of a new program offered by *Middlesex County College* (Edison, N.J.). This program enables mature women to earn college credits while exploring careers. It centers around a *Career Development Seminar* that involves a comprehensive process of self-assessment, aptitude and interest testing, professional counseling and occupational exploration. This seminar also helps to improve the self-confidence of these students and examines the problems related to returning to school and work.

The program includes courses in English, Sociology and Psychology of Women for three credits each and a two credit course in Typewriting. Classes are held between the hours of 10:00 A.M. and 2:00 P.M. to interfere as little as possible with the women's daily family schedules. Further information about this program may be obtained by contacting the Director of Special Projects, Middlesex County College, Edison, N.J. 08817.

The Women's Institute (Bergen Community College, Paramus, N.J.)

The Division of Community Services of *Bergen Community College* (Paramus, N.J.) established *The Women's Institute* in January 1973 as a non-credit educational program for women. This Institute provides a wide variety of educational experiences to women in that community. Career planning workshops, conferences, enrichment courses, refresher courses, seminars and training programs are included. Services and courses are available to women of all ages and backgrounds regardless of the amount of previous formal education.

Courses have been offered in Bookkeeping and Accounting, Fashion Design, Free Lance Writing, Golf, Gregg Shorthand Refresher Course, Investing, Management Training and Development for Women, Photography, Real Estate Salesman's License Course, Tennis, Travel Agency Seminar and Typewriting. A course in Modern Dance as Exercise is open to men and women. Some courses are given on Saturday mornings and afternoons and others during the week, mornings, afternoons and evenings. Child care facilities are available for women who could not otherwise attend classes.

If you would like a brochure giving you information about the Institute and its programs, write to the Director, The Women's Institute, Division of Community Services, Bergen Community College, 400 Paramus Road, Paramus, N.J. 07652.

Women's Center (University of Dayton, Dayton, Ohio)

A *Women's Center* for all women—students, faculty and staff—and for any men interested in helping was established at the *University of*

Dayton (Dayton, Ohio) to improve the status of women on campus. There are three different task forces at work in the Center. The Women's Studies Task Force is setting up courses, in different departments, that are especially relevant to women. A second task force is at work establishing a Day Care Center on campus. The Newsletter Task Force issues a publication at regular intervals to publicize the activities of the Center. Women who need assistance of any kind will find someone to talk to at the Center.

Women's Studies Interdisciplinary Degree Program (Northeastern Illinois University, Chicago, Ill.)

The *Women's Studies Interdisciplinary Degree Program* at *Northeastern Illinois University* in Chicago operates a *Women's Center* on the campus. This Center is a meeting place for women's groups and also houses a library on feminist subjects. During the Summer months, it has a *Kiddie Kollege,* a cooperative play-care center that enables women students to attend classes while their children are vacationing from school.

The Women's Studies Program at Northeastern includes the following three credit courses: American Woman: The Changing Image; Pro-Seminar in Sociology—Sociology of Health Care; Pro-Seminar in Sociology—Special Topics in the Women's Movement; Socialization Processes; and Topics in Literature: Literature By and About Women. Women students at Northeastern are also offered a three credit course in Judo and Self-Defense, in which they are taught the practical application of judo and self-defense techniques with special emphasis on proper training methods, physical conditioning, teaching techniques and rules and regulations in contests. If you would like to have further information, write to: Director, Women's Studies Program, Northeastern Illinois University, 5500 N. St. Louis Ave., Chicago, Ill. 60625.

Continuing Education for Women (Indiana State University at Terre Haute)

Indiana State University at Terre Haute has a special *Continuing Education for Women* program. It is open to women of all ages who may have had some college education in their past or none at all. The women who enroll may take just one course or a full-time college program. They may take non-credit or credit courses depending upon their interests and reasons for returning to college. If you would like details about this program, contact the Director, Continuing Education for Women, Indiana State University, Terre Haute, Ind. 47809.

Continuing Education Program for Women
(Wellesley College, Wellesley, Mass.)

In 1969, *Wellesley College* (Wellesley, Mass.) started its *Continuing Education Program* for women who wish to resume their education on a full- or part-time basis. Unlike many of the women's programs where classes are scheduled at special hours for mature women only, in Wellesley's CEP these women take the same courses as the Wellesley undergraduates and attend classes with them. Women whose academic studies were interrupted have the opportunity to earn their Bachelor of Arts degree through this Continuing Education Program; they may want this to prepare for a new career, or for professional graduate study or study for the enjoyment of learning. For details about this program, write to the Director of Continuing Education, Phi Sigma House, Wellesley College, Wellesley, Mass. 02181.

Programs Directed to Women (Catonsville Community College, Catonsville, Md.)

Among its Community Services Programs, *Catonsville Community College* (Catonsville, Md.) has a number of *Programs Directed to Women* included among which is the *Housewives Program.*

The Housewives Program is especially designed for women returning to school. It aims to update these women's study skills, provide them with information about educational and vocational opportunities open to women, help them gain insight into their own capabilities and thus facilitate their return to the classroom. Essentially, this program consists of: 1) A two-credit course in Communication Skills designed to aid the women in reading faster and better, writing more effectively, taking notes, using resource materials, speaking in class and improving vocabulary; 2) A three-credit liberal arts course of their choice; and 3) Counseling Services to help these housewives to explore the educational curricula and vocations open to them. Child care facilities are available for children from two through five years of age while the mothers are attending classes; these facilities exist on the main campus and in the extension centers at minimal cost.

Other programs designed for women are: 1) Double Standard of Aging, aimed at women over forty who are seeking positive ways to make their lives more meaningful; 2). Setting Life Goals, which is a self-exploration program for women who are interested in looking at new alternatives in their lives; and 3) Starting with Yourself, a program for women interested in physical fitness, health and nutrition.

There are also such courses and seminars as: Current Women's Issues, Divorced and Separated Women, The Challenge of Being Single, The Legal Rights of Women, Women in Sports, Women in the Visual Arts and Women's Weekend.

For details about these programs, write to the Director, Programs Directed to Women, Continuing Education and Community Services, Catonsville Community College, 800 S. Rolling Rd., Catonsville, Md. 21228.

Womanagement (Peirce Junior College, Philadelphia, Pa.)

Peirce Junior College in Philadelphia, Pa., offers its students *Womanagement*. This is a workshop for the potential woman manager. It aims to uncover, assess and develop the executive skills of women who have management potential. The workshop covers such areas as management overview, management functions, principles of motivation, leadership, effective use of time, managerial self-development, how to conduct a meeting, financial statements and budgets and business communication.

Students can earn two college credits upon the successful completion of this two evenings per week, seven and a-half week long concentrated program of executive management concepts. Classes take place at Peirce's Computer Center on Chestnut Street. If you would like further information about this workshop, write to the Admissions Office, Peirce Junior College, 1420 Pine St., Philadelphia, Pa. 19102.

The Center for the Continuing Education of Women in Management (University of California at Los Angeles, Los Angeles, Calif.)

The *University of California at Los Angeles (UCLA) Extension* maintains *The Center for the Continuing Education of Women in Management*. This offers courses and workshops to aid women who seek to enter or advance in management careers. It aids these women as they strive to move up from subordinate to leadership roles. The courses are designed to improve their managerial effectiveness. A course entitled, Managing Your Small Business, aims to aid women who wish to become self-employed; it provides them with the basic principles needed for investing in and maintaining the management of a small business.

Details about the Center, its services and courses may be obtained by writing to the Director, Daytime Programs and Special Projects, University Extension, UCLA, 10995 Le Conte Ave., Los Angeles, Calif. 90024.

Women: Developing Their Role in Management (St. John's University, Jamaica, New York, N.Y.)

St. John's University College of Business in New York City presented a noteworthy, special seminar in October 1974 on Women: Developing Their Role in Management. Essentially, the aims of this seminar were to prepare the participants to fill responsible managerial positions, to aid them in coping with the new pressures and to help them develop good business management techniques. Further information about this and other women's programs may be had by contacting the Seminar Administrator, St. John's University, College of Business, Grand Central and Utopia Parkway, Jamaica, New York, N.Y. 11439.

The Institute for the Career Development of Women in Management (LeMoyne College, Syracuse, N.Y.)

The Institute for the Career Development of Women in Management was initiated at LeMoyne College (Syracuse, N.Y.) in October 1973. This is a workshop series designed to teach management skills, provide a general background in business-related fields and explore the special problems of women in business and industry. It is aimed at women who are eligible for promotion to management positions and at those who have recently been promoted to such positions.

This consists of eight sessions, meeting one afternoon per week for eight weeks. Women who are college graduates or have equivalent experience are given preference in enrollment. All who complete this curriculum are awarded a certificate from LeMoyne College. For more information, write to The Institute for the Career Development of Women in Management, LeMoyne College, LeMoyne Heights, Syracuse, N.Y. 13214.

Major Program in Physical Education (Marywood College, Scranton, Pa.)

In view of the increasingly active participation of women in professional sports, women students may well be interested in the *major program in Physical Education* offered by *Marywood College* (Scranton, Pa.). Marywood is the only Catholic women's college in the East with such a major. Its full array of modern up-to-date facilities include an indoor Olympic-sized swimming pool, basketball court, six outdoor tennis courts illuminated for night tennis, facilities for all indoor sports and soccer, softball and hockey fields.

Students may select their major courses with such special programs as Aquatics, Archery, Basketball, Bowling, Diving, Field Hockey, Golf, Lacrosse, Soccer, Softball and Synchronized Swimming. Successful completion of all of the requirements in this major field of concentration leads to the degree of Bachelor of Science in Physical Education. The job market is good for women as Physical Education teachers in the elementary, middle and secondary schools and as Camping Directors, Recreation Directors and Physical Education Directors with youth groups.

Details about this program may be obtained by writing to the Chairman, Physical Education Department, c/o Admissions Office, Marywood College, Scranton, Pa. 18509.

Council for the Continuing Education for Women (University of Tennessee, Knoxville, Tenn.)

The *University Evening School* of the *University of Tennessee* (Knoxville, Tenn.) organized the *Council for the Continuing Education for Women* in 1972 to serve as a community resource in meeting the educational needs of women. A number of credit and non-credit courses of special interest to women are offered by the University Evening School in the evening, and in the *daytime* too!

The Continuing Education for Women courses presented during the daytime in 1974 by the Evening School included: Gourmet Chinese Cooking, Practical Gourmet Cooking, Painting with Acrylics, Tennis (Beginning) and Yoga. The Cooking courses were repeated in the evening. Other non-credit evening courses were: Be Your Own Decorator, Preventive Self Defense and Wood Applique. Freshman Composition, General Psychology and The Women's Movement were each available for three credits in the mornings through the University Evening School. To make it easier for women to take these courses, the University of Tennessee held classes not only on campus, but also in such off-campus community settings as the Church Street United Methodist Church and the Tennessee Valley Unitarian Church.

For further information about these courses, write to the University

Evening School, Communications and University Extension Building, The University of Tennessee, Knoxville, Tenn. 37916.

Women's Programs (Amarillo College, Amarillo, Texas)

Amarillo College (Amarillo, Texas) has a *Mini Semester* program of courses including special courses for women. The Mini Semester is, as the name implies, shorter than the traditional semester to enable those with limited time to take courses of interest to them. The special courses for women range from two to thirteen weeks in length (the majority are six weeks long) and are held in the mornings, afternoons and evenings. Daytime child care is available through the Amarillo College Child Care Center.

The special courses for women include Cooking with an International Flair, Music Appreciation, Personal Assessment, Powder Puff Mechanic, Preparing for Employment, So You're Going Back to College, The National Constitution Today and Women's Tennis League.

Details about these courses may be obtained from the Office of Women's Programs, Amarillo College, Amarillo, Texas 79178.

Miscellaneous Women's Programs and Courses

As a community service, *Hillsboro Community College* (Tampa, Fla.) offers a non-credit course in Car Care for Women.

Armstrong State College in Savannah, Georgia, offers a non-credit "short course" in its Division of Community Services entitled The American Woman: A History of Feminism and the Changing Status of Women from Colonial Times to the Present. The changing status of the American woman in history, the struggle for equal political and economic opportunity by women and the contributions that women have made in the United States are studied in this course.

Barat College, a private, liberal arts college for women, located in Lake Forest, Illinois, has been expanding to meet the needs of non-college age women who wish to return to college. In the past year, the number of these women at Barat has skyrocketed. A new degree program has been established for these women, a Bachelor of Science in General Scientific Studies. Individual program planning is involved for each of these returning adult learners.

The Division of Continuing Education of the *University of Kansas* (Lawrence, Kans.) has a Committee for Women's Programs which offers credit and non-credit courses and workshops of special interest to women. Most popular among the latter are: Career Exploration Workshop for Women; Women and the Law; and The Women's Movement Today.

Jersey City State College (Jersey City, N.J.) introduced a major degree program in *Women's Studies* into its curriculum in 1974. To improve their future career potential, students are offered the option of a dual major. Thus, for example, a student may major in both a Pre-Law Program and Women's Studies.

The *Evening College of Johns Hopkins University* (Baltimore, Md.) allows a wife to pay only one-half of the registration fee when a husband and wife both register for the same informal, non-credit course. Literature and the Feminine Mystique is one of the stimulating informal courses. (See Chapter 15 for more information about this.)

Being a Woman in Today's World is a non-credit workshop course presented by the Division of Special Studies of *Georgia State University* (Atlanta, Ga.) for women "who wish to discover a stronger, more independent self." Many contemporary problems are discussed. Georgia State also helps the woman of average strength to respond to a threatening situation and protect herself with its course in Basic Self Defense for Women.

The Continuing Education Division of *Indiana University at Kokomo* offers a stimulating non-credit course to help women find themselves. The course is entitled Women in Society: A Search for Identity.

An interdisciplinary program in *Women's Studies* is available at the *State University of New York at Albany* (Albany, N.Y.). Courses pertaining to women may be found in the English, Classics, Sociology, Economics, Recreation, History and Anthropology and Puerto Rican Studies departments.

The Community Service Program of *Austin Community College* (Austin, Minn.) has a Facts on Football course primarily for women who want to become better informed about football all the better to enjoy viewing the game. In view of the increasing popularity of football among women, offering this course is a good idea and other colleges might consider doing likewise—and then too, the doors to sportscasting and sportswriting careers are opening up to women.

Women in Transition is a series of short, stimulating courses for women which was started at *Whitworth College* (Spokane, Wash.) in February 1971. This is a program for women of all ages who are seeking new direction, ideas, interests and purpose. It gives them the opportunity to satisfy their desire for self-development and expression. The theme of the 1974 series was "The Possible You," and classes met on four Fridays in February from 10:00 A.M. to 2:00 P.M.

Sarah Lawrence College (Bronxville, N.Y.) conducted an experimental *Program for Women in Community Activities* for the academic year 1974-75. The purpose of this program was two-fold: 1) to provide resources, space and time for study and reflection to women who have been active in pursuing and/or organizing activities for women, and 2) to conduct a special seminar at which these women might interact with undergraduates and students from the Center for Continuing Education. Participants in this program could audit one or more college courses in addition to attending the seminar. The special seminar, entitled "Women Organizing Women," included historical and theoretical readings on the status of women, reform movement history and theories of feminism. Details may be obtained from the Director, Women's Studies Program, Sarah Lawrence College, Bronxville, N.Y. 10708.

The *Midwestern University* (Wichita Falls, Texas) Division of Continuing Education has a delightfully nontraditional course for women entitled "Housewife (OOPS!) House*person* Physics." The course includes experiments designed to illustrate physics in everyday life. Since a home today is almost like a limited physics lab, this should be of tremendous interest to women. Colleges throughout the country would do well to offer a similar course for "housepersons."

The *Student Husband/Wife Program* at *Indiana State University* (Terre Haute, Ind.) is a welcome addition in the realm of nontraditionality. This program suggests that you "share an educational experience with your spouse." It permits spouses of full-time students to enroll for credit in a maximum of one course for three semester hours of credit during a semester or summer term for only $5.00. Would you like to know more? Then, write or visit the Office of Summer Sessions and Academic Services, Parsons Hall, Room 100, Indiana State University, Terre Haute, Ind. 47809.

"Spouse Tuition" is also an arrangement at *C.W. Post Weekend College* (Greenvale, N.Y.) which permits one spouse to receive a special tui-

tion discount if the other spouse enrolls in the same course and pays full tuition. (See Chapter 3 for information about C. W. Post Weekend College.)

If you would like to learn more about career opportunities for women, you should read this writer's *Nontraditional Careers for Women* (published by Messner Division, Simon & Schuster).

17.

"WHERE THERE IS NO VISION, THE PEOPLE PERISH"

Proverbs, 29:18

"Where there is no vision, the people perish." So says the Good Book, and so true this is. For, where there is no vision, there is no learning—and where there is no learning, there is no life. To learn is to grow, to develop, to live.

The world is moving fast and changing rapidly. Today's complex world is like a treadmill—if you stand still, you go backwards. To go forward with progress, we must continue to learn. Progress calls for the vision to take bold, nontraditional steps in the field of education.

Traditional—Good and Bad; Nontraditional—Bad and Good

Innovations must be made with care, however. Simply because something is innovative does not mean it is good; it may be bad. Change simply for the sake of change is pointless. There are positive changes and negative changes. We must insure that the changes we make are positive, constructive changes.

Not everything that is nontraditional is good. Conversely, not everything that is traditional is bad. There is much that is traditional that is excellent. There is much that is nontraditional that is horrid. I found in my survey of more than 2,000 institutions of higher education that in some schools there is a great deal of activity in the name of nontraditionality, but basically and unfortunately, it is much ado about nothing. Too many are being faddish and doing some silly things so as to say they are doing something nontraditional.

Some of the most ridiculous activities are taking place in the guise of nontraditionality, to such an extent that I was almost tempted to include a chapter in this book entitled, "How to Collect College Credits via a Course in Communing with the Kangaroos in a Kookoo Curriculum at Crazy-Quilt College." Unfortunately, there is all too much of this kind of faddish absurdity going on.

Even some good innovations may be fraught with danger. Excellent examples of this are the self-designed majors and individualized degree programs. Such majors and programs have great potential for bringing out the best in a student's intellectual capacities. However, conversely, if students with self-designed majors and individualized programs do not have the appropriate, competent guidance and supervision of a member of the faculty, these students may be taking a potpourri of nothing much and upon receiving their degrees they will be qualified to do—nothing much!

College Choice

There are many reasons why a student chooses to matriculate at one college rather than at another. Assuming that you have the qualifications to gain admission to the college of your choice, essentially, one college may be more attractive to you than are others because of its superior department in the subject in which you wish to specialize, its geographic location, its student population, whether it is coeducational or all-male or all-female, whether it is a public or private institution (if the latter, whether it is independent or church-related), whether it is a two-year or four-year college, annual tuition and other fees and availability of financial aid. There has to be a certain feeling, a rapport, between the college you wish to attend and yourself. Now, another factor has been added, namely, nontraditionality.

There are many aspects of nontraditionality that are very exciting, very challenging and very rewarding and I have attempted to bring these forth in this book. These can very much enhance your education and your future progress. Therefore, in selecting the college you would like to attend you should first visit it, read its college catalogue and descriptive brochures, speak with its students and professors (if at all possible) and determine whether it is totally traditional, totally nontraditional or has one or more nontraditional characteristics to your liking.

An important matter which you must bear in mind in regard to nontraditional programs is "Caveat emptor" ("Buyer beware!"). Unfortunately, many colleges, afraid to be considered "old-fashioned" and in an attempt to keep up with "fads," have added so-called "nontraditional" features to their curricula which are utter nonsense and a waste of your valuable time and money. So, enter upon nontraditional programs with caution; discuss them with your school counselors and college advisors. If there are aspects of nontraditionality discussed in this book which your college does not have, discuss them with your college administrators and perhaps they will consider adding them to your college.

There is positive, constructive nontradition and there is negative, destructive nontradition. Be sure that you are embarking on a positive nontraditional program and not negative nontraditional nonsense! The positive programs will prove to be of great value. They will enhance your education and your life. So, choose with care.

Tuition Nontradition

College tuition is a matter of importance to all students. Nontradition has even impinged on tuition—and that should be of interest to you. Now, here's something truly nontraditional—a college that gives you a "money back guarantee!" *Mitchell College* (Statesville, N.C.) appears to be the only college in the United States—and probably in the entire world—which stands behind its program of instruction. At Mitchell, if you pass the course, the college keeps your tuition, but if you attended classes conscientiously, studied diligently, prepared your assignments and sought extra help from a member of the faculty and yet do not pass the course, your tuition for that course will be refunded. Hurrah for Mitchell College and may all other colleges do likewise!

At *D'Youville College* in Buffalo, N.Y., families that have two or more full-time students (sisters and/or brothers) attending the same year are allowed a $100 reduction in tuition on each of the student's total tuition. This is with the proviso that neither of the siblings holds a D'Youville College scholarship.

The *Continuing Education and Extension Division* of the *University of Minnesota* has featured a "½ Price Sale" on University Extension Classes. For half of the normal tuition fees, students are permitted to sit in a University Extension class for no credit. There are no examinations or grades to worry about and those who would like to learn something new, attend college for the fun of it or discover how it feels to be a member of a university class have the opportunity to choose from among hundreds of courses for only one-half of the normal price. For a copy of the Bulletin of Information about these courses, write to: Extension Classes, 180 Wesbrook Hall, University of Minnesota, Minneapolis, Minn. 55455.

Surprise, surprise—an institution of higher education that has reduced its tuition fees! The *University of Michigan* reduced its tuition by five per cent for the Winter and Spring terms of 1974.

Those of you who are concerned about college costs might like to read this writer's *Your College Education—How to Pay for It* (published by Messner Division, Simon & Schuster).

Concurrent Character Education

One very important innovation is missing and I would like to suggest it and recommend it to all institutions of higher education. There is no underestimating the importance of career education. But, nothing is of greater importance than character education, and unfortunately that has been absent from the traditional curriculum, which has for many years been preoccupied with the teaching of subjects.

Surely, considering the present state of the world, there is nothing of more importance than morality, compassion, integrity and respect for the rights of all people, and these add up to character education. Education should teach the head, but even more important, it should reach the heart.

A "summa cum laude" award should be bestowed upon Iowa Wesleyan University of Mount Pleasant, Iowa (see Chapter 7) for requiring that all of its students must participate in the Responsible Social Involvement program, a project of volunteer services, before they may receive their baccalaureate degrees. May all other colleges and universities do likewise!

The ultimate in positive nontraditionality is a college education composed of career education concurrent with character education to yield college graduates who not only are knowledgeable and competent in their areas of concentration, but are also kind, cooperative, compassionate human beings. This would go a long way toward making it possible for people of all colors, races and religions to live together in peace and harmony.

Only when character education accompanies career competencies will we be able to meet the challenges of today's complex—and tomorrow's even more complex—world.

Blend the best of tradition with the best of nontradition and then go forth with knowledge, competency and character to enter productive careers and to produce peace in your heart, peace of mind and peace in the world.

SELECTED FURTHER READINGS

Throughout this book, there are references to sources of further information. To obtain further information about specific colleges and their nontraditional characteristics, read the catalogues of these colleges. These catalogues may be found in your school or public libraries and you may obtain copies by writing to the directors of admissions of the individual colleges.

The following recent publications merit reading too. Some concern a particular aspect of nontraditionality which may be of special interest to you.

A Directory of U.S. College and University Degrees for Part-Time Students. Robert J. Pitchell, Editor. 118 pages. 1973. National University Extension Association, Washington, D.C. 20036. $1.95

A Working Woman's Guide to Her Job Rights. 38 pages. 1974. Leaflet 55. U.S. Department of Labor, Employment Standards Administration, Women's Bureau, Washington, D.C. 20210. Free

American Students and Teachers Abroad: Sources of Information about Overseas Study, Teaching, Work and Travel. DHEW Publication No. (OE) 72-196. U.S. Department of Health, Education & Welfare, Office of Education, Institute of International Studies. 38 pages. 1972. Superintendent of Documents, U.S. Government Printing Office, Washington, D.C. 20402. 45¢

CLEP (College-Level Examination Program). Gary R. Gruber. 587 pages. 1973. Simon & Schuster, Inc., Reference, Technical and Review Book Division, New York, N.Y. 10019. $3.95

Get Credit for What You Know. Leaflet 56 (Revised). U.S. Department of Labor, Employment Standards Administration, Women's Bureau. 10 pages. 1974. Superintendent of Documents, U.S. Government Printing Office, Washington, D.C. 20402. 25¢

Going Back to School at 35. Special Labor Force Report 159. 7 pages. 1973. U.S. Department of Labor, Bureau of Labor Statistics, Washington, D.C. 20212. Free

Guide to Independent Study through Correspondence Instruction:

1973-1975. 40 pages. 1973. National University Extension Association, Washington, D.C. 20036. 75¢

Paraprofessions: Careers of the Future and the Present. Sarah Splaver. 192 pages. 1972. Messner Division, Simon & Schuster, Inc., New York, N.Y. 10018. $4.95.

Summer Study Abroad. Institute of International Education, 809 United Nations Plaza, New York, N.Y. 10017. 86 pages. 1974. Unipub, Box 433, New York, N.Y. 10016. $3.00

The New Guide to Study Abroad, 1974-1975 Edition. John A. Garraty, et al. 422 pages. 1974. Harper & Row, Publishers, Inc., New York, N.Y. 10022. $10.95

The New York Times Guide to Continuing Education in America. College Entrance Examination Board. Frances Coombs Thomson, Editor. 816 pages. 1973. Quadrangle Books, New York, N.Y. 10017. $4.95

U.S. College-Sponsored Programs Abroad: Academic Year. Institute of International Education, 809 United Nations Plaza, New York, N.Y. 10017. 89 pages. 1974. Unipub, Box 433, New York, N.Y. 10016. $3.50

What is Cooperative Education? 12 pages. No date. Cooperative Education Association, Drexel University, Philadelphia, Pa. 19104. 10¢

Your Career and Two-Year Colleges. 16 pages. No date. American Association of Community and Junior Colleges, Washington, D.C. 20036. Free

Your College Education—How to Pay For It. Sarah Splaver. 279 pages. 1968. Messner Division, Simon & Schuster, Inc., New York, N.Y. 10018. $4.95

CAREER-COURSE/SUBJECT AREA INDEX

Mechanical Technology, 147, 153
Mechanical Ventilation of the Chronically Ill Patient, 207
Media Arts, 188
Media Studies, 27
Medical Audiovisual Technology, 187
Medical Office Assistant, 207
Medical Preprofessional, 187
Medical Professions, 63
Medical Record Clerk, 36, 207
Medical Record Librarian, 111
Medical Secretary, 111, 148
Medical Technology, 68, 73, 111, 148, 187, 211, 212
Medical Terminology, 207
Medieval & Renaissance Studies, 56
Mental Health, 39, 148, 188
Metallurgical Engineering, 103
Meteorology, 139, 189
Mexican Studies, 42, 43
Microbiology, 190
Microeconomic Analysis, 118
Military Service, 16
Modern Dance, 75, 218, 222
Modern Languages, 28, 55, 73, 177
Modern Management, 142
Modern Western World (European travel seminar), 40
Molecular Biology & Microanatomy, 66
Mortuary Science, 148
Mountaineering, 193, 217
Multicrafts, 216
Museology, 46
Museum Art, 45, 165
Music, 39, 41, 42, 55, 61, 73, 102, 103, 113, 116, 123, 133, 135, 137, 138, 184, 192, 211, 214
Music & Poetry, 39
Music Appreciation, 29, 48, 93, 228
Music History, 130
Music in America, 140
Music in Latin America, 140
Music in Vienna/Salzburg, 131
Music Instrument Technology, 84
Music Literature: From Bach to Rock, 217
Musical Comedy Production, 165
Musical Studies, 56
Mysticism & Spiritual Practices, 46
Mythology, 41

National Constitution Today, 228
Native American Law & Government, 78
Native American Liberation, 78
Native Arts, 106
Natural Health Food Cooking, 215
Natural History—Biological Focus, 197
Natural Resources, 103, 133
Natural Sciences, 24, 58, 73, 123, 157, 165, 190, 192, 193
Nautical Astronomy & Celestial Navigation, 46
Near Eastern Studies, 78
Needlepoint, 31

Needlework, 43, 217
New Math for Parents, 218
New Testament, 78
Newspaper Reporter (assistant), 104
Newspaper Writing, 140
Noise Pollution, 45
Northwest Semitic Languages & Literatures, 78
Norwegian, 137
Novel Workshop, 83
Nuclear Engineering, 63, 66
Numismatics, 31
Nurse Aide, 36, 207
Nursing, 16, 21, 32, 48, 68, 73, 111, 118, 147, 148, 153, 185
Nursing Home Administration, 79, 94
Nutrition, 139, 145

Occult, 40, 41
Occupational Education, 90
Occupational Therapy, 111
Oceanography, 57, 213
Office Administration (or management), 103, 133, 134
Oil Painting, 29, 31, 43
Ojibwa Indian Language, 78
Old Testament, 78
Open Education, 128
Opera (twentieth century), 44
Optics, 135
Orderly Trainee, 36
Organizational Psychology & Management, 45
Oriental Studies, 41, 103, 141
Ornithology, 46
Orthoptics, 81

Painting (and drawing), 32, 69, 163
Painting with Acrylics, 227
Paraprofessions, 16
Parapsychology, 39, 81, 117, 214
Parliament in Contemporary British Politics, 127
Peace Studies, 77
Pentecostal Movements, 46
Perception, 190
Persian, 78, 210
Personal Assessment, 228
Personal Health Science, 141
Personnel Assistant, 104
Personnel Management, 141, 142, 188
Pharmaceutical Sciences, 103
Pharmacology, 135
Pharmacy, 134
Pharmacy Trainee, 104
Philosophies of Life & Living, 29, 203
Philosophies of Punishment, 46
Philosophy, 13, 28, 55, 61, 73, 83, 94, 103, 123, 130, 133, 134, 135, 136, 137, 138, 139, 141, 157, 177, 184, 189, 190, 197, 211
Philosophy of Love, 217
Philosophy of Religion, 56
Photography, 31, 32, 44, 45, 111, 163, 197, 213, 214, 215, 222

INDEX

ABOUT THE AUTHOR

SARAH SPLAVER is a noted guidance consultant and counseling psychologist. She holds a Master of Arts degree from Teachers College, Columbia University, and a Doctor of Philosophy degree from New York University. She served for several years as a high school Director of Guidance. She is nationally and internationally well known as the originator of the socioguidrama, a group guidance technique used as a means of helping young people with their problems.

Dr. Splaver is licensed as a registered psychologist by the Department of Education of the state of New York. She has served as a consultant on psychological and guidance projects to the U.S. Department of Health, Education and Welfare; U.S. Defense Department; Department of the Army; New York Life Insurance Company; International Business Machines Corp.; and various other organizations. She has counseled thousands of college-bound and non-college-bound young people and adults. As a consultant, she has worked on computerized guidance programs.

Her articles on guidance, psychology and career information have appeared in professional journals and other publications. She has authored dozens of *Occupational Abstracts,* prepared the *Guide to Career Literature* for the New York Life Insurance Company's Career Information Service and has written many books and playlets in the field of guidance and psychology. She has lectured at conferences, young people's gatherings and parent-teacher and other meetings. She is the former Director of *Guidance Exchange.*

Dr. Splaver is a Fellow of the International Council of Psychologists and a Life Member of the American Personnel and Guidance Association. Among the other professional organizations in which she holds membership are the National Vocational Guidance Association, American School Counselor Association, American Psychological Association, Institutes of Religion and Health, American Association for the Advancement of Science and the Authors Guild.